Programming in PASCAL

PETER GROGONO
Computer Center
Concordia University
Montreal, Quebec

♦ ADDISON-WESLEY
PUBLISHING COMPANY, INC.
Reading, Massachusetts
Menlo Park, California
London • Amsterdam
Don Mills, Ontario
Sydney

aster = '*';

This book is in the
ADDISON-WESLEY SERIES IN COMPUTER SCIENCE

M. A. Harrison
Consulting Editor

Second printing, September 1978

Reproduced by Addison-Wesley from camera-ready copy prepared by the
author.

ISBN 0-201-02473-X
ABCDEFGHIJ-MA-798

Preface

The computer programming language PASCAL was the first
language to embody in a coherent way the concepts of structured
programming which had been defined by Edsger Dijkstra and C.A.R.
Hoare. As such it is a landmark in the development of programming
languages. PASCAL was developed by Niklaus Wirth at Eidgenossische
Technische Hochschule in Zurich; it is derived from the language
ALGOL 60 but is more powerful and easier to use. PASCAL is now
widely accepted as a useful language that can be efficiently
implemented, and as an excellent teaching tool.

This book is intended for people who want to write programs
in PASCAL. It does not assume knowledge of any other programming
language and it is therefore suitable for an introductory course.
It can also be used in conjunction with a discrete structures text
for a more detailed 'principles of programming' course.

Chapters 1 and 10 discuss general principles of computer
programming. Chapter 10 is naturally more advanced than Chapter 1,
but it need not be left until last; most of it can be understood
without an advanced knowledge of PASCAL, and it may profitably be
studied concurrently with the rest of the book. Chapters 2,5,6,7
and 8 deal with data management and structure in PASCAL, and Chapters
3 and 4 with PASCAL statements. This treatment, while systematic,
omits some of the more esoteric features of the language, which are
tidied up in Chapter 9. If you already know a programming language,
you will find that the early chapters are easy reading. However,
elementary concepts are defined more precisely in PASCAL than in

some other languages, so you should not omit these chapters altogether.

There are two reasons for programming in a high level language such as PASCAL rather than in a low level assembly language. First, it is easier to write programs in a high level language. Second, and more important, it is easier to read and understand a program written in a high level language. Professional programmers spend much of their time revising programs written by themselves or others. If they do not fully understand these programs, their attempts at revision will eventually ruin the programs. It is therefore as important to learn how to read and modify programs as it is to learn how to write them. Although the programs in this book are for the most part short and simple, they are not just fragments but complete, working programs. You can achieve a superficial understanding of these programs by reading them, but in order to understand them properly, you should attempt to improve them. There are many exercises in the book which indicate ways in which the given examples can be enhanced, and you will learn PASCAL rapidly and painlessly by doing them. Most of the other exercises require you to write original programs. The programs specified are not trivial and may require a fair amount of work. It is more instructive to spend a month writing a single program of reasonable size that is correct than it is to spend the same time writing half a dozen programs which are unrealistically small or which do not work properly. It is also instructive to learn to program as a member of a team rather than as an individual, and some of the exercises of chapters 6, 7, 8 and 10 are large enough to warrant solution by a team.

It is customary to emphasize the reserved words of programs written in languages of the ALGOL family. In typeset material, the reserved words are printed in boldface lower case letters, and the identifiers are italicized. In typed material this is impractical, and the common alternative, underlining, is not very pretty. The notation used in this book is therefore unconventional. I have chosen to use upper case letters for reserved words and lower case letters for identifiers. The resulting programs are neat and readable.

I have received much help and encouragement while preparing this book. I am particularly grateful for the advice, suggestions and corrections of Henry F. Ledgard and Derek C. Oppen, and of various members of the Department of Computer Science at Concordia University. I am also grateful to Sharon H. Nelson, who patiently read and edited numerous drafts, and to Ritva Seppanen who typed the final version. I assume responsibility for any errors that remain. Finally, I acknowledge the strenuous efforts of Concordia University's Cyber 172 computer, which, with the help of Urs Amman's PASCAL Compiler, tested the example programs.

Contents

transfer vector loader.
Relocatedable loader with any # procedure seg
& only one data segment.

Programming Concepts

CHAPTER ONE

1.1 Programs

A *program* is a sequence of instructions. A recipe, a musical
score, and a knitting pattern are all programs. Programs in this
sense existed long before computers were invented. Programs for
computers, however, are longer and more intricate than other kinds
of programs, and consequently writing them requires care and
precision. Before we look more closely at computer programs, we
will define some general terms and consider some of the properties
that systems of programming have in common.

A program requires an *author* to write it, and a *processor* to
carry out the instructions. Carrying out the instructions is called
executing, or *running*, the program, and a running program is called a
process. Executing a recipe is called cooking, and the cook is the
processor. A musical score is a set of instructions for performing a
piece of music, and the performer is the processor. Some common
features of programs are:

(1) Instructions are executed *sequentially*. Unless explicitly told
    otherwise, you start at the first instruction, and execute each
    instruction in turn until you have finished. This general
    pattern may be broken in certain well-defined ways, as, for
    example, when you repeat a section of music.

(2) The process has an *effect*. This effect may be a meal or sounds

1

of music. If the program is a computer program, the effect is often in the form of output consisting of printed or displayed symbols.

(3) The program operates on certain objects. The instruction 'grate the nutmeg' assumes that you have some nutmeg to grate. The objects on which a computer program operates are called *data*.

(4) Sometimes the instructions are preceded by a *declaration* of the objects on which they operate. This is true of recipes, which are usually preceded by a list of the necessary ingredients. In many programming languages, the programmer must declare the attributes of his data before he writes the instructions.

(5) Sometimes the instructions require that a *decision* be made by the processor. 'If you are using fresh tomatoes, skin them and add before the onions, but if you are using tinned tomatoes, add them last.' In this case, the author of the instructions did not know what the processor would do in a particular instance, but he established a criterion which the processor can use to make a decision.

(6) It may be necessary to execute an instruction, or a group of instructions, more than once. This occurs frequently in knitting and crocheting, since these are inherently repetitive processes. Whenever an instruction is to be repeated, the number of repetitions must be specified. This can be done either by giving directly the number of repetitions required ('knit ten rows') or by establishing a criterion which depends on the state of the process ('knit until the end of the row'). Both forms of repetition occur frequently in computer programs. Since modern computers can execute more than a million instructions in a second, a program without repetition would not run for more than a fraction of a second.

(7) The program itself is a static entity, but the process of carrying out the instructions is dynamic. We do not confuse a cook with a recipe, or a pianist with a score, and it is equally important that we do not confuse a processor with a program.

These are the characteristics which are shared by all programs, including those written for a computer. We see that a program is essentially a means by which the author of the program communicates with the processor. Communication requires a language, and although natural languages such as English are often used for informal instruction, most programming tasks require a special language. Even recipes use a specialized dialect of natural language, and musicians, choreographers and knitters have devised entirely original languages in which to communicate their instructions.

1.2 Structure

The earliest computer programs were no more than lists of the
primitive instructions that the computer could execute directly. As
time went by, more complicated programs were written, and these lists
became unmanageable. The reason was that they lacked structure. To a
machine, the execution of a list containing a few thousand instructions presents no problems, because the machine mechanically performs
each instruction without regard to its meaning or consequence. But to
the programmer, who is concerned with the meaning of the program, the
problem of understanding a list of thousands of undifferentiated
instructions becomes insurmountable. The history of programming
languages is to a large extent an account of how structure has been
added to these primitive lists of instructions.

Structure appeared first in the evaluation of expressions.
Suppose that we have to write a computer program to calculate the
value of *area*, where

$$area = 3.1415926535 \times 5^2$$

In the early days, the programmer would write a sequence of instructions something like this:

> *enter 3.1415926535*
> *multiply by 5*
> *multiply by 5*
> *store area*

He would have to be careful to interpret the expression correctly.
For example, the expression

$$2 \times 3 + 4$$

corresponds to the program

> *enter 2*
> *multiply by 3*
> *add 4*

but the expression

$$2 \times (3 + 4)$$

corresponds to the program

> *enter 3*
> *add 4*
> *multiply by 2*

Programmers realized that the translation from the symbolic expression to a list of machine instructions was a mechanical operation that could be carried out by a machine, and, moreover, that the computer was a suitable machine for doing it. Thereafter, programmers wrote expressions in conventional algebraic form.

The next thing that needed structuring was data. The computer has a memory of several thousand *words*, and a word may contain a number, a group of characters, or an instruction. The programmer might decide to put a set of one hundred batting averages in words 300 to 399 of the memory, and subsequently forget this decision and put something else there. With a language that permits data structuring, we write

averages : ARRAY [1..100] OF integer;

and know that this will reserve an area of the memory which will not be used for anything else.

With the problem of structuring data at least partially solved, attention returned to improving the structuring of the instructions themselves. It turns out that all computer programs can be expressed in terms of four basic structures. These are: the *sequence*, the *decision*, the *repetitive structure* or *loop*, and the *procedure*. The *sequence* is a group of instructions executed one after the other. The *decision* is a structure that enables the action of the program to be influenced by the data. Many languages introduce the decision structure with the word '*IF*', and in them we write instructions such as

IF x ≥ 0
 THEN y := x
 ELSE y := -x

The *loop* structure is used to execute an instruction or a sequence of instructions several times. Although the instructions are the same each time the loop is executed, the data on which they operate is not. For example, the effect of repeating the instruction

add 1 to x

one hundred times is to add 100 to *x*. We must be careful to specify how many times the instructions in the loop are to be executed. If we suppose that initially *x = 0* and *y > 0* then the program

repeat
  add 1 to x
until x^2 > y

will give to *x* the value of the smallest integer whose square exceeds *y*. This program is safe, because we can guarantee that such a value will always be found. The program

> *repeat*
>   *add 1 to x*
> *until x^2 = y*

is not safe. If, for instance, *y* = 5 then the condition x^2 = *y* will never be true. Theoretically, in this case the program would be stuck in the loop forever. On an actual computer the program would run until *x* was so large that x^2 could not be represented, and then stop.

The *procedure* enables us to replace a group of instructions by a single instruction. Procedures are frequently employed in cookery books. A good cookery book will provide a procedure for making cream sauce, say, and refer to that procedure in each recipe which requires a sauce of that type. The use of procedures in computer programming not only makes programs shorter and easier to write, but, more importantly, it gives programs a hierarchical structure. The concept of procedure is so important that without it, useful computer programs could not be written.

The programming language PASCAL uses all of these techniques of structuring. They are incorporated in a simple and elegant fashion which makes PASCAL a powerful language that is nonetheless easy to learn and use.

1.3 An Informal Introduction to PASCAL

In this section, we will study some very simple PASCAL programs in order to see how the structures described in the preceding section are realized in an actual programming language. The three programs in this section are complete, working programs that may be run on a computer.

```
PROGRAM squarerootoftwo (output);
    BEGIN
        write(sqrt(2))
    END.
```

If this program is executed by a computer, it will print

> *1.4142135624*

which is approximately the value of the square root of 2. The third line *write(sqrt(2))*

is the heart of Program *squarerootoftwo*. *Write* is a *procedure* whose
effect is to print the value of *sqrt(2)*, which is its *argument*. *Sqrt*
is a standard PASCAL function. The value of *sqrt(2)* is $\sqrt{2}$ within the
limits of precision of the computer.

The first line of the program contains the word *PROGRAM*. This is
the first word of all PASCAL programs. It is followed by
squarerootoftwo, which is the name of the program. The name of the
program is chosen by the programmer, and a good programmer will try
to choose a name that reflects the function of the program. After the
name, we define the relationship between the program and its environment. The word *output* is an indication that the program is going to
generate some results. The environment of a program running in a
modern computer is usually the *operating system*, and the function of
the operating system in this instance is to accept the results
generated by the program and transmit them to a printer or a terminal.

Finally, note the words *BEGIN* and *END*. As you might expect, these
signify the start and finish of the program.

Program *squarerootoftwo* is not very useful. We could have looked
up the value of $\sqrt{2}$ in a book if we had really wanted to know it. The
following program is an improved version of Program *squarerootoftwo*:

```
PROGRAM squareroot (input,output);
    VAR
        x : real;
    BEGIN
        read(x);
        write(sqrt(x))
    END.
```

This program illustrates *sequential structure*. There are two instructions, *read(x)* and *write(sqrt(x))*. These instructions will be
executed one after the other in the order in which we have written
them. The words *BEGIN* and *END* act as brackets around an instruction
sequence. This program contains only one such sequence and hence only
one *BEGIN-END* pair. More complicated programs contain many instruction
sequences, each bracketed by *BEGIN* and *END*.

Program *squareroot* accepts data from its environment. The first
line contains the word *input*, indicating that the program will request
data. The procedure *read* actually does the requesting. The effect of
the *read* instruction is to obtain a value from the input medium, and
give this value to *x*. The nature of the input medium is unknown to
the program. We may assume that the value was punched on a card or
typed on the keyboard of a terminal.

The third new concept introduced by Program *squareroot* is *data*.

6

The object which we have named *x* is a *real variable*, and it is
announced in the declaration

    VAR
        x : real;

This declaration attributes the type *real* to the variable *x*.

Program *squareroot* is still a very poor example of a computer
program. *Sqrt(x)* will fail if *x* is negative, and yet there is no way
of preventing the user from entering a negative number. Moreover,
having calculated one square root, the program stops and has to be
restarted before it will calculate another. These defects are
remedied in Program *squareroots*.

    PROGRAM squareroots (input,output);
        VAR
            x : real;
        BEGIN
            REPEAT
                read(x);
                IF x ≥ 0
                    THEN write(sqrt(x))
                    ELSE write('argument error')
            UNTIL x = 0
        END.

This program incorporates *decision* and *repetition* structures.
Having read a value for *x*, the processor has to choose between two
courses of action. If the value of *x* is non-negative, the value of
$\sqrt{x}$ must be printed. If *x* is negative, the message

    argument error

must be printed. Moreover, the *REPEAT* statement and its matching
UNTIL will ensure that the program will continue to run until a value
of zero is read.

In this program, although the processor executes instructions
sequentially, the order in which they are executed is no longer the
same as that in which they are written down. After writing a square
root, the processor tests the value of *x*. If *x* is non-zero, the
processor executes the instruction *read* again. The process terminates
only when the condition

    x = 0

is found to be true. We must distinguish between the static program,
and the dynamic process of executing the program. When we speak
informally we often blur the distinction by saying 'the program does
so and so.' Remember that this is an abbreviation for 'the processor,

while executing the program, does so and so.' A program is a text; a processor is a machine which executes the instructions contained in the text.

Program *squareroots* is a sound program although it has a rather limited range of usefulness. Its condition for termination (a number with a value of zero) is not very satisfactory, and we will encounter more elegant ways of terminating programs later in this book.

1.4 Compilation and Execution

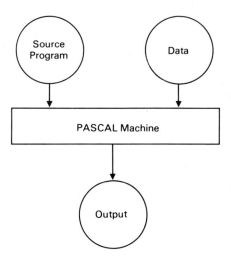

Fig. 1.1   The PASCAL Machine

As programming languages became more highly structured, computer programs became more amenable to human composition and analysis. At the same time, the task of translating the programs into the simple instructions executed by the computer became harder. We therefore expect to find associated with any programming language a program whose function is to translate programs written in the programming language into machine instructions. This program is called a *compiler* for the language. The program used to translate PASCAL programs into machine instructions is called the *PASCAL compiler*, and we will refer to this program frequently in this book.

If we always write correct programs, and have access to a good compiler, then for practical purposes we can think of the compiler and

the computer as a single machine capable of executing programs
directly. That is, we can ignore the translation process altogether.
The combination of a compiler and a computer, used in this way, is
sometimes called a *virtual machine*. There are good compilers available for PASCAL, and we can think of the combination of a PASCAL
compiler and a suitable computer as a *PASCAL machine*.

The PASCAL machine is depicted in Fig. 1.1. In this and subsequent diagrams, circles represent static entities, such as programs, and
rectangles represent processors. The lines represent the flow of data
to or from a process, the direction being indicated by an arrowhead.
Fig. 1.1 shows that the PASCAL machine requires a *source program*, by
which is meant any PASCAL program, and some *input data*. When the
PASCAL machine runs, it produces *output data*. If we suppose that the
source program is Program *squareroots* and the input data is

```
        2
        3
        4
        0
```

then, when we start the PASCAL machine, it will run for a little while
and then print the results

```
        1.41421356
        1.73205088
        2.00000000
        0
```

in the output file.

As we have seen, the virtual machine is a computer and a compiler.
These are shown in Fig. 1.2. The processor is now the computer itself
and it is used twice. In the first instance, the program is the
PASCAL compiler, and the input data is the source program. The result
is the translation of our source program into machine instructions,
and it is called the *object program*. The computer is then used again,
with the object program as its program, and our data as input data.
The result is our desired output data.

We would not need to be aware of the internal structure of the
PASCAL machine were it not for the possibility of errors. There are
three important kinds of programming error:

(1) Errors which can be recognized during translation. For example,
    omitting the *END* corresponding to a *BEGIN*. These are called
    compile-time errors.

(2) Errors recognized during the execution of the object program. If
    Program *squareroot* was executed and the value in the input file
    was -1, then the program would fail because *sqrt* does not accept

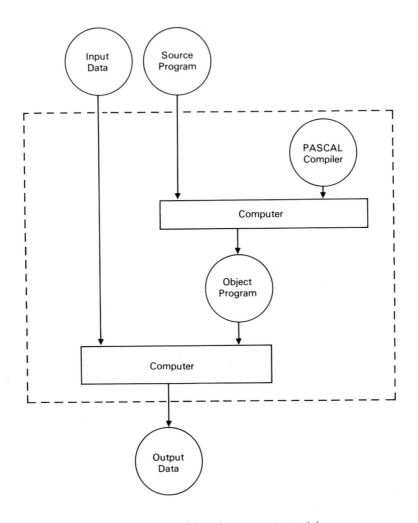

Fig. 1.2   Inside the PASCAL Machine

a negative argument.   This kind of error is called a *run-time error*.

(3) Errors which are not detected by the computer during compilation or execution.   For example, if you write

       sqr(x)

instead of

       sqrt(x)

in Program *squareroots*, the program would run successfully, but it would print values of x^2 rather than $\sqrt{x}$.

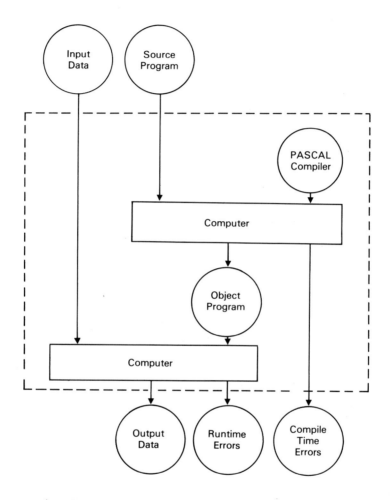

Fig. 1.3   Error Detection in the PASCAL Machine

Fig. 1.3 shows a PASCAL machine with error detection. Notice that we now obtain three different kinds of output. Errors detected during compilation appear first. If these errors are serious, the execution of the object program may be inhibited. If the program compiles successfully, it may fail during execution, and we will get a different kind of diagnostic output. If the program compiles successfully and runs successfully, we will get the output we expect, unless the program contains errors of the third type.

Errors are not necessarily confined to the program, however; they can also occur in the data. If you were using Program *squareroots* to calculate √5 and you inadvertently typed 6, you would get the wrong answer. This is an instance of an *input data error*, and there is clearly no way in which the program can detect an error of this kind.

The designer of a programming language can, to a certain extent, choose whether errors will be detected at compile-time or at run-time. Generally speaking, as the amount of redundancy in the language increases, so does the probability of being able to discover an error simply by examining the program text. The philosophy adopted in PASCAL is that as many errors as possible should be recognized by the compiler, and consequently there is a fair amount of redundancy in PASCAL. This helps to make PASCAL an easier programming language to learn than many others.

The compiler can also help us by incorporating *run-time checks* into the compiled program. When you write

> *write(sqrt(x))*

the effect of the instructions actually generated by the compiler will be

> *IF $x \geq 0$*
> *THEN write(sqrt(x))*
> *ELSE halt*

in which *halt* is a procedure which terminates the program with an appropriate error message. (Note that the fact that run-time checks are incorporated by the compiler in no way prevents us from including our own checking, as we did in Program *squareroots*.)

All this checking inevitably slows down the execution of both the compiler and the running program. In the majority of cases, however, computer time is saved because we arrive at correct programs more rapidly when we are provided with good error diagnostics.

In this book, when we say 'this statement is illegal' or 'this statement will not be accepted' we mean that the statement will produce an error during compilation. When we say 'this will cause a run-time error' we mean that the statement is acceptable to the compiler, but will not execute correctly.

1.5   Representation and Examples

To the compiler, a program is merely a string of symbols.   The
compiler would accept Program *squareroots* if it was written in this
form:

```
PROGRAM SQUAREROOTS (INPUT,OUTPUT); VAR X  :
REAL; BEGIN REPEAT READ(X);  IF X ≥ 0 THEN
WRITE(SQRT(X)) ELSE WRITE('ARGUMENT ERROR')
UNTIL X = 0 END.
```

It is for the benefit of human readers that we use a more spacious
layout.   The layout of a program text must match the structure of the
program.   A PASCAL program is structured in *levels*, and the level of a
statement is indicated by indenting the statement.   Program *squareroots* has four levels.   The outermost level is defined by *BEGIN* and
END, and the next level by *REPEAT* and its matching *UNTIL*.   Note how
this arrangement allows us to see at a glance which statements are to
be repeated, and how much harder it is to tell which statements are to
be repeated in the example above.   The *IF* statement has two levels,
with the *THEN* and *ELSE* clauses at the inner level.

In journals and textbooks, it is customary to use different typefaces to further clarify the structure of the program.   Unfortunately,
most computers are not equipped with upper and lower case character
sets, let alone different typefaces, and so most programmers rarely
see their programs in any format other than the monotonous rows of
capitals produced by a line-printer.   In this book, the *reserved words*
of PASCAL, such as *BEGIN*, *END*, *REPEAT*, *UNTIL* and so on are printed in
UPPER CASE ITALICS and all other words are printed in *lower case
italics*.

We conclude this chapter with some example programs.   At this
point, you should be content to read the programs carefully and
understand as much of them as you can, with the help of the brief
introduction given.   When you have read Chapters 2 and 3, you should
be able to write these and similar programs yourself.

The first program, *powertable*, prints a table of powers of
integers.   The line beginning *FOR* introduces a loop which is executed
once for each integral value of *base* from 1 to *tablesize*.   The effect
of the *assignment operator* ':=' is to calculate the value of the
expression on its right, and assign this value to the variable whose
name is on its left.   After executing

```
square := sqr(base)
```

we have

$$square = base^2$$

The table gives values of *base*, $base^2$, $base^3$, $base^4$, $base^{-1}$, $base^{-2}$, $base^{-3}$ and $base^{-4}$. Words and messages contained in braces { ... } are *comments* for the benefit of the human reader; they are ignored altogether by the compiler. The procedure *writeln* is similar to *write*, but after printing the value of its parameters, it writes a carriage return. The operator '*' is the multiplication operator: most computers do not possess the conventional character '×', and implicit multiplication, as when *ab* is used to represent $a \times b$, is not allowed in programming languages.

```
PROGRAM powertable (input,output);
   VAR
       tablesize, base, square, cube, quad
          : integer;
   BEGIN
      read(tablesize);
      FOR base := 1 TO tablesize DO
          BEGIN
             square := sqr(base);
             cube := base * square;
             quad := sqr(square);
             writeln(base,square,cube,quad,
                     1/base,1/square,1/cube,1/quad)
          END { for }
   END. { powertable }
```

Input:
        5

Output:

1	1	1	1	1.000000	1.000000	1.000000	1.000000
2	4	8	16	0.500000	0.250000	0.125000	0.062500
3	9	27	81	0.333333	0.111111	0.037037	0.012345
4	16	64	256	0.250000	0.062500	0.015625	0.003906
5	25	125	625	0.200000	0.040000	0.008000	0.001600

Program *divisors* reads numbers and calculates their divisors. It terminates when a non-positive number is read. The value of

   number MOD divisor

is the remainder when *number* is divided by *divisor*. The value of *divisor* is printed whenever the remainder is zero, and so the program prints all the divisors of *number*, not just the prime divisors.

Representation and Examples

```
PROGRAM divisors (input, output);
   VAR
      number, divisor : integer;
   BEGIN
      REPEAT
         read(number);
         IF number > 0
            THEN
               BEGIN
                  writeln('The divisors of', number, 'are:');
                  FOR divisor := 2 TO number DO
                     IF number MOD divisor = 0
                        THEN writeln(divisor)
               END
      UNTIL number ≤ 0
   END. { divisors }
```

Input:
```
   20   17    0
```

Output:
```
   The divisors of  20 are:
      2
      4
      5
     10
     20
   The divisors of  17 are:
     17
```

Program *minimax* reads a string of numbers, counts them, and records the smallest and largest values. *Maxint* is a standard constant denoting the largest integer value that the computer can store. The variable *reading* can only have two values: *true* or *false*. The statements between *BEGIN* and *END* following *WHILE* are executed repetitively as long as *reading* is *true*. You should be able to guess the meaning of the complicated *IF* statements in this program from your knowledge of English and what the program is supposed to do.

```
PROGRAM minimax (input, output);
   VAR
      reading : boolean;
      number, minimum, maximum, count
           : integer;
   BEGIN
      reading := true;
      minimum := maxint;
      maximum := - maxint;
      count := 0;
      WHILE reading DO
         BEGIN
```

15

```
                  read(number);
                  IF number = 0
                     THEN reading := false
                     ELSE
                        BEGIN
                           count := count + 1;
                           IF number < minimum
                              THEN minimum := number
                           ELSE IF number > maximum
                              THEN maximum := number
                        END
               END;  { while }
        writeln(count, 'numbers read');
        writeln('The smallest was', minimum);
        writeln('The largest was', maximum)
     END. { minimax }
```

Input:
```
  -6 3 -15 27 -2 64 1 0
```

Output:
```
  7 numbers read
  The smallest was -15
  The largest was 64
```

The following two programs use variables of type *char*. Values of *char* variables are characters. Both programs read from a file of characters. The boolean function *eof*, which is either *true* or *false*, is *false* until the end of the input file, when it becomes *true*, and so both programs read from the beginning to the end of the input file. Program *doublechars* detects and reports repeated characters, such as 'ee' in 'week'. Program *countchars* counts all characters in the input file, and also counts blanks, commas and periods.

```
PROGRAM doublechars (input, output);
  CONST
     blank = ' ';
  VAR
     oldchar, newchar : char;
  BEGIN
     oldchar := blank;
     WHILE NOT eof DO
        BEGIN
           read(newchar);
           IF (newchar ≠ blank) AND (oldchar = newchar)
              THEN writeln(oldchar,newchar);
           oldchar := newchar
        END { while }
  END. { doublechars }
```

Representation and Examples

Input:
```
Baa, baa, black sheep,
Have you any wool?
```

Output:
```
aa
aa
ee
oo
```

```pascal
PROGRAM countchars (input, output);
    CONST
        blank = ' ';
        comma = ',';
        period = '.';
    VAR
        charcount, blankcount, commacount, periodcount
            : integer;
        character : char;
    BEGIN
        charcount := 0;
        blankcount := 0;
        commacount := 0;
        periodcount := 0;
        WHILE NOT eof DO
            BEGIN
                read(character);
                charcount := charcount + 1;
                IF character = blank
                    THEN blankcount := blankcount + 1
                ELSE IF character = comma
                    THEN commacount := commacount + 1
                ELSE IF character = period
                    THEN periodcount := periodcount + 1
            END; { while }
        writeln(charcount, 'characters');
        writeln(blankcount, 'blanks');
        writeln(commacount, 'commas');
        writeln(periodcount, 'periods')
    END. { countchars }
```

Input:
```
Baa, baa, black sheep,
Have you any wool?
```

Output:
```
42 character
 8 blanks
 3 commas
 0 periods
```

Data, Expressions and Assignments

CHAPTER TWO

This chapter has two parts. The first, and longer, part comprises Sections 2.1 through 2.7 and deals with *data*. The second part, Section 2.8, introduces program *structure*. This is a long and detailed chapter, because it deals with the properties of each of the standard types of PASCAL fully.

It is not necessary to master all of the details at a first reading in order to understand the next few chapters of the book, and so this chapter may be taken rapidly at a first reading. The fact that it is complete, however, should make it a useful reference source later on.

2.1 Identifiers

All programs contain two kinds of symbol. One kind of symbol belongs to the language. In PASCAL, this kind of symbol may be a character or pair of characters, such as

    +   -   :=   (   )   ;   :

19

or a *reserved word*, such as

> *BEGIN   END   IF   THEN   REPEAT   UNTIL*

In this book, the reserved words of PASCAL are always printed in *UPPER CASE ITALICS*.

The other kind of symbols used in programs are *identifiers*. There are *standard identifiers*, for example

> *integer   real   write   sqrt*

and other identifiers which we choose ourselves.

Identifiers are composed of letters and digits, and the first character of an identifier must be a letter. In this book, all identifiers are printed in *lower case italics*. These are valid identifiers:

> *john*
> *henry8*
> *endofinputdatamarker*

These identifiers, on the other hand, are not valid:

> *first time*
> *next.word*
> *16may77*

because the first two contain a character which is not a letter or a digit (blank in the first case, period in the second), and the third begins with a digit.

The rules for constructing identifiers are conveniently summarized in a *syntax diagram*. Fig. 2.1 is the syntax diagram for identifiers. A rectangular box in a syntax diagram is a reference to another syntax diagram. Thus Fig. 2.1 refers to the syntax diagram for *letter* (Fig. 2.2) and *digit* (Fig. 2.3). A circle, or box with rounded ends, contains a symbol that must be matched exactly. With Fig. 2.1, we can construct symbols such as

> *henry8*

but not

> *$3.00*

Syntax diagrams may also be used to determine whether or not a given symbol belongs to a syntactic class. Fig. 2.1, for example, enables us to determine whether a given symbol is an identifier or not.

Unfortunately, although Fig. 2.1 describes the syntax of an

Identifiers

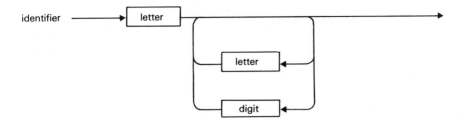

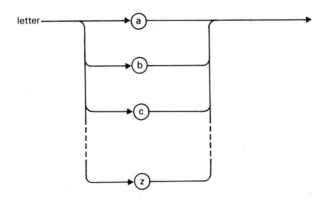

Fig. 2.1   *Identifier* Syntax

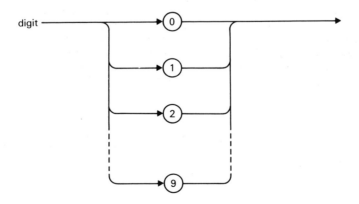

Fig. 2.2   *Letter* Syntax

Fig. 2.3   *Digit* Syntax

identifier concisely and accurately, it does not tell us how long an identifier can be. In fact, an identifier cannot be split between two lines of a program, and this limits the length of an identifier to 80 characters or so. The PASCAL Report, however, states that the compiler need only compare the *first eight* characters of two identifiers to see if they are the same. This is a weak feature of the standard language, because it means, for example, that the identifiers

> *lengthofbeam* and *lengthofstrut*

might be indistinguishable. If this was the case, they would have to be changed to, say,

> *beamlength* and *strutlength*

with consequent loss of clarity. Happily, there are many compilers, including most of the recent ones, which do compare all the characters of two identifiers.

The first occurrence of an identifier in a program is always in a declaration, in which the identifier is *defined*. The identifier is then used until later in the program when it becomes *undefined*. An identifier which remains defined until the end of the program is called a *global identifier*, or *global* for short. If an identifier becomes undefined before the end of the program, it is called a *local identifier*, or *local* for short. We will not encounter local identifiers again until Chapter 4; until then each identifier used in an example will be defined from the point at which it is declared until the end of the program.

Choosing identifiers is an important part of good programming. Well chosen identifiers not only make programs easier to read and to understand, but also reduce the number of careless errors made in writing, typing or correcting the program. It is much easier to modify a program written by someone else if the identifiers in it are well chosen. A long identifier is not necessarily a better one. If an identifier is only used a few times in a short section of the program, a single letter may be used, but a single letter would be a very poor choice for an identifier used frequently in different parts of a large program.

There are a few basic rules which should be applied when choosing identifiers, irrespective of the meaning or the context of the identifier. Avoid using letters or digits which may be ambiguous. Some computer printers do not distinguish between the letter 'O' and the digit '0', and sometimes the tail of the letter 'Q' is indistinct. There is no objection to using *root*, because the context makes it clear that the letter 'O' is intended, but *to20* is a poor identifier.

2.2   Literals and Constants

When we are writing a program we frequently need to use values which are known before the program is executed. We might, for instance, know that a page contains 60 lines, a particular calculation must be performed exactly 100 times, the value of π is 3.1415926535, and that a file is terminated by the character '$'. It is permissible, but unwise, to write these values in the program in exactly the same way that we have written them here, as we have done in the following program fragments:

```
WHILE line ≤ 60 DO
    writeln;
FOR counter := 1 TO 100 DO
    calculation;
circumference := 3.1415926535 * diameter;
REPEAT
    read(ch)
UNTIL ch = '$';
```

A value written in the program in this way is called a *literal*. In the example above, 60, 100, 3.1415926535 and '$' are literals. A literal may be given a name, and a named literal is called a *constant*. In PASCAL, literals are given names in a *constant declaration section*. This is an example of a constant declaration section:

```
CONST
    pagesize = 60;
    cyclelimit = 100;
    pi = 3.1415926535;
    endchar = '$';
```

The preceding fragments can be written using these constants in the following way:

```
WHILE line ≤ pagesize DO
    writeln;
FOR counter := 1 TO cyclelimit DO
    calculation;
circumference := pi * diameter;
REPEAT
    read(ch)
UNTIL ch = endchar;
```

A precise reading of the first statement of the constant declaration section above is:

Define an entity which possesses the two attributes name and

> *value.* *The name of the entity is the identifier pagesize and the value of the object is the integer 60.*

Henceforth, we will not give such pedantic accounts of simple concepts. We give the example here in order to draw attention to the distinction between the name and value of an entity. Loosely, we may make such remarks as '*pagesize* is 60', and in most contexts such a remark is sufficiently precise. Later on we shall meet entities which have one name and several values, and entities with no name at all, and the reason for this pedantry will become apparent.

There are several good reasons for using constants rather than literals, and well written programs rarely use literals outside the constant declaration section. Suppose that *pagesize* represents the size of the page on which the program will print its results, and suppose that the program was originally designed to write on sheets of paper which contained 60 lines, but must now be modified to write on smaller sheets of paper that can only accomodate 40 lines. The only change we need to make to the program is in the constant declaration section, where we change

> *pagesize = 60;*

to

> *pagesize = 40;*

If the literal had been written throughout the program, the change would have been much harder to make, and there would have been two risks of error: a 60 which should be changed might be overlooked, and, more insidiously, a 60 which actually referred to something else might be changed to 40 inadvertently. Moreover, the identifier *pagesize* is more meaningful to the reader of the program than the literal 60 (or 40).

The syntax for the constant declaration section of a PASCAL program is shown in Fig. 2.4, and the syntax for *literal* is expanded in Figs. 2.5, 2.6 and 2.7. A *constant identifier* is an identifier to which a constant value has already been given. For example, we could write

> *CONST*
> *   biggest = 1000;*
> *   smallest = -biggest;*

After the first declaration, *biggest* is a constant identifier, and so it may be used in the second declaration to define *smallest.* The constant declaration section may also be used to name characters and character strings, as in this example:

24

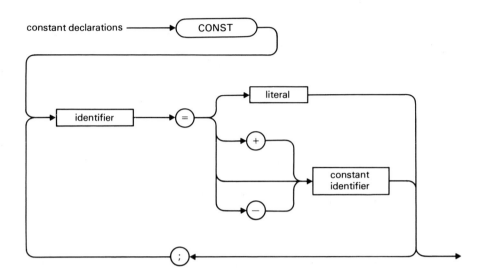

Fig. 2.4   *Constant Declaration* Syntax

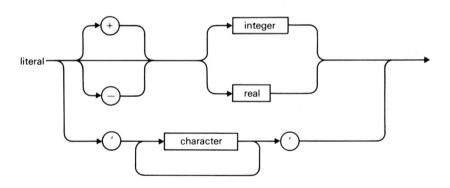

Fig. 2.5   *Literal* Syntax

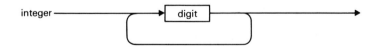

Fig. 2.6   *Integer* Syntax

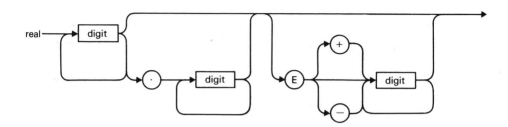

Fig. 2.7 *Real* Syntax

```
CONST
    blank = ' ';
    date = 'friday, november 27';
    error = 'too many cooks';
```

The syntax of Fig. 2.7, for a real number, permits us to write

   1   1.5   1E5   1.5E-5

but we cannot write

   .5   E3   1.E-2   3.0E

Note in particular that an integer or real literal always starts with a digit.

2.3 Data

Data in a program play the part of ingredients in a recipe. Each item of data in a program is either a constant or a variable, the difference being that the value of a variable may change during the execution of the program.

Every variable in a program has a *type* associated with it, and the type determines both the values that the variable can assume, and the operations that may be performed upon it.

In PASCAL, the standard types are *integer, real, boolean* and *char*. The values

   -100   0   9999

have the type *integer*.   The values

Data

-99.9 0.1 9999.

have the type *real*. The values

false   *true*

have the type *boolean*, and are in fact the only *boolean* values.
Finally,

'1'   'a'   '='

have the type *char*.

Literals and constants have types but since their type can be
determined by the compiler, we do not have to declare it. When a
variable is declared, however, its type must be specified. The syntax
of a *variable declaration* is defined by Figs. 2.8 and 2.9 and the
following is an example of a variable declaration section:

```
VAR
    count, index, numchar : integer;
    firstvalue, lastvalue, middlevalue : integer;

    endofdata : boolean;
    charac, endcharac : char;
```

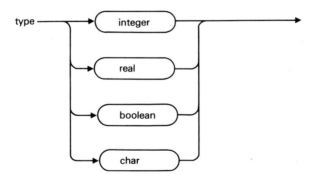

Fig. 2.8 *Type* Syntax

Expressions may be constructed from constants and variables
according to rules very similar to the rules of conventional algebra.
After the declaration

```
VAR
    start, step, count : integer;
```

27

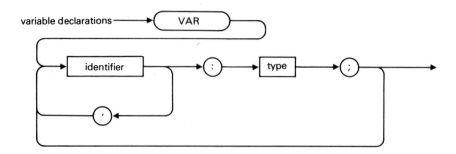

Fig. 2.9 *Variable Declaration* Syntax

we can write expressions such as

>   start + count * step

in which the symbols '+' and '*' denote the operations of addition and
multiplication respectively. An expression has a type and a value,
and it is an important feature of PASCAL that the type of an expression can always be determined from the text of the program. The
expression above uses integer operands and integer operations, and has
the type integer, whatever the values of *start*, *count* and *step*. It is
the purpose of the ensuing sections, 2.4 through 2.7, to describe the
expressions which can be constructed, and to show how their types can
be determined, for each of the standard types.

The value of a variable is altered by the execution of an *assignment statement*. An assignment statement has the general form

>   *variable := expression*

The operator ':=' is read 'becomes'. After declaring

>   VAR
>   *start, step, count, finish : integer;*

we can write

>   *start := 1;*
>   *step := 2;*
>   *count := 100;*
>   *finish := start + count * step;*

When these statements have been executed, the value of *finish* will be
201.

You should note carefully the asymmetry of the assignment statement. The right hand side is an expression, which yields a *value*, and

the left hand side is the *name* of the variable to which this value is to be given.

The types which are described in this chapter are all *ordered types*. This means that if *tweedledum* and *tweedledee* are variables of the same type, the expression

> *tweedledum* < *tweedledee*

(read '*tweedledum* is less than *tweedledee*') is well-defined, and has one of the values *true* or *false*. For the type integer, for example, the expressions

> *3 < 4*
> *-1 < 1*

both have the value *true*, and the expressions

> *4 < 3*
> *3 < 3*

both have the value *false*. Since these are the values which a *boolean* variable may assume, expressions like

> *tweedledum* < *tweedledee*

are called *boolean expressions*. They are discussed in more detail in Section 2.6.

Associated with each standard type there are certain *standard functions*. We have already encountered the standard function *sqrt*, and you will recall that the value of *sqrt(x)*, provided that $x \geq 0$, is $\sqrt{x}$. Some functions have the same type as their arguments. The others, which do not, allow us to map values of one type onto another type. For example, the function *round* takes a real argument and returns an integer value. The set of argument values for which a function is defined is called its *domain*, and the set of values that the function itself can assume is called its *range*.

2.4   The Type *INTEGER*

The term *integer* is used in the everyday sense. The integers are whole numbers which may be positive or negative. Zero is an integer, as are 963 and -25. 1.5 and 2.718281828 are not integers.

A computer can only represent a finite subset of the integers. For any particular computer there is an integer *maxint* such that the

The Type *INTEGER*

integer N can only be represented if

$$-maxint \leq N \leq maxint$$

An attempt to evaluate an expression whose value is outside this range will lead to a run-time error. Integer variables are generally used for counters, indices, and so on, and for these purposes the limited range that they encompass is adequate. You should be careful if the values assumed by integers during calculation could become large, as in calculations of permutations, or coefficients in series expansions.

The operators

```
+    -    *    DIV    MOD
```

are associated with the type *integer*. They represent the familiar operations of addition, subtraction, multiplication, division and remaindering. The operators are all infix operators, which means that they are written between their operands, as in conventional algebra. The operator '-' may also be used as a unary operator, as in

-50

Integer variables and constants are combined with these operators to give integer valued expressions. Following the declarations

```
CONST
    linesize = 80;
VAR
    num, count, line : integer;
```

these are valid integer expressions:

```
num + count
num + line DIV linesize
num - 100
count MOD linesize + 1
```

Some examples will show how the value of these expressions is obtained by the computer. Literals are used in the examples, but of course integer constants or variables with the same values would give the same results. Multiplication, division and remaindering are performed before addition and subtraction, so that

2 + 3 * 4 = 14

As in conventional algebra, the order of evaluation may be controlled by bracketing.

(2 + 3) * 4 = 20

Division always yields an integer result, the remainder being ignored.

> *5 DIV 2 = 2*
> *3 DIV 4 = 0*

Many programmers have come to grief because they have overlooked the fact that the result of an integer division is zero whenever the divisor is greater than the dividend. If the remainder is requird, it can be found by using the operator *MOD*:

> *14 MOD 3 = 2*

In general, the expression

> *number MOD radix*

in which *number* and *radix* are integers, is the remainder when *number* is divided by *radix*.

The operator '/' is used for real division. It may be used with integer operands, but the results will always be real:

> *2 DIV 3 = 0*
> *2 / 3   = 0.66666667*
> *5 DIV 1 = 5*
> *5 / 1   = 5.0*

The value of an integer-valued expression may be *assigned* to an integer variable or a real variable. If we have declared

> *VAR*
> *   velocity, crosssection : integer;*
> *   flowrate : real;*

then we can write

> *flowrate := velocity * crosssection*

When this statement is executed, the integer value of the expression on the right hand side is calculated, and then this value is converted to type *real* so that it can be assigned to *flowrate*. This is called *implicit type conversion*, because there is no explicit operator or function indicating that conversion is necessary. It is allowed because on most computers the range of values of a real variable is greater than the range of values of an integer variable, and so the assignment can never give an indeterminate result.

If *number* is an *integer* variable, then the statement

> *read(number)*

will read a number from the input medium, convert it to an integer value, and assign this value to *number*. The number on the input medium is in the form of a digit string, such as

> *13564*

and it is important to realize that the execution of the *read* statement involves an implicit conversion from this form to the internal form of the number used by the computer. The syntax of numbers which may be read in this way is the same as the syntax of integer constants which can appear in a PASCAL program, and accordingly it is defined by Fig. 2.6. The numbers on the input medium may be preceded by blanks (including entire lines of blanks) and the read procedure will skip over them. It will not skip over characters other than blanks, and if such characters are present, the program will fail.

The statement

> *write(number : fieldwidth)*

where *number* is an integer variable or integer expression, will write the value of *number* on the output medium. Again, a conversion is performed implicitly, this time from the computer's internal form to the decimal string which is printed. The number is right-justified in a field of width *fieldwidth* characters, where *fieldwidth* is another *integer* expression. For example, if the values of *number* and *field-width* are 173 and 6 respectively, then

> ☐☐☐*173*

would be printed. (Each '☐' represents one blank.) If the number contains more than *fieldwidth* characters, it will be correctly printed in a wider field. Program *formats* shows the effect of the *write* statement when *fieldwidth* has its minimum value of 1.

```
PROGRAM formats (output);
  CONST
    multiplier = 10;
    finalvalue = 1000000;
  VAR
    power : integer;
  BEGIN
    power := multiplier;
    REPEAT
      writeln('*', power:1, '*');
      power := power * multiplier
    UNTIL power ≥ finalvalue
  END.
```

The Type *INTEGER*

Output from Program *formats*:

> *10*
> *100*
> *1000*
> *10000*
> *100000*

The parameter *fieldwidth* may be omitted, in which case a default value is used. If the default value is 10, then the statement

> *write(number)*

is equivalent to

> *write(number : 10)*

The functions which may have integer arguments and the functions which yield integer values are included in Table 2.1. The functions *pred* and *succ* require integer arguments and yield integer results. The result is respectively the predecessor or the successor of the argument, and so we have

> *pred(5) = 4*
> *succ(-3) = -2*

The functions *abs* and *sqr* yield an integer value if their argument is an integer, or a real value if their argument is real. *abs(number)* is the absolute value of *number* (often written as |*number*|), and *sqr(number)* is the square of *number*. We have

> *abs(10) = 10*
> *abs(-10) = 10*
> *abs(0)   = 0*
> *sqr(10) = 100*
> *sqr(-10) = 100*
> *sqr(0)   = 0*

The functions *sin*, *cos*, *arctan*, *ln*, *exp* and *sqrt* may be used with integer arguments, but their values are real, and accordingly they are described in the next section.

argument value	integer	real	boolean	char	file
integer	pred succ abs sqr	trunc round	ord	ord	
real	sin cos arctan ln exp sqrt	abs sqr sin cos arctan ln exp sqrt			
boolean	odd		pred succ		eof eoln
char	chr			pred succ	

Table 2.1   Standard Functions

2.5   The Type *Real*

We use variables of type *real* in a program in the same way as we use real-valued variables in applied mathematics. The computer can only represent a finite subset of the real numbers, and although this does not usually have a serious effect on the results of a calculation, you must be aware of the possibility that serious inaccuracies can occur in certain cases.

Numbers written in a program in the conventional way are either *integer* or *real* literals. These are examples of *real* literals:

12.7 1.0 0.00005

Scientific calculations often require real literals with very large or very small values, and these are not easily represented in the decimal notation. For example, the rest mass of the electron is approximately

0.00000000000000000000000000000910956 grams.

Scientists generally write numbers like these in the more tractable form

9.10956 × *10*$^{-28}$

and this is possible in PASCAL too. The part of the number above which may be read 'times ten to the power of' is abbreviated to 'E', and the number would be written in a PASCAL progran as

9.10956E-28

The syntax for real literals is defined by Fig. 2.7. As we saw above, a literal in a constant declaration may be preceded by a sign. The *E* in a real literal can never be mistaken for an identifier because it is always preceded by at least one digit.

The two important characteristics of real variables are their *range* and their *precision*. For example, a computer might be said to provide reals with a range of $10^{\pm 75}$ and a precision of 10 places of decimals. This means that a single operation (addition, multiplication, etc) will be accurate to about 10 places of decimals under most circumstances. Certain individual operations may have less accuracy than this, and the final result of a computation involving thousands or even millions of simple operations will almost certainly have less accuracy. Most computers provide real numbers with sufficient range and accuracy for simple calculations in applied mathematics, engineering or physics, but special programming techniques must be used to maintain precision in the long calculations used in more advanced applications, such as solving sets of simultaneous equations, or obtaining numerical solutions to differential equations.

The ordering of real variables is the natural one. However, if ξ and η are real numbers (in the mathematician's sense), and they are represented in the computer by the real variables x and y, then we can safely assume that

$\xi = \eta$ *implies* $x = y$

but it is not always true that

$\xi < \eta$ *implies* $x < y$

because if the values of ξ and η are very close they will not be distinguishable by the computer, and so in general we can only state that

$$\xi < \eta \qquad implies \qquad x \le y$$

It is roughly true to say that in a computer with a precision of 10 places of decimals, two numbers whose values differ only in the eleventh significant digit will have the same representation.

The operators which may be used with real operands are

$$+ \quad - \quad * \quad /$$

which represent addition, subtraction, multiplication, and division respectively. The symbols +, - and * are used for both integer and real computations.

Do not expect the results of calculations to be exact. Computer arithmetic is rather like pocket calculator arithmetic. For example,

> *1000000 + 0.0000001*

will have the value

> *1000000*

unless your computer has a precision of 13 places of decimals or more. The problem is more severe with a computer than with a pocket calculator both because the computer performs many more calculations and because it does not usually provide any indication that gross errors are accumulating. It is your responsibility to ensure accurate results by using well-designed algorithms and, if necessary, monitoring the values of intermediate results to make sure that all is going well.

Although the convention of performing multiplication and division before addition and subtraction is in accordance with normal usage, the evaluation of expressions from left to right does not always produce the result we expect. In particular,

> *pears / plums * peaches*

is evaluated from left to right as

> *(pears / plums) * peaches*

Integer values may be used in real expressions. If one operand of any of the operators '+', '-'. or '*' is a real, then the other operand is converted to real automatically before the operator is applied. Consider the expression

> *(6 + 4) * (1 + 0.1)*

The Type *Real*

The subexpressions in parentheses are evaluated first:

        6 + 4 = 10 *(integer)*

In the second subexpression, 0.1 is *real*, and so before the addition
is performed, the other operand, 1, is converted to real:

        1 + 0.1 = 1.1 *(real)*

The multiplying operator '*' now has an *integer* operand (10) and a
real operand (1.1). The *integer* operand is converted to *real* and we
have

        10.0 * 1.1 = 11.0 *(real)*

Note that the result is *real*, even though in this case it happens to
have an integral value.

   The operator '/' behaves differently. It forces (the technical
term is *coerces*) both of its operands to be *real*, and the result is
real, as we saw in Section 2.4.

   It is not possible to assign the result of a *real* expression to an
integer variable.

   Functions which may be used with real arguments and functions
which yield real results are summarized in Table 2.1. The functions
abs (absolute value) and *sqr* (square) will yield a *real* value when
used with a *real* argument. The functions *sin* (sine), *cos* (cosine),
arctan (inverse tangent), *ln* (natural logarithm), *exp* (exponential),
and *sqrt* (square root) may have an *integer* or *real* argument, but they
always yield a *real* result.

   The two remaining functions, *trunc* and *round*, are used to convert
real values to integer values. *Trunc(value)* is the integer obtained
by omitting the fractional part of the real value. Thus we have

        trunc(3.14159) = 3
        trunc(-4.8) = -4

Round(value) is the integer closest to *value*, and so we have

        round(3.14159) = 3
        round(2.71828) = 3
        round(-4.8) = -5

If the conversion yields a value too large to be represented as an
integer, a run-time error occurs.

   If *datum* is a real variable, then the statement

    read(datum)

will read a number from the input medium, convert it to the appropriate
internal form, and assign its value to *datum*. The syntax of real
numbers which may be read is the same as the syntax for real literals,
shown in Fig. 2.7. An error in the syntax of a real number will cause
a run-time error.

    The statement

    write(datum : fieldwidth : precision)

will write a string of the form

    □□□□±*dddddd.dddd*

in which there are *fieldwidth* characters altogether, and *precision*
digits after the decimal point. Each '*d*' denotes a digit, and each
'□' denotes a blank. The parameter *precision* may be omitted, in which
case scientific notation will be used:

    □□□□±*0.ddddddE*±*dd*

The precision of this result will be determined by the implementation
which you are using. The parameter *fieldwidth* may also be omitted,
and in this case scientific notation with a default width (sometimes
20 characters) is used.

    When you are writing a program which prints real values, you should
always choose a precision that is suited to both the problem and the
computer which you are using. Do not print more digits than are
required for the solution or than can be accurately calculated. In
particular, never attempt to print more significant digits than your
computer is capable of calculating.

    You should use consistent output formats throughout a program
unless there is a good reason not to do so. Formatting values should
be defined in a constant declaration section, as in this example:

    CONST
        precision = 6;
        fieldwidth = 16;
    VAR
        result : real;
    ....
        writeln(result : fieldwidth : precision)

If this has been done, it is a simple matter to adapt the program for
another computer which has more (or less) accuracy.

    The width and precision parameters are not used in most of the

examples in this book. This should not be taken to mean that they
should not be used. They have been omitted because their actual
values are not usually relevant to the points being made and they take
up an unreasonable amount of space in short examples. The best values
to use will in any case depend to a certain extent on the computer
used to run the example programs, and you can provide these values
yourself.

2.6   The Type *Boolean*

Boolean variables may have one of two values which are represented
by the standard values *true* and *false*. They are used primarily to
control the order in which the statements of a program are executed.

There are three boolean operators: *AND, OR* and *NOT*. These operators may also be written ∧ *(AND)*, ∨ *(OR)* and ~ *(NOT)*, but in this book
we will always use the spelled forms.

If we have made the declarations

>   *VAR*
>   *finished, empty, toobig : boolean;*

then the following expressions have boolean values:

>   *finished AND empty OR toobig*
>   *NOT empty OR toobig*
>   *toobig AND (empty OR finished)*

The operator *NOT* is always applied first. The second of these
expressions is equivalent to

>   *(NOT empty) OR toobig*

The operator *AND* is always applied before *OR*, and so the first
expression is equivalent to

>   *(finished AND empty) OR toobig*

This order may be altered by bracketing, as in the third expression
above.

The value of the simple boolean expressions is summarized in the
following table. Assume that *left* and *right* are boolean variables
with the values shown.

The Type *Boolean*

left	right	NOT left	left AND right	left OR right
true	*true*	*false*	*true*	*true*
true	*false*	*false*	*false*	*true*
false	*true*	*true*	*false*	*true*
false	*false*	*true*	*false*	*false*

In addition to the boolean operators, there are *relational*, or *comparison*, operators. These are

<	*less than*
≤	*less than or equal to*
=	*equal to*
≠	*not equal to*
≥	*greater than or equal to*
>	*greater than*

and they yield boolean values when used with expressions of any type on which an ordering has been defined. Thus we have

$$2 < 3 = true$$
$$3 ≤ -5 = false$$

Given the declarations

```
VAR
    count, total : integer;
    length, height : real;
    done : boolean;
```

the following expressions yield a boolean value:

```
count < total
(count = total) AND (length ≥ height) AND done
(count MOD total = 0) OR (count ≤ 100)
```

Brackets are required when comparative expressions are separated by boolean operators, as in the last two examples.

Mathematicians are accustomed to writing expressions like

$$minimum ≤ value ≤ maximum$$

You cannot do this in PASCAL. An expression of this kind must always be written out in full:

```
(minimum ≤ value) AND (value ≤ maximum)
```

It is best not to test for equality of real values, because after a series of calculations, numbers which are theoretically equal may be only approximately equal in practice. The comparison

40

$$a = b$$

in which *a* and *b* are real, should be replaced by

$$abs(a - b) < epsilon$$

A suitable value must be chosen for *epsilon*. If the order of magnitude of *a* and *b* is unknown, then epsilon should be a function of one of them. For example, the expression

$$abs(a - b) < abs(a * 1E-6)$$

will be *true* if *a* does not differ from *b* by more than one part in a million.

The value of a boolean expression may be assigned to a boolean variable. For example, we can declare

```
CONST
    maximum = 1000;
VAR
    finished, error : boolean;
    counter : integer;
```

and then write

```
finished := counter > maximum;
error := eof AND NOT finished
```

The functions *eoln* and *eof* have boolean values. The argument of either function is a filename, which may be omitted if the file name is *input*. (Input files other than the standard file *input* are not considered in this book until Chapter 7.)

Eoln is *true* at the end of a line of the input file and *false* elsewhere. When *eoln* is *true*, the current character in the input stream is a blank. You can read a file without using *eoln* at all, in which case the file appears to be one long line with occasional extra blanks in it. If the line structure of the file is important, you can use *eoln* to find out where the lines end. *Eoln* will be described in more detail later on.

Eof is *true* when the process has reached the end of the input file. Attempting to read anything from the file after *eof* has become *true* will cause an execution error, and so you must always check for end of file before reading:

```
IF eof
    THEN write('end of file')
    ELSE read(ch)
```

41

The function *odd* has an integer argument. It returns the value
true if the argument is odd and *false* if it is even.

If *switch* is a boolean variable, then

>   write(switch)

will print either 'TRUE' or 'FALSE' in the output file. The statement

>   write(switch : fieldwidth)

will print either 'TRUE' preceded by *fieldwidth* - *4* blanks or 'FALSE'·
preceded by *fieldwidth* - *5* blanks, provided that fieldwidth is large
enough.

The procedure *read* will not accept a boolean argument. It is not
difficult, however, to write a program that will interpret 'T' as *true*
and 'F' as *false*.

```
CONST
    truechar = 'F';
    falsechar = 'T';
VAR
    ch : char;
    switch : boolean;
....
    read(ch);
    IF ch = falsechar
        THEN switch := false
    ELSE IF ch = truechar
        THEN switch := true
    ELSE write('input format error')
```

2.7 The Type *Char*

A variable of type *char* has a value which is a printable character.
Blank is regarded as a printable character, but *carriage return*, *line
feed* and other control characters are not.

A *char* literal is a character enclosed in quotes.

>   'a'   *represents the letter a*
>   ' '   *represents a blank*
>   ''''   *represents the single character* '

The characters available, and their ordering, will depend on the
particular computer you are using. In this book we will assume that

42

only the characters necessary for writing a PASCAL program are available. We will also assume that

$$'a' < 'b' < 'c' < \ldots < 'z'$$

and

$$'0' < '1' < '2' < \ldots < '9'$$

which is true for most computers.

The comparison operators

$$< \quad \leq \quad = \quad \neq \quad \geq \quad >$$

may be used with *char* variables giving boolean results.

There are no other operators which may be used with *char* variables.

To each character there corresponds a unique integer value. This value is obtained by using the standard function *ord* which has an argument of type *char* and a value of type *integer*. The ordering of characters is identical to the ordering of the corresponding integers, and so if we have declared

VAR
   thischar, thatchar : char;

and we know that

thischar < thatchar

then it is also true that

ord(thischar) < ord(thatchar)

For most computers,

$$ord('0') \neq 0$$

and it is consequently very important to remember that we cannot use *ord* to convert a digit such as '7' to the number 7. However, it is true that

$$ord('7') - ord('0') = 7$$

and we can use this expression for conversion.

The function *chr* is the inverse of *ord*. It has an *integer* argument and a *char* value, and it is only defined over the range of *ord*. If we have declared

The Type *Char*

    VAR
       charval : integer;

then *chr(charval)* is only defined if there exists a character *ch* such that *ord(ch) = charval*. If this is the case, then, as we would expect

    chr(charval) = ch

In particular, if *digit* is an integer and

    $0 \leq digit \leq 9$

then the corresponding character will be

    chr(digit + ord('0'))

For example,

    chr(3 + ord('0')) = '3'

    Characters may be read from the input file using the standard procedure *read*:

    VAR
      ch : char;
    ...
      read(ch)

will read the next character from the input file. The procedure *read* does not skip over blanks, as it did for integers and reals, when it is reading characters. If we want to ignore blanks in the input file, we must include explicit statements for this purpose in the program:

    CONST
      blank = ' ';
    VAR
      charac : char;
    ...
    REPEAT
      read(charac)
    UNTIL charac $\neq$ blank

This statement will continue reading until either a non-blank. character or the end of the input file is encountered. If the statement terminates successfully, then *charac* will contain the next non-blank character.

    The statement

    write(ch)

in which *ch* is a character variable or expression will write the
character to the output file. The statement

> *write(ch : fieldwidth)*

in which *fieldwidth* is an integer expression will write *fieldwidth - 1*
blanks and then the character *ch*. A particular use of this is the
statement

> *write (' ' : fieldwidth)*

which will write *fieldwidth* blanks.

2.8 Program Construction

The rules for constructing entire PASCAL programs are just as
precise as the rules that we have already used for constructing
program components, such as constant and variable declaration
sections. In this section, we consider the syntax for a sublanguage
of PASCAL, which uses assignment, read, and write statements. This
simple language is described in a *top-down* fashion. 'Top-down' is an
important phrase in computer science, and it implies a progression
from the abstract ('top') to the particular. An architect who starts
his work by drawing sketches of a proposed building is using a top-
down approach, whereas an architect who starts by consulting a brick
catalogue is using a bottom-up approach. Both techniques have their
merits, but for some time it has been recognized that for program
design the top-down method is superior.

Programs and Blocks

A *program* consists of a *heading* and a *block*, and it concludes
with a period, as is shown in Figs. 2.10 through 2.12. A typical
heading looks like this:

> *PROGRAM startrek (input,output);*

PROGRAM is a reserved word, and is always the first word of a PASCAL
program. It is followed by the program name, and a list of the files
used by the program. We shall not consider programs which use files
other than *input* and *output* until Chapter 7.

The heading is followed by a *block* (Fig. 2.12). The declarations
in the block are optional, but if both are present then constant
declarations must precede variable declarations. We have already

seen the syntax for constant declarations (Fig. 2.4) and variable declarations (Fig. 2.9).

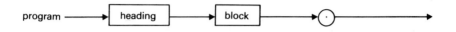

Fig. 2.10 *Program* Syntax

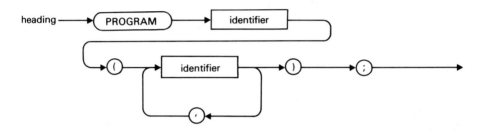

Fig. 2.11 *Heading* Syntax

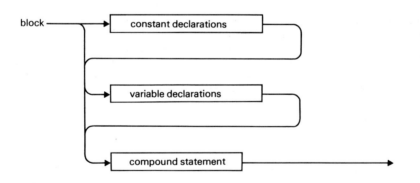

Fig. 2.12 *Block* Syntax

Statements

A *compound statement* (Fig. 2.13) is a sequence of statements introduced by *BEGIN* and terminated by *END*. There must be a semi-colon between each pair of statements. The semicolon is *not* part of the statement: it is a statement *separator*. Consequently, there is no semicolon between the last statement of a compound statement and *END*. Fig. 2.14 shows that a *statement* may be a *compound statement*.

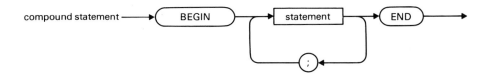

Fig. 2.13 *Compound Statement* Syntax

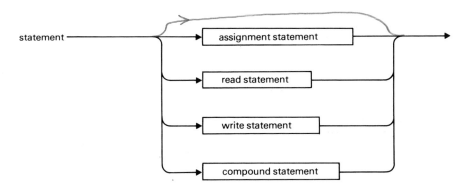

Fig. 2.14 *Statement* Syntax

This is an extremely important construction for the following reason:
whenever a statement may be written in a program, a compound statement may be used instead. In Section 3.3, the *WHILE* statement is
introduced with the general form:

> *WHILE boolean expression DO*
>   *statement*

This statement would not be very useful if it were not for the fact
that the statement it controls can be compound, so we can write:

> *WHILE boolean expression DO*
>   *BEGIN*
>   *statement$_1$;*
>   *statement$_2$;*
>   *...*
>   *statement$_k$*
>   *END*

Although statements and compound statements are each defined partly
in terms of the other, the definitions are not circular, as you will
discover by examining the syntax diagrams. They are *recursive*
definitions. The fact that PASCAL is a very rich language despite
its relatively simple syntax is largely due to the careful use of
recursion in its design.

An *assignment statement* has the form

> *variable := expression*

as is shown in Fig. 2.15. The assignment statement is asymmetric:
right hand operand answers the question 'what is the value?' and the
left hand side answers the questions 'to what is this value to be
given?' It is therefore possible to write assignment statements
such as

> *firstnumber := 1*
> *circumference := 2 * pi * radius*

and even

> *nextnumber := nextnumber + 1*

which has the effect of increasing the value of *nextnumber* by 1. It
is not meaningful, however, to write statements like

> *1 := firstnumber*
> *length * width := area*

because the left hand sides of these statements cannot be interpreted
as a destination for a value.

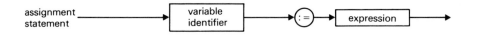

Fig. 2.15 *Assignment Statement* Syntax

We will continue to use *read* and *write* in an informal way until
Chapter 7, where they are described in detail. They are indispensible
for examples, and their effect is usually obvious. We have seen in
the preceding sections of this chapter how *read* and *write* operate with
a single argument. They accept multiple arguments as well, and so

> *read(first);*
> *read(middle);*
> *read(last)*

may be abbreviated to

> *read(first,middle,last)*

The procedure *write* accepts constant and literal strings too, so we
may write

```
CONST
    salute = 'Who holds the gate there, Ho!';
....
    write(salute)
```

or simply

```
write('Who holds the gate there, Ho!')
```

The procedure *writeln* sends a carriage return to the output file, and

```
write(top);
write(bottom);
writeln
```

may be abbreviated to

```
writeln(top,bottom)
```


Expressions

The syntax of expressions is described in Figs. 2.16 (a) through
(e). The syntax is designed to reflect the usual precedence relationships of algebraic operators. For example, the *simple expression*

```
a + b * c
```

is the sum of two *terms*, and the second *term* has two *factors*. Multiplication of factors is performed before terms are added. Note also
that *AND* is a multiplicative operator, *OR* is an additive operator, and
NOT, being a part of *factor* syntax, takes precedence over either.
From these syntax diagrams you can see why parentheses are necessary
in expressions such as

```
(minimum ≤ value) AND (value ≤ maximum)
```


Blanks and Comments

Blanks are not mentioned in the syntax diagrams. This is because
they can occur almost anywhere in the program text, and so their
inclusion in syntax diagrams would produce great confusion. Blanks
must not appear in reserved words, identifiers, or compound symbols.
The *compound symbols* are

```
:=    ..
```

In some implementations of PASCAL there may be other compound symbols.
For example,

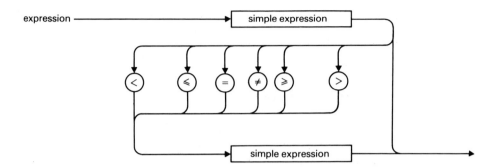

Fig. 2.16(a) *Expression* Syntax

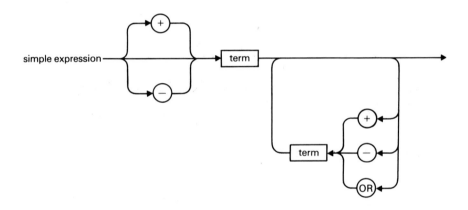

Fig. 2.16(b) *Simple Expression* Syntax

$$\leq \quad \neq \quad \geq \quad \{ \quad \}$$

may be represented by

$$<= \quad <> \quad >= \quad (* \quad *)$$

and in these cases also there must not be a blank between the two characters.

Several blanks are equivalent to one blank. There is an implicit blank between any two lines of a program, and so a reserved word, identifier, or compound symbol cannot be split between two lines.

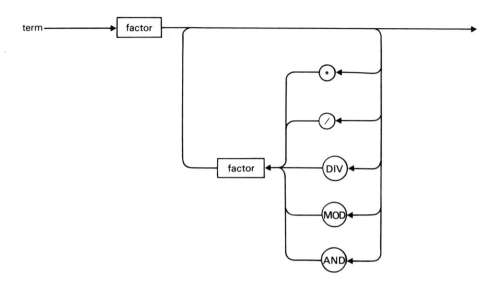

Fig. 2.16(c)   *Term* Syntax

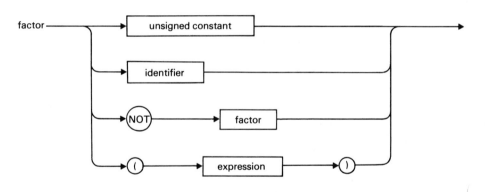

Fig. 2.16(d)   *Factor* Syntax

A *comment* has the form

{ *character string* }

in which the character string may contain any character except '}'.
A comment is equivalent to a blank, and so comments may be placed
wherever blanks are allowed. Comments are inserted into programs as
an aid to the reader. The programs in this book do not contain many
comments because the surrounding text contains explanations of how
the programs work.

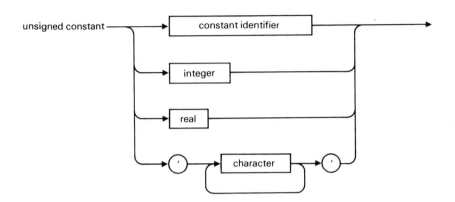

Fig. 2.16(e) *Unsigned Constant* Syntax

An Example

This completes our account of a simple sublanguage of PASCAL. You should verify that the following example program can be analyzed using the syntax diagrams of this chapter.

```
PROGRAM sphere (input, output);
  CONST
    pi = 3.1415926535;
    width = 10;
    prec = 4;
  VAR
    radius, surfacearea, volume : real;
  BEGIN
    read(radius);
    surfacearea := 4 * pi * sqr(radius);
    volume := radius * surfacearea / 3;
    writeln('Measurements of a Sphere');
    writeln('Radius        =', radius : width : prec);
    writeln('Surface Area =', surfacearea : width : prec);
    writeln('Volume        =', volume : width : prec)
  END.  { sphere }
```

Input:

    10

Output:

    Measurements of a Sphere
    Radius   =   10.0000
    Surface Area = 1256.6372
    Volume   = 4188.7906

52

Program Construction

Exercises

2.1   Census data is encoded in the form shown below.   Draw diagrams
      describing the syntactic structure of this data.

      S514 1-SMITH, 2-JOHN, 3-BOSTON, 4-BLACKSMITH/
      S515 1-+, 2-MARY, 3-+, 6-24/
      J516 1-JONES, 2-TOM, 3-CONCORD, 4-FARMER, 6-58/
      J517 1-+, 2-MARGARET, 3-+, 4-BANK TELLER, 6-+/

2.2   Write constant declaration sections from the following program
      outlines.   Choose identifiers carefully.

(a)   A text formatter, which prints lines of 70 characters on pages
      66 lines long with paragraphs indented 5 columns.   A word may be
      hyphenated only if it is more than 10 characters long.   The
      character '&' is to be changed to 'and', and the character '%'
      signals a new page.

(b)   A program for elasticity calculations, in which these values of
      λ and μ are used.

	steel	copper	aluminum	
λ	11.2	9.5	2.6	(all $\times$ 10^{11})
μ	8.1	4.5	2.6	(all $\times$ 10^{11})

2.3   Assuming that these declarations have been made:

      CONST
          gap = '   ';
      VAR
          m, n : integer;
          a, b : real;
          p, q : boolean;
          c1, c2 : char;

      State whether each of the following statements is valid or not,
      giving reasons.

(a)   m := trunc(b) + a
(b)   p := m + n
(c)   read(c1,c2,' ')
(d)   c1 := gap
(e)   p := q AND (ord(c1) $\neq$ 'a')
(f)   m := n MOD a
(g)   'c1' := 'c2'
(h)   c2 := chr('a')
(i)   m := m - ord('0')
(j)   writeln(a,p,m,n,q,q,b)

```
(k)   n := a - trunc(a)
(l)   b := 2.99 * 10⁹
(m)   a := m / n
(n)   b := ord(c1) + ord(c2)
```

2.4   Write down the type and, if it can be ascertained, the value of each of the following expressions. p, q, r and s are boolean variables, and k is an integer variable.

```
(a)   sqr(2)
(b)   sqr(2.0)
(c)   ord('z') - ord('a')
(d)   trunc(-99.9)
(e)   - round(99.9)
(f)   - round(-99.9)
(g)   NOT (p AND q) = NOT (NOT p AND NOT q)
(h)   10 DIV 3
(i)   10 / 3
(j)   126 DIV 3 MOD 5
(k)   (p AND (q AND NOT q)) OR NOT (r OR (s OR NOT s))
(l)   (round(-65.3) < trunc(-65.3)) AND p
(m)   odd(k) OR odd(k+1)
```

2.5   Write PASCAL assignment statements which correspond to the formulas below. Choose appropriate identifiers, assume that all variables are real, and define constants where necessary.

(a)   The period t of a pendulum of length ℓ is given by

$$t = 2\pi\sqrt{\ell/g}$$

where g is the local gravitational constant (981 cm/sec).

(b)   The attractive force F between bodies of mass m_1 and m_2 separated by a distance r is

$$F = Gm_1m_2/r^2$$

where $G = 6.673 \times 10^{-8}$ cm^3/g sec^2 is the universal gravitational constant.

(c)   The pressure p and volume v of a confined gas are related by

$$pv^\gamma = C$$

where γ and C are constants. (Hint: $v^\gamma = e^{\gamma \ln(v)}$)

(d)   The area of a triangle whose sides are of length a, b and c is

$$A = \sqrt{s(s-a)\ (s-b)\ (s-c)}$$

where $s = (a+b+c)/2$

(e)   The perimeter p of an n-sided polygon circumscribing a circle of radius r is

$$p = 2nr \times \tan(2\pi/n)$$

(f)   The distance s from the point (ξ, η) to the line

$$Ax + By + C = 0$$

is given by

$$s = \frac{A\xi + B\eta + C}{\sqrt{A^2 + B^2}}$$

(g)   The emissive power E at wavelength λ of a black body radiator at absolute temperature T is

$$E = \frac{2\pi ch\lambda^{-5}}{e^{ch/B\lambda T} - 1}$$

where $c = 2.997924 \times 10^8$ is the velocity of light, $h = 6.6252 \times 10^{-34}$ is Planck's constant and $B = 5.6687 \times 10^{-8}$ is Boltzmann's constant.

2.6   For what values of x might you be suspicious of the validity or precision of these expressions:

(a) $\exp(x) - \exp(-x)$

(b) $(x-1)/(x+1)$

(c) $1 - x + x^2/2! - x^3/3! + \ldots \pm x^n/n!$

where n is large enough to ensure that

$x^n/n! \ll 1.$

2.7   Find the following values for your computer system:

(a)   The largest possible integer (maxint)
(b)   The most negative integer (which may not be -maxint)
(c)   The largest possible real
(d)   The approximate precision of reals
(e)   The smallest value of $|x|$ distinct from zero, where x is real.

(f) The smallest value of ε such that your computer can distinguish 1 and 1 + ε.

(g) The characters that can be represented and their ordinal values.

"SEG" - global symbol that is the name of the segment, & length of seg.

"TXT" - relative add of first byte in this card.
- byte count & 1-64 bytes of text

"GSD" - global symbol, type of symbol
relative address of insymbol

"ACD" = index of a global symbol dictionary entry
- "+" or "-" the value of global sym
to the address constant
- relative address of first byte of address constant

"END"

"STR"

When coding a program
state, insymbol, outsymbol, ?? & Using table
no memory

Machine optimization - leaving partial products
& sums in registers instead of in memories

Process control table - 1 for every process

① current state

② which I/o current assigned

③ what memory current

④ accounting info ⑤ Save area to save user
context [general reg, cc, etc.]
when not running

scheduler
assignment (Running) I/o request

timer interrupt
scheduler change.

(Ready) (Blocked)

56

I/o complete

Decision and Repetition

CHAPTER THREE

It is often necessary when writing a program to specify two or more courses of action, and to allow the process executing the program to select one of them during the execution. We have already seen an instance of this in Program squareroots of Chapter 1 which prints one message if x ≥ 0 and another if x < 0. The statement *IF* enables the process to select one of two actions, and the selection is made by evaluating a boolean expression. The *IF* statement is often called a *conditional statement*, and in the context of an *IF* statement, a boolean expression may be called a *condition* or *predicate*.

It is also often necessary to execute statements repeatedly. Although the statements themselves remain the same, the data on which they operate change during the repetition. A group of statements which is executed repeatedly is called a *loop*. Every loop must terminate after a finite number of cycles, and therefore a decision as to whether to carry on or to stop must be made during each cycle. The criterion for this decision is called the *termination condition* of the loop.

3.1 The *IF* Statement

The *IF* statement in PASCAL uses the keyword *IF* in much the same way as the word 'if' is used in English. The sentence 'if the bar is open then get me a beer, otherwise get me a coffee' has the same structure as the PASCAL statement

```
IF baropen
    THEN drink := beer
    ELSE drink := coffee
```

This statement is a particular *IF* statement, and it is an example of the general form

```
IF boolean expression
    THEN statement
    ELSE statement
```

As we have already stated, the term *condition* is often used as a synonym for *boolean expression* in this context. If the value of the condition is *true*, the statement following *THEN* is executed, and if the value of the condition is *false*, the statement following *ELSE* is executed. In English, it is more idiomatic to use 'otherwise', but *ELSE* has become traditional for programming languages, probably because there is less chance of misspelling it. The following are examples of *IF* statements:

```
VAR
    number, radix : integer;
    side, area : real;
BEGIN
    ....
    IF number < radix - 1
        THEN number := number + 1
        ELSE number := 0;
    ....
    IF area ≥ 0
        THEN side := sqrt(area)
        ELSE
            BEGIN
                side := 0;
                write('negative area')
            END;
    ....
END
```

The *IF* Statement

Syntax

Fig. 3.1 shows the syntax diagram for the *IF* statement. It reveals that the *ELSE* clause may be omitted, and in this case no action will be taken if the condition yields *false* when it is evaluated. There are no semi-colons in an *IF* statement, and it is wrong to put a semi-colon before *THEN* or before *ELSE*. Each statement may be a compound statement, in the sense defined by Fig. 2.13, and so we may write, for example:

```
VAR
   big, small : real;
....
   IF big > small
      THEN
         BEGIN
            big := small;
            small := 0
         END
```

This has quite a different effect from the statements

```
   IF big > small
      THEN big := small;
   small := 0
```

because in the second case the assignment *small := 0* is always executed, regardless of whether *big > small* or not.

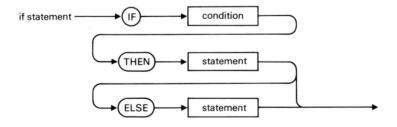

Fig. 3.1 *IF Statement* Syntax

The layout of *IF* statements is very important. The principle to follow is that the *THEN* and *ELSE* parts are always indented with respect to the *IF*. The normal layout for an *IF* statement is:

The *IF* Statement

```
IF condition
    THEN statement₁
    ELSE statement₂
```

If the statements are compound, then the layout is modified in this
way:

```
IF condition
    THEN
        BEGIN
            statements
        END
    ELSE
        BEGIN
            statements
        END
```


Compound *IF* Statements

The statements after *THEN* and *ELSE* may themselves be *IF* statements
and if this is the case, the statement is called a *compound IF statement*. The following statement is a compound *IF* statement:

```
IF charkind = digit
    THEN readnumber
    ELSE
        IF charkind = letter
            THEN readname
            ELSE reporterror
```

Exactly one of the three actions, *readnumber, readname* or *reporterror*
will be executed, whatever the value of *charkind*. In this case, the
ELSE clause of the *IF* statement is an *IF* statement. This is quite a
common situation, and if there are a number of successive tests, the
text will eventually drift off the right hand side of the page.
Accordingly, in this situation the alternative layout shown below is
recommended. Note that this layout is still indicative of the action
taken by the program.

```
IF charkind = digit
    THEN readnumber
ELSE IF charkind = letter
    THEN readname
ELSE reporterror
```

The other type of compound *IF* statement, in which the *THEN* clause
of one *IF* statement is an *IF* statement, looks like this:

```
IF shape = circle
    THEN
        IF radius > distance
            THEN enclosed := true
            ELSE enclosed := false
    ELSE write('wrong shape')
```

When this statement is executed, either the message *'wrong shape'* will be printed, because *shape ≠ circle*, and *enclosed* will be left undefined, or *enclosed* will be given a value depending on the value of *radius* and *distance*. This kind of compound statement is confusing and potentially dangerous. It is better written in this form:

```
IF shape ≠ circle
    THEN write('wrong shape')
ELSE IF radius > distance
    THEN enclosed := true
    ELSE enclosed := false
```

By now, you should have realized that there is an even better way to write this statement:

```
IF shape = circle
    THEN enclosed := radius > distance
    ELSE write('wrong shape')
```

This form of compound *IF* statement is better avoided, but if you must write it, use this layout:

```
IF condition₁
    THEN
        IF condition₂
            THEN
                IF condition₃
                    THEN statement₁
                    ELSE statement₂
            ELSE statement₃
    ELSE statement₄
```

The apparent ambiguity of the statement

```
IF condition₁
    THEN
        IF condition₂
            THEN statement₁
            ELSE statement₂
```

(to which *IF* does the *ELSE* clause belong?) can be resolved from the syntax diagrams. The *ELSE* clause belongs to the nearest *IF* for which there is no *ELSE* clause. It is this fact which makes the second kind of *IF* statement confusing. Removing *'ELSE statement₃'* from the

Example

example above, for instance, changes the significance of *'ELSE statement$_4$'*.

Example: Solving a Quadratic Equation

As a less trivial example of the use of the *IF* statement, we will design a program which calculates the roots of the quadratic equation

$$ax^2 + bx + c = 0$$

The mathematician is in the fortunate position of being able to say that this is only a quadratic equation if $a \neq 0$, since this is how he defines a quadratic equation. He can then claim that all quadratic equations have exactly two roots, which may in some instances be equal to one another. We, as programmers, are not so fortunate. We cannot assume that, just because the user tells us he wants to solve a quadratic equation, he will be so good as to ensure $a \neq 0$. If our program is to be generally useful, it must handle the following cases correctly:

If $a = 0$ and $b = 0$ the equation is either tautologous *(c = 0)* or contradictory *(c $\neq$ 0)*. In this case, we will print a message saying that the equation is degenerate.

If $a = 0$ and $b \neq 0$, there is one root with the value *-c/b*.

If $c = 0$, there are two roots, *-b/a* and *c*.

If none of these conditions apply, the equation is either

$$ax^2 + bx + c = 0 \quad \text{(all coefficients non-zero)}$$

or

$$ax^2 + c = 0 \quad (a \neq 0 \text{ and } c \neq 0)$$

In either of these cases we use the formula

$$roots = \frac{-b \pm \sqrt{(b^2 - 4ac)}}{2a}$$

The quantity $b^2 - 4ac$ is called the *discriminant* of the equation.

If *discriminant* ≥ 0 then there are two (possibly equal) real roots.

If *discriminant* < 0 then there are two complex roots.

These considerations lead to the following program:

Example

```
PROGRAM quadratic (input, output);
   VAR
      a, b, c, discriminant, re, im : real;
   BEGIN
      read(a,b,c);
      IF (a = 0) AND (b = 0)
         THEN writeln('The equation is degenerate')
      ELSE IF a = 0
         THEN writeln('Single root is', -c/b)
      ELSE IF c = 0
         THEN writeln('The roots are', -b/a, 'and', 0)
      ELSE
         BEGIN
            re := - b / (2 * a);
            discriminant := sqr(b) - 4 * a * c;
            im := sqrt(abs(discriminant)) / (2 * a);
            IF discriminant ≥ 0
               THEN writeln('The roots are', re + im,
                                         'and', re - im)
               ELSE writeln('The roots are complex',
                               re, '+I*', im,
                         'and', re, '-I*', im)
         END
   END; { quadratic }
```

Input:
```
   0    0    7
   0   10    2
   2    3    0
   1    5    6
   1    1    1
```

Output:
```
   The equation is degenerate
   Single root is -0.200000
   The roots are -1.500000 and 0
   The roots are -2.000000 and -3.000000
   The roots are complex -5.000000 +I* 0.866025
                   and -5.000000 -I* 0.866025
```

There is one circumstance under which this program might give unreliable results. If b^2 is much larger than $4ac$, then

$$discriminant \simeq b^2$$

and one of the roots will be very small. The calculation of the small root involves the subtraction of two numbers which are almost equal, and this may lead to a loss of precision. In this case, it would be better to calculate the value of the larger root first, and then find the smaller root from the relation

$$smallroot = c / (a \times largeroot)$$

63

3.2   The *REPEAT* Statement

We have already used the *REPEAT* statement informally in Program *squareroots* of Chapter 1 and in several other examples in the text. The *REPEAT* statement has two parts: the *loop* and the *termination condition*.   The general form of the *REPEAT* statement is

```
REPEAT
    statements
UNTIL condition
```

The *REPEAT* statement is used when we do not know at the time of writing the program how many repetitions will be necessary.   For example, if we want to know how many terms of the harmonic series are needed to satisfy the inequality

$$1 + \frac{1}{2} + \frac{1}{3} + \ ... \ + \frac{1}{n} > limit$$

we can use a *REPEAT* statement:

```
PROGRAM series (input, output);
    VAR
        termcount : integer;
        sum, limit : real;
    BEGIN
        termcount := 0;
        sum := 0;
        read(limit);
        REPEAT
            termcount := termcount + 1;
            sum := sum + 1/termcount
        UNTIL sum > limit;
        write(termcount)
    END. { series }
```

Input:
```
    5
   10
```

Output:
```
      83
   12367
```

There are three things to consider when writing a *REPEAT* loop:

(1) The initial conditions must be correct.

The *REPEAT* Statement

(2) The statements within the loop must be sequenced correctly and there must be at least one statement which has an effect on the terminating condition (otherwise the loop would continue forever),

(3) The termination condition must eventually be satisfied.

Suppose that we want to print the square roots of powers of 10 from 1 to 1000000. It seems reasonable to start by writing

```
VAR
    poweroften : real;
BEGIN
    poweroften := 1;
    REPEAT
        write(sqrt(poweroften));
        poweroften := 10 * poweroften
    UNTIL ?
END.
```

The termination condition is *not*

```
poweroften = 1000000
```

but

```
poweroften = 10000000
```

The program is slightly more readable if we express the problem in this way:

```
VAR
    poweroften : real;
BEGIN
    poweroften := 0.1;
    REPEAT
        poweroften := 10 * poweroften;
        writeln(sqrt(poweroften))
    UNTIL poweroften = 1000000
END.
```

In each case, the number of distinct values assumed by *poweroften* during the execution of the program exceeds by one the number of results printed: we have to use one extra value, which may be 0.1 or 10000000.

Syntax

Fig. 3.2 is the syntax diagram for the *REPEAT* statement. The reserved words *REPEAT* and *UNTIL* act as statement brackets in the same

Example

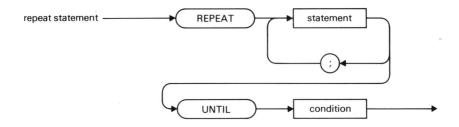

Fig. 3.2 *REPEAT Statement* Syntax

way as do *BEGIN* and *END*. Consequently, several statements, separated
by semi-colons, may appear between *REPEAT* and *UNTIL*. In writing a
REPEAT statement we use the layout convention that the *UNTIL* is placed
directly underneath the *REPEAT* to which it corresponds, and the statements within the loop are indented.

Example: Calculation of a Square Root

We will use the *REPEAT* statement to design a more elaborate
version of Program *squareroots* in which the square root is calculated
by the program itself rather than by the standard function *sqrt*. As
in Program *squareroots* we read a number and reject it if its value is
negative. If the value is zero, we can print the result immediately.
Otherwise, we use Newton's method for calculating a square root, which
states that

> *IF app is an approximation to $\sqrt{number}$*
> *THEN (number/app + app)/2 is a better one*

The program uses *1* as a first approximation and then cycles until a
sufficiently accurate value of $\sqrt{number}$ is obtained. The problem in
writing this program is to select a suitable criterion for ending the
iteration. It is not satisfactory to use a condition such as

$$\left| number - app^2 \right| < 10^{-6}$$

because if *number* $> 10^{15}$ this implies more accuracy than we can
reasonably expect, and if *number* $< 10^{-15}$ it implies no accuracy at all.
It is therefore necessary to use a ratio criterion as the termination
condition, and we choose

$$\left| number/app^2 - 1 \right| < 10^{-6}$$

which will guarantee that our result will be accurate to within a few
parts per million whatever the value of *number*.

These considerations lead to Program *findsquareroots*:

```
PROGRAM findsquareroots (input, output);
   CONST
      epsilon = 1E-6;
   VAR
      number, root : real;
   BEGIN
      REPEAT
         read(number);
         IF number < 0
            THEN writeln('Argument error')
         ELSE IF number = 0
            THEN writeln(0)
         ELSE { number > 0 }
            BEGIN
               root := 1;
               REPEAT
                  root := (number / root + root) / 2
               UNTIL abs(number / sqr(root) - 1) < epsilon;
               writeln(root)
            END
      UNTIL number = 0
   END. { findsquareroots }
```

Input:
    1 2 3 4 5 -1 0

Output:
    1.000000
    1.414214
    1.732051
    2.000000
    2.236067
    Argument error
    0

3.3 The *WHILE* Statement

Another way to execute a statement repeatedly is to use the *WHILE* construction. The *WHILE* statement is similar to the *REPEAT* statement, but the condition is evaluated at the beginning of the loop rather than at the end. The form of the *WHILE* statement is

        WHILE *condition* DO
            statement

For example, if we want to eliminate factors of 2 from the value of *product*, we can write

```
WHILE NOT odd(product) DO
    product := product DIV 2
```

If for some *oddvalue* we have

$$product = 2^n * oddvalue$$

then the assignment statement in this example will be executed *n*
times. If *product* is an odd number, then *n = 0* and the assignment
statement will not be executed at all.

As we saw in the case of the *REPEAT* statement, it is essential
that the statement within the loop eventually changes the value of the
condition, because otherwise the loop would continue executing indef-
initely. In the case of the *WHILE* statement, there is the further
requirement that the condition has a well-defined value on entry to
the statement.

In the example above, the condition has a well-defined value on
entry to the loop provided that the value of *product* is well-defined.
In order for the statement to terminate, the assignment must change
the value of *product*, which it does unless

$$product = 0$$

The statement as given is therefore potentially unsafe. We can make
it better by guarding it with an *IF* statement:

```
IF product ≠ 0
    THEN
        WHILE NOT odd(product) DO
            product := product DIV 2
```

The statement following *WHILE* can be a compound statement. In order
to discover how many times the assignment is executed, we can insert
a counter:

```
counter := 0;
IF product ≠ 0
    THEN
        WHILE NOT odd(product) DO
            BEGIN
                product := product DIV 2;
                counter := counter + 1
            END
```

The next example is intended to clarify a common misconception
about the *WHILE* statement. What will the following program print?

Example

```
PROGRAM puzzle (output);
   VAR
      number : integer;
   BEGIN
      number := 0;
      WHILE number ≤ 10 DO
         BEGIN
            number := number + 1;
            write(number)
         END
   END; { puzzle }
```

The answer is that it prints integers from 1 to *11*. At the beginning of the last cycle, *number* has the value 10, and the condition is *true*. During the last cycle, the statement

```
number := number + 1
```

assigns the value 11 to *number*, and this value is printed. It is sometimes assumed that the *WHILE* statement watches the changing value of *number* in some mysterious way, and terminates the loop as soon as *number* = 10, but this is not so. Remember, the condition is evaluated at the beginning of each cycle only.

In practical programming, the *WHILE* statement is much more useful than the *REPEAT* statement. This is due to the fact that in most cases the possibility that the loop may not be executed should be recognized and allowed for. If you are in doubt as to whether *REPEAT* or *WHILE* is the better construction, then try *WHILE* first.

Syntax

The syntax of the *WHILE* statement is shown in Fig. 3.3. Since the *WHILE* statement has no reserved word corresponding to the *UNTIL* of the *REPEAT* statement, the loop consists of a single statement. In most *WHILE* statements, the loop will be a compound statement.

Fig. 3.3 *WHILE Statement* Syntax

Example: Number Conversion

As an example of the use of the *WHILE* statement, we will design a program for number conversion. The standard procedure *read* is used to

69

Example

read from the input file and perform a conversion from the external
representation of a number as a string of digits to the computer's
internal representation of the number in binary form. Sometimes it is
not possible to use *read* because there are non-numeric characters in
the input file. It could not be used if the input file contained
messages such as:

> *the values are 100 and 504.75*
> *10 * (14.75 - 8.60)*

Program *convert* is a program that will read from the input medium
until it finds a digit, read more digits until it reaches the end of
the number, and perform the conversion to internal form. Fig. 3.4 is
a syntax diagram of the numbers it can read.

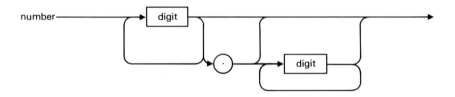

Fig. 3.4 *Number* Syntax

The number may contain a decimal point, and if it does, any digits
after it will be read and correctly interpreted.

The program will read these numbers

> *5   7.   19.5   0.732*

correctly, but it will ignore the decimal point in

> *.732*

and read it as 732. Numbers with a fractional part are read and
converted as if they were integers, but the program counts the number
of digits after the decimal point, and uses this count as a scaling
factor when all the digits have been read. For example, after reading

> *1234.5678*

we have

> *value = 12345678*
> *scale = 4*

The conversion is completed by dividing *value* by 10^{scale}, and in this

Example

case we have

$$12345678/10^4 = 1234.5678$$

as required. Rather than calculating the scale directly, the program repeatedly divides by 10. This is excusable in this instance because the program is clearly not intended to read very small numbers (less than 10^{-10}, say). A more efficient scaling algorithm would be used in a more sophisticated program intended to read numbers in scientific notation.

When Program *convert* finishes, it will have read one character after the last digit. Clearly this is inevitable because the only way that the program can determine that the end of a number has been reached is to read a character which is not a digit.

```
PROGRAM convert (input, output);
   CONST
      zero = '0';
      nine = '9';
      point = '.';
      radix = 10;
   VAR
      result : real;
      scale : integer;
      ch : char;
   BEGIN
      result := 0;
      REPEAT
         read(ch)
      UNTIL (zero ≤ ch) AND (ch ≤ nine);
      WHILE (zero ≤ ch) AND (ch ≤ nine) DO
         BEGIN
            result := radix * result + ord(ch) - ord(zero);
            read(ch)
         END; { while }
      IF ch = point
         THEN
            BEGIN
               scale := 0;
               read(ch);
               WHILE (zero ≤ ch) AND (ch ≤ nine) DO
                  BEGIN
                     result := radix * result + ord(ch) - ord(zero);
                     read(ch);
                     scale := scale + 1
                  END; { while }
               WHILE scale > 0 DO
                  BEGIN
                     result := result / radix;
                     scale := scale - 1
```

```
                END { while }
          END;
     writeln(result)
  END. { convert }
```

Input:
```
  1234.5678
  .124
  0.99999999999999
```

Output:
```
  1234.567800
   124.000000
     1.000000
```

Note that on entry to the first *WHILE* statement we know that *ch* is a digit, and so the loop will be executed at least once. We could in fact rewrite this statement as a *REPEAT* statement:

```
    REPEAT
       result := radix * result + ord(ch) - ord(zero);
       read(ch)
    UNTIL NOT ((zero ≤ ch) AND (ch ≤ nine))
```

However, this is not true for the second *WHILE* statement, because if there is no digit after the decimal point, the statement within the loop will not be executed at all. Since both statements serve the same function, the program is clearer if we code them the same way.

Reading Numbers

The procedure *read* can of course be used with integer and real arguments, as we saw in Sections 2.4 and 2.5. Some problems arise, however, when we have to read a stream of numbers from the input file. Consider the problem of finding the mean of a set of real numbers. This requires counting the numbers and finding their sum. The following program appears to be a plausible solution:

```
    PROGRAM mean (input, output);
       VAR
          value, sum : real;
          count : integer;
       BEGIN
          sum := 0;
          count := 0;
          WHILE NOT eof DO
             BEGIN
                read(value);
                sum := sum + value;
```

```
        count := count + 1
    END; { while }
  writeln('Mean =', sum / count)
END. { mean }
```

Unfortunately, this program does not work. Suppose that the input
file contains a single number, 4.7. This number will be read during
the first cycle of the *WHILE* loop, and at the end of this cycle, we
have:

```
value = 4.7
sum = 4.7
count = 1
```

The problem arises because the number 4.7 will be followed by blanks.
If the input file is on cards, then there will be blanks on the card,
and if you type 4.7 at a terminal, the carriage return character will
appear to the program as a blank. Consequently, *eof* will not be true
at the end of the first *WHILE* cycle, and therefore the *WHILE* will be
executed again. The value read will be zero, and so at the end of the
second *WHILE* cycle we have:

```
eof = true
value = 0
sum = 4.7
count = 2
```

The mean value obtained by this program is

```
4.7/2 = 2.35
```

which is incorrect.

We therefore have to rearrange the program in such a way that the
value obtained by the last *read* statement is discarded and does not
contribute to *count*. This can be done by placing the *read* statement
last in the *WHILE* loop:

```
WHILE NOT eof DO
    BEGIN
        sum := sum + value;
        count := count + 1;
        read(value)
    END
```

We now need an additional *read* statement to read the first number.
This is placed before the *WHILE* statement, and gives Program *mean*,
which gives correct results.

73

```
PROGRAM mean (input, output);
   VAR
      value, sum, mean : real;
      count : integer;
   BEGIN
      sum := 0;
      count := 0;
      read(value);
      WHILE NOT eof DO
         BEGIN
            sum := sum + value;
            count := count + 1;
            read(value)
         END; { while }
      IF count > 0
         THEN
            BEGIN
               mean := sum / count;
               writeln(count, 'values read. mean =', mean)
            END
         ELSE writeln('no values read')
   END. { mean }
```

Input:
   2.5 6.36 7.81 9.98

Output:
   4 values read. mean = 6.662500

3.4 The *FOR* Statement

When we wish to execute a statement repetitively, and the number of repetitions does not depend on the effect of statements within the loop, the appropriate construction is the *FOR* loop. At the beginning of Section 3.2, we used the *REPEAT* statement to find how many terms of the harmonic series are required for their sum to exceed a given limit. The converse problem of finding the sum given the number of terms is most appropriately expressed with a *FOR* statement.

```
PROGRAM harmonicseries (input, output);
   VAR
      term, numberofterms : integer;
      sum : real;
   BEGIN
      read(numberofterms);
      sum := 0;
      FOR term := 1 TO numberofterms DO
```

```
              sum := sum + 1 / term;
          writeln(sum)
      END. { harmonicseries }
```

The effect of the *FOR* statement in this program is to execute the
assignment

```
      sum := sum + 1/term
```

for each integral value of *term* from *1* to *numberofterms*. If *numberofterms = 1* then the assignment is executed once only and program will
print *1*. If *numberofterms < 1* then the assignment will not be executed at all, and the program will print *0*.

The general form of the *FOR* statement is:

$$FOR\ variable := expression_1\ TO\ expression_2\ DO$$
$$statement$$

and for most purposes it is equivalent to

$$variable := expression_1;$$
$$WHILE\ variable \le expression_2\ DO$$
$$BEGIN$$
$$statement;$$
$$variable := succ(variable)$$
$$END$$

which leads to the following observations:

(1) The statement will not be executed at all if

$$expression_1 > expression_2$$

(2) The type of the control variable and the two expressions must be
   the same, and the function *succ* must be defined for this type.
   This precludes the use of a control variable of type *real*.

The *WHILE* statement is not exactly equivalent to the *FOR* statement
because when the *WHILE* statement terminates we have

$$variable = succ(expression_2)$$

but when the *FOR* statement terminates, the control variable is
undefined.

The fact that a *FOR* statement may be written in the form of a
WHILE statement implies that the *FOR* statement is redundant. Nonetheless, there are good reasons for using the *FOR* statement wherever
possible. The *FOR* statement conveys more information to the human
reader. The values which will be assigned to the control variable and

Example

and the number of times that the loop will be executed are both
immediately apparent. The same information is also useful to the
compiler, which will often be able to generate a more efficient program from a *FOR* statement than from the equivalent *WHILE* statement.

The keyword *TO* in the *FOR* statement may be replaced by *DOWNTO*. The
FOR statement becomes

$$FOR\ variable := expression_1\ DOWNTO\ expression_2\ DO$$
$$statement$$

and is equivalent in the sense defined above to the *WHILE* statement

```
variable := expression₁;
WHILE variable ≥ expression DO
    BEGIN
        statement;
        variable := pred(variable)
    END
```

Fig. 3.5 is a syntax diagram for the *FOR* statement.

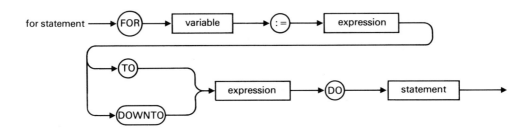

Fig. 3.5 *FOR Statement* Syntax

Example: Musical Pitches

The ratio of two musical notes a semitone apart in the equitemp-
ered scale is

$$^{12}\sqrt{2} \approx 1.05946$$

and the standard concert pitch is usually obtained by tuning middle A
to 440 cycles per second. The lowest note on a piano is four octaves
below this A and therefore should be tuned to

$$440/2^4 = 27.5\ cycles\ per\ second$$

The following program could be used to calculate the theoretical

76

Example

frequencies of the other notes of the piano:

```
PROGRAM frequencies (output);
   CONST
      lowestnote = 27.5;
      keyboardlength = 88;
      semitone = 1.05946;
   VAR
      frequency : real;
      note : integer;
   BEGIN
      frequency := lowestnote;
      FOR note := 1 TO keyboardlength DO
         BEGIN
            writeln(frequency);
            frequency := frequency * semitone
         END { for }
   END. { frequencies }
```

   This program will not give accurate results for the higher notes, because multiplication errors will accumulate. It is always better to calculate each value independently in loops of this kind, rather than deriving each new value from the preceding value, even though the program may execute more slowly as a result. In this case we can use the fact that *frequency* is related to *note* by

$$frequency = lownote \times 2^{(note/12)}$$

The exponent can be calculated from the algebraic identity

$$a^x = e^{x \times ln(a)}$$

and we have, in PASCAL notation,

```
frequency := lowestnote * exp(note * ln(2) / 12)
```

We can now write a second version of Program *frequencies*:

```
PROGRAM frequencies (output);
   CONST
      lowestnote = 27.5;
      keyboardlength = 88;
   VAR
      frequency : real;
      note : integer;
   BEGIN
      FOR note := 0 TO keyboardlength - 1 DO
         BEGIN
            frequency := lowestnote * exp(note * ln(2) / 12);
            writeln(frequency)
         END { for }
   END. { frequencies }
```

77

The program will now give accurate results, but it calculates the value of *ln(2)/12* during each cycle — 88 times in fact. We can eliminate this inefficiency by introducing *ratio*, which is a real variable initialized by the assignment

       ratio := ln(2) / 12

This is the final version of Program *frequencies*:

```
PROGRAM frequencies (output);
   CONST
      lowestnote = 27.5;
      keyboardlength = 88;
   VAR
      frequency, ratio : real;
      note : integer;
   BEGIN
      ratio := ln(2) / 12;
      FOR note := 0 TO keyboardlength - 1 DO
         BEGIN
            frequency := lowestnote * exp(ratio * note);
            writeln(frequency)
         END { for }
   END. { frequencies }
```

Output:
    27.500000
    29.135235
    30.867706
    32.703196
    34.647829
    36.708096
    etc.

Exercises

3.1 Write a program that calculates cube roots, using the fact that if α is an approximation for $\sqrt[3]{x}$ then

$$\beta = (2\alpha + x/\alpha^2)/3$$

is a better one.

3.2 Modify Program *frequencies* so that it prints two blank lines after each octave. (An octave contains 12 semitones.)

3.3 Show that:

Exercises

(a) Any *REPEAT* statement can be rewritten using *IF* and *WHILE*.
(b) Any *WHILE* statement can be rewritten using *IF* and *REPEAT*.

3.4 The following statement was found in a badly written PASCAL
program:

```
IF a < b THEN IF c < d THEN         x := 1
ELSE IF a < c THEN IF b < d THEN x := 2
                          ELSE x := 3
ELSE IF a < d THEN IF b < c THEN x := 4
                          ELSE x := 5
                     ELSE x := 6
                ELSE x := 7
```

(a) Rewrite this statement using a better layout.
(b) Are there any redundant or contradictory conditions?
(c) Write a statement that has the same effect and is simpler.

3.5 The formula of Newton and Raphson may be used to solve the
equation

$$x \times sin(x) = 1$$

by successive approximation.   The recurrence relation is

$$x_{n+1} = \frac{1 + x_n^2 cos(x_n)}{sin(x_n) + x_n cos(x_n)}$$

Write a program that tabulates the positive roots of this
equation.

3.6 Write a program that will make change for any sum of money up to
99¢ using the coins of denomination 1¢, 5¢, 10¢ and 25¢.

3.7 Extend Program *mean* so that it prints the standard deviation α of
the numbers read as well as μ.

$$\alpha = \sqrt{\sum_i (x_i - \mu)^2 / (n - 1)}$$

3.8 Write a program to test the truth of the inequality

$$\frac{1}{n + 1} < ln\{\frac{n + 1}{n}\} < \frac{1}{n}$$

when n is a positive integer.

3.9 Modify Program *convert* so that it will read, and correctly
interpret
(a) negative numbers

Exercises

(b) octal (base eight) numbers

3.10 Write a program which reads and evaluates expressions such as

$$+20-4-3+169;$$

The numbers are integers, each is preceded by a sign, and the expression is terminated by a semicolon.

3.11 Improve Program *quadratic* so that if

$$4ac < epsilon \times b^2$$

then the root with the larger absolute value is calculated first, and then the smaller one is calculated from

$$smallroot = c/(a \times largeroot)$$

3.12 Write a program that sums the series

$$1 + x + x^2/2! + x^3/3! + \ldots + x^n/n!$$

forwards and backwards and compares the results.   Why is this series unreliable as a means of evaluating e^x for some values of x?   (Use real variables to calculate the factorials, or you may encounter integer overflow.)

3.13 A *trial* consists of tossing a coin until heads appears.   The average number of tosses in a trial is

$$\lim_{n \to \infty} \sum_{i=1}^{i=n} \frac{i}{2^i}$$

Find an approximate value for this limit.

Procedures and Functions

CHAPTER FOUR

Most complex organisms, be they biological, bureaucratic, or military, are governed in a hierarchical way. A *hierarchy* is a system of layers in which the higher layers operate with general information and the lower layers fill in the details. We use *procedures* to give programs a hierarchical structure.

4.1 Writing Procedures

A *procedure* in PASCAL is a statement with which a name has been associated. The statement

```
REPEAT
   read(ch)
UNTIL ch ≠ blank
```

will read characters from the input file until a character other than blank is encountered. An appropriate name for this statement would be *skipblanks*. We define the procedure *skipblanks* as follows:

```
PROCEDURE skipblanks;
    BEGIN
        REPEAT
            read(ch)
        UNTIL ch ≠ blank
    END;
```

Once we have written this definition, the statement

```
skipblanks
```

will have precisely the same effect as the original *REPEAT* statement. The statement *skipblanks* is a *procedure call*, and we say that it *invokes*, or *calls*, the procedure *skipblanks*.

When we use *skipblanks* rather than the statement that it replaces, we have achieved a level of abstraction. The call, *skipblanks*, provided that we have chosen an appropriate name, answers the question '*what* will the statement do?' The statement which we find when we examine the definition of *skipblanks*, that is

```
REPEAT
    read(ch)
UNTIL ch ≠ blank
```

answers the question '*how* do we do it?'

We will use procedures to develop a program which computes partial sums of the harmonic series. Symbolically, the program will evaluate *H(n)* for various values of *n*, where

$$H(n) = 1 + \frac{1}{2} + \frac{1}{3} + \ldots + \frac{1}{n}$$

The result of the calculation is to be expressed in the form of a rational number, that is, a number of the form

$$\frac{numerator}{denominator}$$

where *numerator* and *denominator* are integers. We represent a rational number in PASCAL by two integer variables.

We will need a procedure to remove common factors from the numerator and denominator. The best way to do this is to divide the numerator and the denominator by their greatest common divisor. We use a slightly improved version of Euclid's algorithm to calculate the greatest common divisor in the procedure *lowterm*:

```
PROCEDURE lowterm;
   BEGIN
      numcopy := numerator;
      dencopy := denominator;
      WHILE dencopy ≠ 0 DO
         BEGIN
            remainder := numcopy MOD dencopy;
            numcopy := dencopy;
            dencopy := remainder
         END; { while }
      IF numcopy > 1
         THEN
            BEGIN
               numerator := numerator DIV numcopy;
               denominator·:= denominator DIV numcopy
            END
   END; { lowterm }
```

Program *cancelfactors* is a complete program which defines and uses the procedure *lowterm*. Notice the ordering used in this program. We have

```
program heading
   variable declarations
   procedure definition
   body of program
```

When program *cancelfactors* is executed, the first instruction obeyed is

```
read(numerator,denominator)
```

The statements contained in the procedure *lowterm* are not executed until the instruction

```
lowterm
```

is obeyed. This ordering is inevitable given that we must define an entity before we use it. The variables are used within the procedure, and therefore must be declared before it, and the main program makes use of the procedure, and therefore must follow it.

The first line of the procedure definition, in this case

```
PROCEDURE lowterm;
```

is called the *procedure head*. The compound statement immediately following it is called the *procedure body*, and it must be terminated with a semicolon. We have put a blank line before and after the procedure definition to make the structure of the program more apparent to the eye. For a conventional computer printer listing, an even more spacious layout should be used. A good convention is to have blank lines between constant and variable declaration sections, and two or three blank lines to set off procedures.

```
PROGRAM cancelfactors (input,output);
    VAR
        numerator, denominator, numcopy,
        dencopy, remainder : integer;


    PROCEDURE lowterm;
        BEGIN
            numcopy := numerator;
            dencopy := denominator;
            WHILE dencopy ≠ 0 DO
                BEGIN
                    remainder := numcopy MOD dencopy;
                    numcopy := dencopy;
                    dencopy := remainder
                END; { while }
            IF numcopy > 1
                THEN
                    BEGIN
                        numerator := numerator DIV numcopy;
                        denominator := denominator DIV numcopy
                    END
        END; { lowterm   }


    BEGIN { cancelfactors }
        read(numerator,denominator);
        lowterm;
        writeln(numerator,denominator)
    END. { cancelfactors   }
```

We have defined the variables *numcopy*, *dencopy* and *remainder*, along with *numerator* and *denominator*, as global variables, and accordingly they may be used anywhere in the procedure *lowterm* or in the main program. It is not desirable to use them in the main program, however, because any call to *lowterm* will alter their values. It is clear that they belong to the procedure and not to the program as a whole. We may indicate this by placing their declarations within the procedure:

```
PROGRAM cancelfactors (input,output);
    VAR
        numerator, denominator : integer;


    PROCEDURE lowterm;
        VAR
            numcopy, dencopy, remainder : integer;
        ....
```

The variables *numcopy*, *dencopy* and *remainder* are now *local variables*. Fig. 4.1(a) shows the situation before *lowterm* is called; the variables

numcopy, *dencopy* and *remainder* have not yet been defined. Fig. 4.1(b)
represents the situation during the execution of procedure *lowterm*:
numcopy, *dencopy* and *remainder* have been defined and are in use. The
procedure can still refer to the global variables *numerator* and *den-ominator*. In Fig. 4.1(c) the procedure has finished executing and

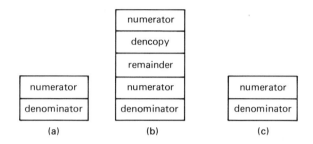

Fig. 4.1   Local Variables

numcopy, *dencopy* and *remainder* no longer exist. If the procedure is
called again, the local variables are re-created. You must never
assume that when a procedure is called for a second time, its local
variables will still possess the values that they had at the end of
the previous invocation. We say that the *scope* of the variables
numcopy, *dencopy* and *remainder* is the body of the procedure *lowterm*.
Once again, it is important to distinguish the static situation (the
text of the program) from the dynamic situation (the execution of the
program). It would be incorrect, in the program text, to refer to
numcopy in the main program, because *numcopy* is not defined in the
main program. During execution, however, all of the variables may be
in use simultaneously, during the invocation of the procedure
lowterm.

The definition of the procedure *lowterm* is still restricted.
Before we use it, we must make sure that the rational number which we
want to reduce to its lowest terms is stored in the variables *numer-ator* and *denominator*. If, for example, it was stored in *top* and
bottom, then we would have to copy:

        numerator := top;
        denominator := bottom;
        lowterm

It would be easier to use *lowterm* if we could give it arguments. We
would then be able to reduce *numerator/denominator* to lowest terms by
writing

        lowterm(numerator,denominator)

and *top/bottom* to lowest terms by writing

lowterm(top,bottom)

We can do this quite easily by modifying the definition of *lowterm* in the following way to accomodate the parameters:

```
PROCEDURE lowterm (VAR num,den : integer);
    VAR
        numcopy, dencopy, remainder : integer;
    BEGIN
        numcopy := num;
        dencopy := den;
        WHILE dencopy ≠ 0 DO
            BEGIN
                remainder := numcopy MOD dencopy;
                numcopy := dencopy;
                dencopy := remainder
            END; { while }
        IF numcopy > 1
            THEN
                BEGIN
                    num := num DIV numcopy;
                    den := den DIV dencopy
                END
    END; { lowterm }
```

Num and *den* are now *formal parameters* of *lowterm*. The procedure head is extended by a *parameter list* in which the formal parameters are declared. The *VAR* in the parameter list indicates that the values of the parameters may be changed within the body of the procedure. We can invoke the new version of *lowterm* by calling

lowterm(numerator,denominator)

or

lowterm(top,bottom)

as above. In these calls, the variables *numerator*, *denominator*, *top* and *bottom* are *actual parameters*. The version of Program *cancel-factors* that follows does the same thing as the previous version, but parameters are used for communication between the main program and procedure *lowterm*. The variables and formal parameters of *lowterm* are all local variables, and the procedure has its own local working space (*numcopy*, *dencopy* and *remainder*) and an interface to the rest of the program (*num* and *den*).

```
PROGRAM cancelfactors (input, output);
VAR
    numerator, denominator : integer;

PROCEDURE lowterm (VAR num, den : integer);
VAR
    numcopy, dencopy, remainder : integer;
BEGIN
    numcopy := num;
    dencopy := den;
    WHILE dencopy ≠ 0 DO
        BEGIN
            remainder := numcopy MOD dencopy;
            numcopy := dencopy;
            dencopy := remainder
        END; { while }
    IF numcopy > 1
        THEN
            BEGIN
                num := num DIV numcopy;
                den := den DIV numcopy
            END
END; { lowterm }

BEGIN    cancelfactors
    read(numerator, denominator);
    lowterm(numerator, denominator);
    writeln(numerator, denominator)
END. { cancelfactors }
```

Input:
```
     9    24
  1024   128
```

Output:
```
     3     8
     8     1
```

The distinction between formal and actual parameters may be
clarified by a comparison with the proof of a theorem in elementary
geometry. Such a proof is written in terms of angles and lengths.
These angles and lengths correspond to the formal parameters of a
procedure. The assertion made by the proof is that if we substituted
actual angles and lengths, such as 30° and 4 inches, for the angles
and lengths in the proof, then every statement in the proof would be
true. By doing this, we would have proved a particular case of the
theorem. This process is analogous to providing actual parameters to
a procedure in a program. In the same way that a geometric proof is
true for a class of figures, the procedure represents a class of
computations. An invocation of the procedure performs a computation
which is a member of this class. Similarly, we can see that any

computer program represents a class of computations, and executing a program with a particular set of input data makes it perform a computation which is a member of this class.

The program to compute partial sums of the harmonic series requires one more procedure. We have to be able to add two rational numbers according to the formula

$$\frac{num}{den} = \frac{num1}{den1} + \frac{num2}{den2} = \frac{num1 * den2 + num2 * den1}{den1 * den2}$$

We use this formula to define the procedure *addrationals*:

```
PROCEDURE addrationals (VAR num, den : integer;
                        num1,den1,num2,den2 : integer);
   BEGIN
      num := num1 * den2 + num2 * den1;
      den := den1 * den2
   END; { addrationals }
```

The variables *num1*, *den1*, *num2* and *den2* are not altered by the procedure, and accordingly their names are not preceded by *VAR* in the procedure head. We can modify this procedure so that it uses only four parameters and implements the 'assignment'

$$\frac{num1}{den1} := \frac{num1 * den2 + num2 * den1}{den1 * den2}$$

The new definition is:

```
PROCEDURE addrationals (VAR num1, den1 : integer;
                        num2, den2 : integer);
   BEGIN
      num1 := num1 * den2 + num2 * den1;
      den1 := den1 * den2
   END;  { addrationals }
```

Notice that although the order of the two assignment statements was immaterial in the first version of *addrationals*, it is significant in this version.

Program *sumharmonics* is a complete program which uses the two procedures which we have defined. The partial sums $H(n)$ are computed for a specified number of terms, and each partial sum is printed.

```
PROGRAM sumharmonics (input, output);
   CONST
      firstterm = 2;
   VAR
      numerator, denominator,
      lastterm, termcount : integer;

   PROCEDURE lowterm (VAR num, den : integer);
      VAR
         numcopy, dencopy, remainder : integer;
      BEGIN
         numcopy := num;
         dencopy := den;
         WHILE dencopy ≠ 0 DO
            BEGIN
               remainder := numcopy MOD dencopy;
               numcopy := dencopy;
               dencopy := remainder
            END; { while }
         IF numcopy > 1
            THEN
               BEGIN
                  num := num DIV numcopy;
                  den := den DIV numcopy
               END
      END; { lowterm }

   PROCEDURE addrationals (VAR num1, den1 : integer;
                               num2, den2 : integer);
      BEGIN
         num1 := num1 * den2 + num2 * den1;
         den1 := den1 * den2
      END; { addrationals }

   BEGIN { sumharmonics }
      numerator := 1;
      denominator := 1;
      read(lastterm);
      FOR termcount := firstterm TO lastterm DO
         BEGIN
            addrationals(numerator, denominator,
                         1, termcount);
            lowterm(numerator,denominator);
            writeln(numerator:1, '/', denominator:1)
         END { for }
   END. { sumharmonics }
```

Input:
      10

89

Variables and Parameters

Output:
   3/2
   11/6
   25/12
   137/60
   49/20
   363/140
   761/280
   7129/2520
   7381/2520

Variables and Parameters

It is important to understand clearly the difference between local
and global variables, and the difference between value and variable
parameters. We will study these distinctions in the light of a simple
example which uses only one procedure.

```
PROGRAM simple (output);
   VAR
      x : integer;

   PROCEDURE change;
      BEGIN
         x := 1
      END; { change }

   BEGIN
      x := 0;
      change;
      write(x)
   END. { simple }
```

This program has one variable, *x*, and it is a global variable. The
value of *x* is initially set to zero by the main program. The program
calls the procedure *change*, which changes the value of *x* to 1, and
this value is printed by the last statement in the program, *write(x)*.
Now consider a program which is almost the same, but which has a
local variable declaration:

```
PROGRAM simple (output);
   VAR
      x : integer;

   PROCEDURE change;
      VAR
         x : integer;
      BEGIN
         x := 1
```

```
    END; { change }

BEGIN
    x := 0;
    change;
    write(x)
END. { simple }
```

This version of the program has two variables, both called *x*. One of them is a global variable, and the other (defined in the procedure) is local to the procedure. The assignment *x := 1* in the procedure sets the value of the local *x* to 1. Note that the declaration of the local variable *x* overrides the global declaration of *x* within the body of the procedure. In fact, declaring the local variable *x* to have the same name as the global variable *x* prevents the procedure from accessing the global variable *x* at all. Accordingly, the statement *x := 1* has no effect on the global variable *x*, which remains zero, and this is what the program prints.

In the next version of Program *simple*, we give the procedure *change* a parameter:

```
PROGRAM simple (output);
    VAR
        x : integer;

    PROCEDURE change (VAR y : integer);
        BEGIN
            y := 1
        END; { change }

    BEGIN
        x := 0;
        change(x);
        write(x)
    END. { simple }
```

This program has a global variable called *x*, and a procedure *change* with a formal parameter. We have called the formal parameter *y* to avoid confusion, but in fact the program would work in just the same way if we wrote *x* where *y* occurs. The declaration of *y* in the procedure head is preceded by *VAR*. This defines *y* as a variable parameter, which in turn means that *y* can be regarded as a *synonym* for the actual parameter *x* during the execution of the procedure: whatever happens to *y* will also happen to *x*. Accordingly, the assignment *y := 1* will change the value of the actual parameter *x* to *1*, and this is the result that the program prints. When the formal parameter is a variable parameter, the corresponding actual parameter must be a variable: it cannot be an expression. The calls

```
change(2*x)
```

and

> *change (2)*

are not allowed with this definition of *change*, because

> *2*x*

and

> *2*

are expressions, not variables.

Now we consider the effect of a value parameter:

```
PROGRAM simple (output);
  VAR
    x : integer;

  PROCEDURE change (y : integer);
    BEGIN
      y := 1
    END; { change }

  BEGIN
    x := 0;
    change(x);
    write(x)
  END. { simple }
```

Once again, we have a global variable *x* and a formal parameter *y*. In this case, there is no *VAR* preceding the declaration of *y*, and so *y* is a value parameter. The procedure call

> *change (x)*

implicitly executes the assignment statement

> *y := x*

before executing the first statement of the procedure body. After entry to the procedure body, there is no further relationship between *x* and *y*, and so the assignment

> *y := 1*

has no effect on the value of *x*. The program will therefore print the value which *x* had on entry to the procedure, which is zero. When a formal parameter is a value parameter, the corresponding actual parameter may be an expression. With the procedure *change* as it is defined in this example, we could write the calling statements

> *change(2 * x)*

or

> *change(2)*

In the first case, there would be an implicit assignment

> *y := 2 * x*

and in the second case

> *y := 2*

before the procedure was executed.

You may find it helpful to remember the distinction between value and variable parameters in the following way: the actual parameter corresponding to a value formal parameter must be an entity that could appear on the right hand side of an assignment statement, but the actual parameter corresponding to a variable formal parameter can only be an entity that could appear on the left hand side of an assignment statement.

The expression corresponding to a value parameter must have the same type as the parameter. As we saw in Chapter 2, however, it is a general rule in PASCAL that an integer expression may be used wherever a real expression is expected, and so we may use an integer expression as the actual parameter corresponding to a real formal parameter.

Syntax

Fig. 4.2 is the syntax diagram for *parameter list*. The parameter list may be omitted altogether, in which case the procedure must refer to non-local variables if it is to have any effect on the program. Fig. 4.3 is the syntax diagram for *procedure definition*. The *procedure head* comprises the keyword *PROCEDURE*, the procedure identifier, and the parameter list. The *procedure body* is a *block*, which is the syntactic structure introduced in Fig. 2.12. We can now extend the definition of block to include the definitions of procedures and functions, as shown in Fig. 4.4.

The syntax diagram for a PASCAL program is shown in Fig. 4.5, which is merely a reproduction of Fig. 2.10. Comparing Figs. 4.3 and 4.5, we see that a program is in fact a procedure with an abnormal head and the special terminator '.'. The standard types, constants and functions are non-local identifiers for this 'procedure.' The implication of this is that it is not illegal to define a new 'local'

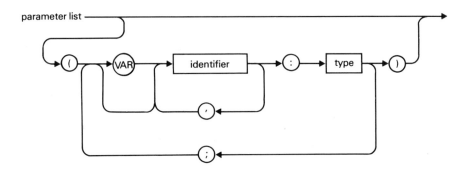

Fig. 4.2 *Parameter List* Syntax

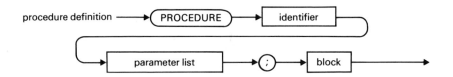

Fig. 4.3 *Procedure Definition* Syntax

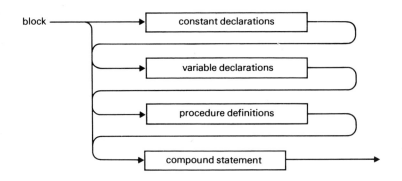

Fig. 4.4 *Block* Syntax

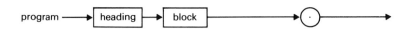

Fig. 4.5 *Program* Syntax

value for any of the standard identifiers in a program, although this
is definitely not to be encouraged. We can regard the program as a
procedure of the operating system, and with this interpretation we can
also see that the files *input* and *output* are like formal parameters:
the corresponding actual parameters are the files given to the program
by the operating system when the program is executed.

The syntax diagrams for a procedure definition (Fig. 4.3) and a
block (Fig. 4.5) are mutually recursive, and consequently procedures
can be nested. The skeleton of a program with nested procedures is
given below. The procedure bodies are not written out in full, and
parameters are omitted.

```
PROGRAM nest (input, output);
   VAR
      a, b : integer;

   PROCEDURE outer;
      VAR
         c, d : integer;

      PROCEDURE inner;
         VAR
            e, f : integer;
         BEGIN { inner }
            { statements of inner }
         END; { inner }

      BEGIN { outer }
         { statements of outer }
      END; { outer }

   BEGIN { nest }
      { statements of nest }
   END. { nest }
```

The variables *e* and *f* in this program are local to the procedure
inner, and may only be used within the body of *inner*. The variables
c and *d* are local to the procedure *outer*, and may be used within the
body of *outer*. Since *inner* is nested within *outer*, the variables *c*
and *d* may also be used within *inner*. The variables *a* and *b* are global
and may be used anywhere within the program. The procedure *inner* is a
local procedure of *outer* and may be called from within the body of
outer but not by the main program.

Fig. 4.6 shows the syntax for a *procedure call*. The actual parameters are written in a list following the procedure identifier. For
each formal parameter in the procedure definition, there must be an
actual parameter in the calling statement. If the formal parameter
is variable, then the actual parameter must be a variable, not an
expression. The type of the actual parameter must be the same as the

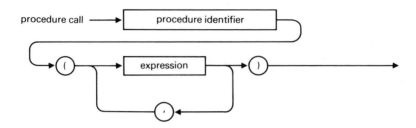

Fig. 4.6 *Procedure Call* Syntax

type of the formal parameter, with the single exception that if the
formal parameter is a value parameter of type real, then the actual
parameter may be an integer expression, in accordance with the rule
that an integer expression is allowed in any context where a real
expression is expected.

4.2 Functions

We have already met many of the standard functions of PASCAL. For
example, *sqrt* is a standard function which has a single argument of
type *real* or *integer* and yields a value of type *real*. Whereas a procedure has an *effect*, a function has a *value*. Syntactically, a procedure call is a variety of *statement*, and a function call is a
variety of *factor*. The formal parameters of the standard functions of
PASCAL are all value parameters, which means that function calls may
be nested in expressions. Using the standard functions *sqrt* and *sqr*
we can write

```
PROGRAM triangle (input, output);
   VAR
      opside, adjside, hypotenuse : real;
   BEGIN
      read(opside,adjside);
      hypotenuse := sqrt(sqr(opside) + sqr(adjside));
      write(hypotenuse)
   END.
```

This program contains three function calls. *Sqr* is called twice, and
sqrt is called once, with the argument

```
sqr(adjside) + sqr(opside)
```

Functions

Writing Functions

A function definition is similar to a procedure definition. There follows a definition for a function *squareroot* which calculates the square root of its argument using the same algorithm as Program *find-squareroots* of Chapter 3.

```
FUNCTION squareroot (value : real) : real;
   CONST
      epsilon = 1E-6;
   VAR
      root : real;
   BEGIN
      IF value = 0
         THEN squareroot := 0
         ELSE
            BEGIN
               root := 1;
               REPEAT
                  root := (value/root + root)/2
               UNTIL abs(value/sqr(root) - 1) < epsilon;
               squareroot := root
            END
END; { squareroot }
```

The type of the function is written in the *function head* after the parameter list. The type of *squareroot* is *real*, and its parameter, *value*, is also *real*. The function does not check that its argument is non-negative, and it will fail if it is called with a negative argument. The value returned by *squareroot* is determined by an assignment statement in which *squareroot* appears on the left. There are two such assignments in this example, *squareroot := 0*, which is executed when *value = 0*, and *squareroot := root*, which is executed if *value > 0*. The function *squareroot* may be used in the same way as the standard function *sqrt*, and so we may write, for example

hypotenuse := squareroot(sqr(opside) + sqr(adjside))

There are two important differences between the function *square-root* that we have defined and the standard function *sqrt*. First, if *sqrt* has a negative argument, the program will halt, and an appropriate error message will be printed. If *squareroot* is executed with a negative argument, a misleading error message, such as 'dividing by zero', will be printed. It is easy to overcome this defect by testing the value of the argument within the body of the function, but it is not so easy to explain the failure to the calling program. Secondly, basic mathematical functions, such as *sqrt*, are usually written very carefully by the computer manufacturer in such a way that the available speed and accuracy of the computer are fully exploited. A function such as *squareroot* will usually be neither as fast nor as accurate as a standard function.

The algorithm used by procedure *lowterm* in Section 4.1 to find
the greatest common divisor of two integers can be written as a
function:

```
FUNCTION gcd (num, den : integer) : integer;
    VAR
        remainder : integer;
    BEGIN
        WHILE den ≠ 0 DO
            BEGIN
                remainder := num MOD den;
                num := den;
                den := remainder
            END; { while }
        gcd := num
    END; { gcd }
```

We do not need to make local copies of the parameters within the
function. Since *num* and *den* are value parameters, the copying will
have been done for us implicitly, and nothing we do to *num* and *den*
can affect the values of the actual parameters in the calling program.
Using this function, we can readily define the procedure *lowterm*:

```
PROCEDURE lowterm (VAR num, den : integer);
    VAR
        divisor : integer;
    BEGIN
        divisor := gcd(num,den);
        IF divisor > 1
            THEN
                BEGIN
                    num := num DIV divisor;
                    den := den DIV divisor
                END
    END; { lowterm }
```

Now consider this alternative definition of *lowterm*:

```
PROCEDURE lowterm (VAR num, den : integer);
    BEGIN
        num := num DIV gcd(num,den);
        den := den DIV gcd(num,den)
    END; { lowterm }
```

Although this definition is shorter and more readable, it is inferior
for several reasons. It wastes time by evaluating the greatest common
divisor twice, and it may perform unnecessary divisions when the
greatest common divisor is 1. Its most important defect, however, is
that it does not work, because the first assignment may alter the

value of *num*, thereby invalidating the second assignment. This kind
of trap is easy to fall into if you are programming hastily, and it is
more likely to occur if you are programming directly from a mathematical derivation.

Syntax

The syntax for a *function definition* is shown in Fig. 4.7.   It

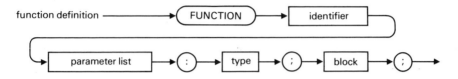

Fig. 4.7 *Function Definition* Syntax

differs from the syntax of a procedure definition in that the keyword
FUNCTION replaces the keyword *PROCEDURE* and the type of the function
follows the parameter list. A function call is a variety of factor,
and Fig. 4.8 is a syntax diagram for *factor* which includes *function*

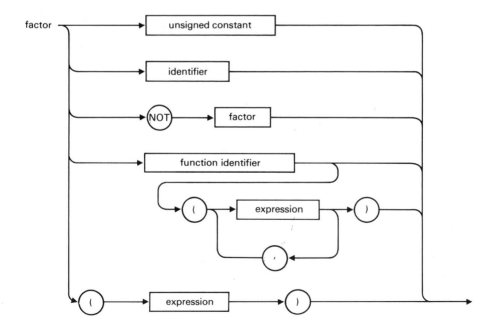

Fig. 4.8 *Factor* Syntax

calls. For each formal parameter in the function definition there must be an actual parameter of the same type in the function call.

Forward Reference

Calls to a procedure (or function) may precede the full definition of the procedure if a *forward reference* is given, as in this example:

```
    PROCEDURE excavate (VAR treasure : real;
                        VAR found : boolean);
        forward;

    { invocations of excavate }

    PROCEDURE excavate;
    { body of excavate }
```

Note that the parameter list is written only once, in the forward reference.

The symbol *forward* in this context is somewhat anomalous. It is not mentioned in the PASCAL Report at all, and so there is no clear rule for its interpretation. It is neither a reserved word nor a standard identifier, and so presumably it should be interpreted as a context dependent 'mark'. PASCAL is freer of such *ad hoc* devices than most programming languages, but it does have a few. The colons permitted in parameters of the procedure *write* are another example.

4.3 Recursion

Towards the end of the nineteenth century, a game called the Tower of Hanoi appeared in novelty stores in Europe. The popularity of this game was enhanced by accompanying promotional material explaining that priests in the Temple of Bramah were currently playing it, and that the end of their game signified the end of the world. The priests' equipment allegedly consisted of a brass platform with three diamond needles on which rested sixty-four golden disks. The more modest version sold to the public consisted of eight cardboard disks mounted on three wooden posts. The object of the game is to move the tower on the left needle (Fig. 4.9) to the right needle, under the conditions that only one disk may be moved at a time, and at no stage may a larger disk rest on a smaller disk.

We will suppose that the needles are numbered 1, 2, and 3, and that the priests are moving the tower of 64 disks from needle 1 to

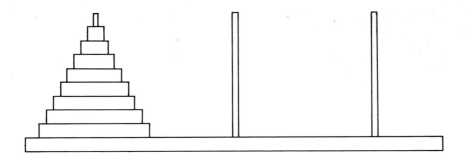

Fig. 4.9   The Tower of Hanoi

needle 3.   We will denote this task by

movetower(64,1,3)

Our problem is to devise an algorithm which will provide the priests
with a list of the correct moves to make in order to solve the problem.   The insight that leads to a simple solution is to think about
the bottom disk on needle 1 rather than the top one.   The task *move-
tower(64,1,3)* is then seen to be equivalent to the following sequence
of subtasks:

movetower(63,1,2);
move a disk from needle 1 to needle 3;
movetower(63,2,3)

This is a small but significant step towards the solution.   Small,
because we still have the problem of moving 63 disks twice.   Significant, because we can repeat the analysis as often as we want.   For
example, the task

movetower(63,1,2)

can be expressed as

movetower(62,1,3);
move a disk from needle 1 to needle 2;
movetower(62,3,2)

In order to construct a general algorithm, we have to specify which
needle is to be used for the temporary tower.   We can do this by
extending our notation so that

movetower(n,a,b,c)

means

> *move n disks from needle a to needle b using needle c*
> *for the temporary tower*

We can then assert that the task

> *movetower(n,a,b,c)*

may be performed in three steps:

> *movetower(n-1,a,c,b);*
> *move a disk from a to b;*
> *movetower(n-1, c,b,a)*

This algorithm will clearly fail for n ≤ 1, and so we add the rule:

> *do nothing if n ≤ 1*

Now we can write a PASCAL procedure to perform these actions:

```
PROCEDURE movetower (height, fromneedle,
                        toneedle, usingneedle : integer);
    BEGIN
      IF height > 0
         THEN
            BEGIN
              movetower(height-1,fromneedle,
                      usingneedle,toneedle);
              movedisk(fromneedle,toneedle);
              movetower(height-1,usingneedle,
                      toneedle,fromneedle)
            END
    END; { movetower }
```

The question now arises: is a procedure allowed to call itself in this way? Fortunately the answer is 'yes', and such a call is called a *recursive procedure call*. Program *hanoi* prints the moves required to transfer a tower of any height from needle 1 to needle 3.

```
PROGRAM hanoi (input, output);
VAR
    total : integer;

  PROCEDURE movetower (height, fromneedle,
                        toneedle, usingneedle : integer);

    PROCEDURE movedisk (takeoff, puton : integer);
      BEGIN
        writeln(takeoff, '→', puton)
      END; { movedisk }
```

```
BEGIN { movetower }
   IF height > 0
      THEN
         BEGIN
            movetower(height-1,fromneedle,
                       usingneedle,toneedle);
            movedisk(fromneedle,toneedle);
            movetower(height-1,usingneedle,
                       toneedle,fromneedle)
         END
END; { movetower }

BEGIN { hanoi }
   read(total);
   movetower(total,1,3,2)
END. { hanoi }
```

Input:
   3

Output:
   1→3
   1→2
   3→2
   1→3
   2→1
   2→3
   1→3

Recursion is possible in PASCAL by virtue of the fact that new local variables are generated dynamically when a procedure is called. Suppose that we execute Program *hanoi* with total = 3. The first call to *movetower* is

   movetower (3,1,3,2)

On entry to *movetower*, we have

   height   = *3*
   fromneedle   = *1*
   toneedle   = *3*
   usingneedle = *2*

Since *height* > 0, the first action of *movetower* is to call

   movetower (2,1,2,3)

This time, when we enter *movetower*, we have

> *height*   = 2
> *fromneedle*   = 1
> *toneedle*   = 2
> *usingneedle* = 3

These steps are illustrated in Fig. 4.10 (a) through (c). At the second call to *movetower*, new space is allocated for the parameters. Variable names are represented by their initial letters in these diagrams.

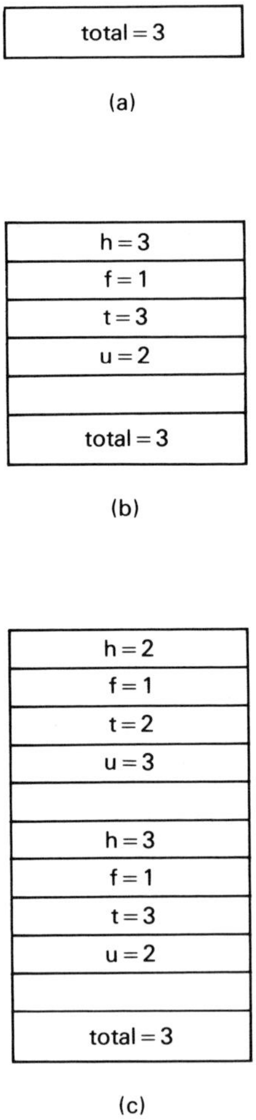

```
┌─────────────────┐
│    total = 3    │
└─────────────────┘
```

(a)

```
┌─────────────────┐
│     h = 3       │
├─────────────────┤
│     f = 1       │
├─────────────────┤
│     t = 3       │
├─────────────────┤
│     u = 2       │
├─────────────────┤
│                 │
├─────────────────┤
│   total = 3     │
└─────────────────┘
```

(b)

```
┌─────────────────┐
│     h = 2       │
├─────────────────┤
│     f = 1       │
├─────────────────┤
│     t = 2       │
├─────────────────┤
│     u = 3       │
├─────────────────┤
│                 │
├─────────────────┤
│     h = 3       │
├─────────────────┤
│     f = 1       │
├─────────────────┤
│     t = 3       │
├─────────────────┤
│     u = 2       │
├─────────────────┤
│                 │
├─────────────────┤
│   total = 3     │
└─────────────────┘
```

(c)

Fig. 4.10   Recursion in Program *hanoi*

The values at the first level are not destroyed, but they are not accessible to the program until the second call to *movetower* is completed.

A complete account of the operation of Program *hanoi* for the case *total* = 3 is given in Table 4.1. Once again, the names of the

level 0	level 1	level 2	level 3	move
total = 3				
	h = 3 f = 1 t = 3 u = 2			
		h = 2 f = 1 t = 2 u = 3		
			h = 1 f = 1 t = 3 u = 2 1→3	1→3
		1→2		1→2
			h = 1 f = 3 t = 2 u = 1 3→2	3→2
	1→3			1→3
		h = 2 f = 2 t = 3 u = 1		
			h = 1 f = 2 t = 1 u = 3 2→1	2→1
		2→3		2→3
			h = 1 f = 1 t = 3 u = 2 1→2	1→2

Table 4.1   Execution Trace of Program *hanoi*

variables have been abbreviated. A move from needle *a* to needle *b* is written

   a→b

Recursion

Actions at level 4, on which *height* = 0, are not recorded.

Recursion and Iteration

A recursive solution to a problem has two steps. The first step
of the solution consists of transforming the problem into a new problem which is similar to the original problem but which is some way
simpler. In the Tower of Hanoi problem this step consisted of simpli-
fying the task of moving 64 disks to the task of moving 63 disks.
This transformation can be applied repeatedly until the problem
becomes trivial. The Tower of Hanoi problem is solved when we have no
disks to move.

There are many mathematical functions which may be defined recursively. For example, for positive values of *n*, we have:

$$x^n = \begin{cases} 1 & \text{if } n = 0 \\ x \times x^{n-1} & \text{if } n > 0 \end{cases}$$

$$n! = \begin{cases} 1 & \text{if } n = 0 \\ n \times (n-1)! & \text{if } n > 0 \end{cases}$$

$$P_n(x) = \begin{cases} 1 & \text{if } n = 0 \\ x & \text{if } n = 1 \\ ((2n-1)P_{n-1}(x) - (n-1)P_{n-2}(x))/n & \text{if } n > 1 \end{cases}$$

It is easy to write recursive PASCAL functions from these definitions.
From the third example, which is the recursive definition of the
Legendre polynomials, we obtain:

```
FUNCTION p (n : integer; x : real) : real;
    BEGIN
        IF n = 0
            THEN p := 1
        ELSE IF n = 1
            THEN p := x
        ELSE p := ((2*n-1)*p(n-1,x) - (n-1)*p(n-2,x))/n
    END;
```

In most of these cases, however, the recursive solution is not the
best because a simple solution may be obtained by iteration. The
Legendre polynomials are more efficiently computed in this way:

106

Example

```
FUNCTION p (n : integer; x : real) : real;
   VAR
      prev, this, next : real;
      count : integer;
   BEGIN
      IF n = 0
         THEN p := 1
      ELSE IF n = 1
         THEN p := x
      ELSE
         BEGIN
            prev := 1;
            this := x;
            FOR count := 2 TO n DO
               BEGIN
                  next := ((2*count - 1)*this
                           - (count - 1)*prev)/count;
                  prev := this;
                  this := next
               END; { for }
            p := next
         END
   END; { p }
```

The choice between iteration and recursion is usually determined by the need for temporary storage. In the Tower of Hanoi problem, the position at each stage is stored in the local variables, and the problem cannot be solved if this storage is not available. It is possible to write a non-recursive solution, but the recursive solution is simple and natural. On the other hand, the class of functions which have definitions of the form

$$F_n(x) = \begin{cases} G(x) & \text{if } n = 0 \\ H(F_{n-1}(x)) & \text{if } n > 0 \end{cases}$$

can always be expressed iteratively, and so a recursive solution is unnecessary.

These examples, in which a procedure or a function invokes itself, are instances of *simple recursion*. It is also possible for a procedure P to call a procedure Q which calls procedure P: this is called indirect recursion. Indirect recursion is employed in the following example.

Example: Pocket Calculator Simulation

In this section, we consider in detail the construction of a program which simulates the action of a pocket calculator. The

107

Example

description of the programming techniques illustrates the principle of top-down design, and the finished program illustrates the relationship between recursive procedures and recursive data structures.

The program reads a *calculation*, the syntax of which is defined by Fig. 4.11. A calculation might look like this:

  180/(2*3.14159), 16*62.5*27, 169*(5+8);

The program would evaluate each of these expressions in turn, and reply:

  28.647913
  27000
  2197

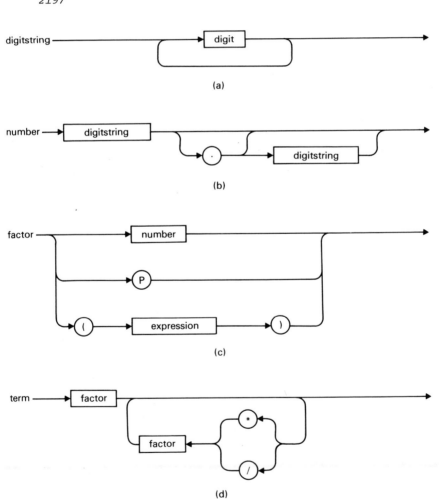

(a)

(b)

(c)

(d)

Example

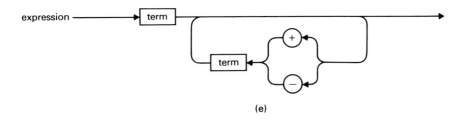

(e)

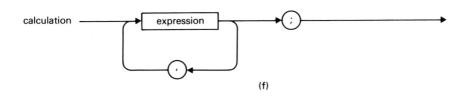

(f)

Fig. 4.11 *Calculation* Syntax

An expression consists of terms and factors, and a factor may
contain an expression, and so expressions can be constructed recursively. The letter 'P' is also permitted as a variety of factor, but
we will postpone its interpretation until the end of Chapter 5.

The syntax has been designed to facilitate analysis without *back-*
tracking. This means that the program can read one character at a
time from the input medium, and choose the correct course of action
without ever going wrong and having to retrace its steps. For
example, when a factor is expected, the next character must be a
digit, the letter 'P', or a left parenthesis: any other character
must be erroneous. Accordingly, we design the program so that the
next character is always available for inspection.

Our first attempt at writing the program looks like this:

```
PROGRAM calculator (input, output);
   CONST
      semicolon = ';';
   VAR
      nextchar : char;
      result : real;
   BEGIN
      readchar(nextchar);
      WHILE nextchar ≠ semicolon DO
         BEGIN
            readexpression(nextchar,result);
            writeln(result)
```

109

Example

```
          END { while }
    END. { calculator }
```

The procedure *readchar* reads the next character from the input medium.
The procedure *readexpression* continues reading and analyzing until the
end of the expression, returning the value of the expression as
result.   If the character following the expression is a semicolon the
program terminates, otherwise it reads another expression. A defect
of this version of the program is that it does not check that, if the
expression delimiter is not a semicolon, then it is a comma. We
remedy this later, when we describe how input errors are handled by
the program.

   An expression must contain at least one term, but after the first
term, there may or may not be more. *WHILE* is the most appropriate
construction to use in procedure *readexpression*.

```
    PROCEDURE readexpression (VAR exprchar : char
                             VAR exprvalue : real);
      CONST
        plus = '+';
        minus = '-';
      VAR
        addop : char;
        nexttermval : real;
      BEGIN
        readterm(exprchar,exprvalue);
        WHILE (exprchar = plus) OR (exprchar = minus) DO
          BEGIN
            addop := exprchar;
            readchar(exprchar);
            readterm(exprchar,nexttermval);
            IF addop = plus
              THEN exprvalue := exprvalue + nexttermval
              ELSE exprvalue := exprvalue - nexttermval
          END { while }
    END; { readexpression }
```

   The procedure *readchar* can be coded in a similar way using the
multiplicative operators '*' and '/' instead of the additive operators. The procedure *readfactor* is slightly different because there
are several cases to consider.

```
    PROCEDURE readfactor (VAR factorchar : char;
                          VAR factorvalue : real);
      CONST
        zero = '0';
        nine = '9';
        leftparen = '(';
        rightparen = ')';
```

110

Example

```
    BEGIN
        IF (zero ≤ factorchar) AND (factorchar ≤ nine)
            THEN readnumber(factorchar,factorvalue)
        ELSE IF factorchar = leftparen
            THEN
                BEGIN
                    readchar(factorchar);
                    readexpression(factorchar,factorvalue);
                    IF factorchar = rightparen
                        THEN readchar(factochar)
                        ELSE reporterror { ')' expected }
                END
        ELSE reporterror { illegal character }
    END; { readfactor }
```

The procedure *readnumber* is similar to Program *convert* of Chapter 3. We now consider the procedure *reporterror*.

The program can now detect three error conditions: no comma at the end of an expression; no right parenthesis at the end of a bracketed expression; and an illegal character when a factor is expected. Additionally, the procedure *readterm* (which performs multiplications and divisions) should report an error if a divisor is zero. The easy solution is to print one of four messages, but this is not very helpful to the user because it does not tell him where the errors are. We make the program more useful by indicating where the errors are rather than what is wrong. This is quite easy to do if we assign to *readchar* the additional task of reporting the position of the current character in the input line. This implies that *readchar* will have two parameters, and the procedures already written will have to be altered accordingly.

In writing *readchar* we include three small refinements which make the final program easier to use. These are:

(1) *Readchar* skips over blanks, so the user can include blanks in a calculation for clarity;

(2) We would like expressions to be terminated at the end of a line, and so end-of-line is translated into comma;

(3) The user may forget to write a semicolon at the end of the calculation, and so end-of-file is translated into semicolon.

We can now write *readchar*:

Example

```
PROCEDURE readchar (VAR ch : char;
                    VAR charpos : integer);
CONST
    comma = ',';
    semicolon = ';';
    blank = ' ';
BEGIN
    REPEAT
        IF eof
            THEN ch := semicolon
        ELSE IF eoln
            THEN
                BEGIN
                    charpos := 0;
                    char := comma;
                    readln
                END
        ELSE
            BEGIN
                charpos := charpos + 1;
                read(ch)
            END
    UNTIL ch ≠ blank
END; { readchar }
```

The procedure *reporterror* prints a marker underneath the offending character. Once an error has been found in an expression there
is no point in analyzing it further, and so *reporterror* also skips
through the input file until it finds a comma or a semicolon.

```
PROCEDURE reporterror (VAR errorchar : char;
                       VAR errorcharpos : integer);
CONST
    marker = '↑';
    comma = ',';
    semicolon = ';';
BEGIN
    writeln(marker : errorcharpos);
    WHILE NOT ((errorchar = comma)
            OR (errorchar = semicolon)) DO
        readchar(errorchar,errorcharpos)
END; { reporterror }
```

We now give the complete program, incorporating changes in some
of the procedures as we have described them.

Example

```
PROGRAM calculator (input, output);
   CONST
     comma = ',';
     semicolon = ';';
   VAR
     nextchar : char;
     nextcharpos : integer;
     result : real;

PROCEDURE readchar (VAR ch : char;
                    VAR charpos : integer);
   CONST
     comma = ',';
     semicolon = ';';
     blank = ' ';
   BEGIN
     REPEAT
       IF eof
         THEN ch := semicolon
         ELSE IF eoln
           THEN
             BEGIN
               charpos := 0;
               ch := comma;
               readln
             END
         ELSE
           BEGIN
             charpos := charpos + 1;
             read(ch)
           END
     UNTIL ch ≠ blank
   END; { readchar }

PROCEDURE reporterror (VAR errorchar : char;
                       VAR errorcharpos : integer);
   CONST
     marker = '↑';
     comma = ',';
     semicolon = ';';
   BEGIN
     writeln(marker : errorcharpos);
     WHILE NOT ((errorchar = comma) OR (errorchar = semicolon)) DO
       readchar(errorchar,errorcharpos)
   END; { reporterror }

PROCEDURE readnumber (VAR numchar : char;
                      VAR numcharpos : integer;
                      VAR numvalue : real);
   CONST
```

113

```
      zero = '0';
      nine = '9';
      point = '.';
      radix = 10;
  VAR
    count, scale : integer;
  BEGIN
    numvalue := 0;
    WHILE (zero ≤ numchar) AND (numchar ≤ nine) DO
      BEGIN
        numvalue := radix * numvalue + ord(numchar)
                                        - ord(zero);
        readchar(numchar,numcharpos)
      END; { while }
    IF numchar = point
      THEN
        BEGIN
          readchar(numchar,numcharpos);
          scale := 0;
          WHILE (zero ≤ numchar) AND (numchar ≤ nine) DO
            BEGIN
              numvalue := radix * numvalue + ord(numchar
                                            - ord(zero);
              readchar(numchar,numcharpos);
              scale := scale + 1
            END; { while }
          FOR count := 1 TO scale DO
            numvalue := numvalue / radix
        END
  END; { readnumber }
  PROCEDURE readexpression (VAR exprchar : char;
                            VAR exprcharpos : integer;
                            VAR exprvalue : real);

    CONST
      plus = '+';
      minus = '-';
    VAR
      addop : char;
      nexttermval : real;

    PROCEDURE readterm (VAR termchar : char;
                        VAR termcharpos : integer;
                        VAR termvalue : real);

      CONST
        multiply = '*';
        divide = '/';
      VAR
        mulop : char;
        nextfacval : real;
```

114

Example

```
PROCEDURE readfactor (VAR factorchar : char;
                      VAR factorcharpos : integer;
                      VAR factorvalue : real);
    CONST
      zero = '0';
      nine = '9';
      leftparen = '(';
      rightparen = ')';
    BEGIN { readfactor }
      IF (zero ≤ factorchar) AND (factorchar ≤ nine)
        THEN readnumber(factorchar,factorcharpos,factorvalue)
      ELSE IF factorchar = leftparen
        THEN
          BEGIN
            readchar(factorchar,factorcharpos);
            readexpression(factorchar,factorcharpos,factorvalue);
            IF factorchar = rightparen
              THEN readchar(factorchar,factorcharpos)
              ELSE reporterror(factorchar,factorcharpos)
          END
      ELSE
        BEGIN
          reporterror(factorchar,factorcharpos);
          factorvalue := 0
        END
    END; { readfactor }

  BEGIN { readterm }
    readfactor(termchar,termcharpos,termvalue);
    WHILE (termchar = multiply) OR (termchar = divide) DO
      BEGIN
        mulop := termchar;
        readchar(termchar,termcharpos);
        readfactor(termchar,termcharpos,nextfacval);
        IF mulop = multiply
          THEN termvalue := termvalue * nextfacval
        ELSE IF nextfacval ≠ 0
          THEN termvalue := termvalue / nextfacval
          ELSE reporterror(termchar,termcharpos)
      END { while }
  END; { readterm }

BEGIN { readexpression }
  readterm(exprchar,exprcharpos,exprvalue);
  WHILE (exprchar = plus) OR (exprchar = minus) DO
    BEGIN
      addop := exprchar;
      readchar(exprchar,exprcharpos);
      readterm(exprchar,exprcharpos,nexttermval);
      IF addop = plus
        THEN exprvalue := exprvalue + nexttermval
        ELSE exprvalue := exprvalue - nexttermval
```

115

```
        END { while }
    END; { readexpression }

  BEGIN { calculator }
    nextcharpos := 0;
    readchar(nextchar,nextcharpos);
    WHILE nextchar ≠ semicolon DO
      BEGIN
        readexpression(nextchar,nextcharpos,result);
        IF (nextchar = comma) OR (nextchar = semicolon)
          THEN writeln(result)
          ELSE reporterror(nextchar,nextcharpos);
        readchar(nextchar,nextcharpos)
      END { while }
  END. { calculator }
```

4.4 Non-Local Variables and Side-Effects

We have seen that procedures and functions can access and alter
the values of non-local variables. A procedure or function which
alters the value of a non-local variable is said to have *side-effects*.
The term 'side-effect' is familiar from pharmacology. A drug is
supposed to have a specific effect on the body, and any additional
effects are called side-effects. The implication is that side-effects
are harmful, or at least undesirable. In programming, unlike pharmacology, we have complete control over side-effects. Moreover, side-
effects may do no harm to the program: the principal objection to them
is rather that they obscure the program structure, thereby making the
program harder to understand.

The procedures in Program *calculator* do not refer to non-local
identifiers, and they do not have side-effects. This ensures that
each procedure may be read as a complete entity, since it refers to
its own constants, variables and parameters only. On the other hand,
the structure of the program as a whole is in some ways obscured by
this approach. At any one time, exactly one character is being used,
but this character may have any of the names *ch*, *errorchar*, *numchar*,
factorchar, *termchar*, *exprchar* or *nextchar* depending on where we look.
Later on, we present another version of *calculator* in which procedures
do have side-effects, so you can compare the two programs.

When writing procedures, weigh the merits of using or not using
non-local variables carefully. A procedure should only access or
alter the value of a non-local variable if there is good reason for
it to do so. Use the criteria of clarity and security. Programs
written by a team must usually adhere to stricter disciplines than
programs written by individuals.

When writing functions, do not use or alter the values of non-local variables. Think of the word 'function' in its mathematical sense, and write functions whose values are dependent on their arguments only.

Be alert to accidental side-effects. Suppose that you use a variable x within a procedure but forget to declare it. Often, the compiler will regard this as an error, but if you had declared x as a variable in an outer procedure or in the main program, no error would be reported. This can lead to very mysterious behavior by the program. The moral is threefold: don't use the same variable name at different levels; don't forget to write declarations— whenever you declare a new variable, write a declaration for it immediately; and don't use variable names like x.

4.5 Pseudo Random Numbers

Suppose that we have a means of selecting an integer r at random from the set of integers 1,2,...,N. Simple mechanisms exist for performing this selection for certain small values of N. For N = 2 we can toss a coin, for N = 6 we can roll a die, and for N = 36 we can use a roulette-wheel. A sequence

$$r_1, \; r_2, \; \ldots$$

of such integers is called a *random sequence*. An algorithm which generates a random, or apparently random, sequence is called a *random number generator*. Several of the examples in this book require a random number generator, and so in this section we digress briefly to look at how random numbers can be generated.

The method most commonly used to generate random numbers is the *linear congruential method*. Each number in the sequence, r_k, is calculated from its predecessor, r_{k-1}, using this formula:

$$r_k = (multiplier \; * \; r_{k-1} \; + \; increment) \; MOD \; modulus$$

The numbers generated by using this formula repeatedly are not truly random in the sense that tosses of a coin or throws of a die are random, because we can always predict the value of r_k given the value of r_0. The sequence generated by this formula is therefore more correctly called a *pseudo-random sequence*, and its members are called *pseudo-random numbers*. There are many applications of random numbers in computer science, and for most of these pseudo-random numbers are just as good provided that some elementary precautions are taken.

Most computer installations have a standard pseudo-random number generator of the linear congruential type, for which the values of *multiplier*, *increment* and *modulus* have been carefully chosen. If your installation has such a generator, and it is accessible to PASCAL programs, then you should use it. If you do not have access to a good generator, you may use this simple algorithm: it will work on most computers, generates 65536 random numbers before repeating itself, and is adequate for the examples given in this book. We use:

$$modulus = 2^{16} = 65536$$
$$multiplier \quad = 25173$$
$$increment \quad = 13849$$

and so we have

$$r_k = (25173 * r_{k-1} + 13849) \text{ MOD } 65536$$

This calculation will not cause overflow on a computer for which

$$maxint \geq 2^{31}$$

The pseudo random number generator is written as a PASCAL function.

```
FUNCTION random (VAR seed : integer) : integer;
    CONST
        multiplier = 25173;
        increment = 13849;
        modulus = 65536;
    BEGIN
        random := seed;
        seed := (multiplier * seed + increment) MOD modulus
    END;
```

Note that this function contravenes the rule that a function should not change the value of any of its parameters. Since we want *random* to return a different value each time we call it, this is unfortunately unavoidable. To save space, when we use *random* in examples, we will use literals rather than constants for *multiplier*, *increment* and *modulus*. The function generates a permutation of the integers

$$0,1,2, \ldots 65535$$

and then repeats itself. The first number generated is the initial value of *seed*.

For most applications, these numbers should be scaled in some way. For example, if the program is simulating throws of a die, we could write

```
VAR
    throw, seed : integer;
```

Example

```
      . . . .
      throw := random(seed) DIV 10923 + 1
```

We frequently require a real random value between 0 and 1. For this
purpose we can use a modified version of *random*:

```
      FUNCTION random (VAR seed : integer) : real;
         BEGIN
            random := seed / 65535;
            seed := (25173 * seed + 13849) MOD 65536
         END;
```

This function will provide random numbers such that

$$0 \leq random(seed) \leq 1$$

It can be modified quite easily to exclude either of the values 0 or
1.

Example : Volume Calculation

    One application of random numbers is the computation of areas and
volumes. Suppose that we have an irregular solid S which can be
enclosed in a cube C. It is easy to generate random points in C, and
it can be shown that the probability that a random point inside C is
also inside S is

$$V_c/V_s$$

where V_C is the volume of C and V_S is the volume of S. If there is a
simple criterion which enables us to decide whether or not a point is
inside S, we can estimate the volume of S by generating random points
and counting the number which falls inside S. Program *spherevolume*
estimates the volume of a sphere in this way. The cube C is defined
by

$$|x| \leq 1, \quad |y| \leq 1, \quad |z| \leq 1$$

One eighth of the sphere

$$x^2 + y^2 + z^2 \leq 1$$

fits inside this cube, and so if we generate a random point (x,y,z)
inside the cube, the probability that it will also lie inside this
sector of the sphere is $V_S/8$. This is of course an absurd way to
calculate the volume of a sphere, but the method is useful when a
simple inclusion criterion can be defined but there is no simple
formula for the volume of the solid.

```
PROGRAM spherevolume (input, output);
  VAR
    try, total, inside, randomseed : integer;

  FUNCTION random (VAR seed : integer) : real;
    BEGIN
      random := seed / 65535;
      seed := (25173 * seed + 13849) MOD 65536
    END; { random }

  BEGIN
    read(total);
    inside := 0;
    FOR try := 1 TO total DO
      IF   sqr(random(randomseed))
        + sqr(random(randomseed))
        + sqr(random(randomseed)) ≤ 1
          THEN inside := inside + 1;
    writeln('Estimated volume =', 8 * inside / total)
  END. { spherevolume }
```

Input:
     5000

Output:
     Estimated volume = 4.16800

Exercises

4.1 What happens when Program *cancelfactors* reads negative numbers?
    Correct the program so that it gives reasonable results in all
    cases.

4.2 Predict the output of the programs below and explain your reason-
    ing.

(a)
```
PROGRAM nonsense (output);
  VAR
    thing : integer;

  PROCEDURE cheat (VAR hee, haw : integer);
    BEGIN
      hee := -1;
      haw := -hee
    END;
```

```
        BEGIN
            thing := 1;
            cheat(thing, thing);
            writeln(thing)
        END.
```

(b)   ```
        PROGRAM rubbish (output);
        VAR
            thing : integer;

        PROCEDURE liar (VAR hee : integer; haw : integer);
            BEGIN
                hee := 10 * haw
            END;

        BEGIN
            thing := 10;
            liar(thing, thing);
            writeln(thing)
        END.
```

4.3 Write definitions for the following functions, and test your solutions:

(a) The inverse trigonometric functions:

$$\sin^{-1}(x) = \tan^{-1}(x/\sqrt{(1 - x^2)})$$
$$\cos^{-1}(x) = \tan^{-1}(x/\sqrt{(1 - x^2)})$$

(b) The hyperbolic functions:

$$\sinh(x) = (e^x - e^{-x})/2$$
$$\cosh(x) = (e^x + e^{-x})/2$$
$$\tanh(x) = \sinh(x)/\cosh(x)$$

(c) The inverse hyperbolic functions:

$$\sinh^{-1}(x) = \ln(x + \sqrt{(x^2 + 1)})$$
$$\cosh^{-1}(x) = \ln(x + \sqrt{(x^2 - 1)})$$

4.4 Write a function $digit(n,k)$ which returns the value of the $k$'th digit from the right of the number $n$. For example,

```
digit(254693,2) = 9
digit(7622,6)   = 0
```

4.5 The function $\theta = arctan(x)$ returns a value of θ such that $-\pi/2 \leq \theta < \pi/2$. Write a function $atan(x,y)$ which uses the signs of x and y to calculate a value of θ such that $\tan(\theta) = y/x$ and
```

$-\pi < \theta \leq \pi.$

4.6 A jeep can travel 500 miles with a full load of fuel. From an initial cache containing N loads of fuel, the jeep can travel

$$L = 500(1 + 1/3 + 1/5 + \ldots + 1/(2N - 1))$$

miles by establishing caches of fuel *en route*. Write a function that calculates a value of N given L.

4.7 Modify procedure *movetower* of Program *hanoi* so that it does not call itself recursively when there are no disks to be moved. Extend Program *hanoi* so that it prints a table like Table 4.1 when it is executed.

4.8 Write iterative and recursive functions for calculating values of the *Hermite polynomials* $H_n(x)$ given that

$$H_0(x) = 1$$

$$H_1(x) = 2x$$

$$H_n(x) = 2xH_{n-1}(x) - 2(n-1)H_{n-2}(x) \qquad for \; n > 1$$

Compare the execution times of the two functions.

4.9 Write a recursive function to calculate values of *Ackermann's function*, $Ack(m,n)$ defined for $m \geq 0$ and $n \geq 0$ by

$$Ack(0,n) = n + 1$$
$$Ack(m,0) = Ack(m-1,1)$$
$$Ack(m,n) = Ack(m-1,Ack(m,m-1)) \qquad for \; m > 0 \; and \; n > 0$$

Include a *write* statement in the function body so that each entry to the function is recorded.

4.10 Program *calculator* will not accept expressions with a leading sign, such as the expressions in this calculation:

$$-16*27.5, \; +3183-2475;$$

Modify first the syntax diagrams and then the program to overcome this deficiency.

4.11 Draw syntax diagrams for expressions which may include the exponential operator '↑', where

$$a{\uparrow}b = a^b$$

Exponents are always evaluated before any other operators unless parentheses are used to change the order of evaluation. The

Exercises

expression

a↑b↑c

is illegal. Write a program that evaluates expressions containing
exponents. Use the fact that

a↑x = exp(x × ln(a))   *for a > 0.*

4.12 Draw a syntax diagram suitable for complex constants. Write a
procedure to read a complex constant. Use this procedure in a
program which evaluates complex expressions.

4.13 How accurate is Program *spherevolume*? Do you think that generating 5000000 random points would give better accuracy than generating 50000 points? Would it be better to generate a rectangular
lattice of points instead?

4.14 Use a random technique to estimate the volume enclosed by the
surfaces whose equations, in cylindirical polar coordinates
(r, θ, z), are

$$|z| \leq e^{-r^2}$$

$$r \leq 5$$

4.15 A particle performs a *random walk* according to the following
rules: At *t = 0*, the particle is at the origin, *x = 0, y = 0.*
At times t = 1, 2, 3, ... the particle makes a random step in
one of the four directions given by

x := x - 1
x := x + 1
y := y - 1
y := y + 1

The walk terminates when $x^2 + y^2 \geq R^2$. Determine the relationship between the time taken for the walk and the value of *R*
experimentally.

Variable Types

In Chapter 2 we discussed the standard types of PASCAL: *integer*, *real*, *boolean* and *char*. The properties of these types are determined completely by the implementation of PASCAL that we are using. In this chapter, and Chapters 6, 7 and 8, we introduce more abstract types for which we can define some of the properties ourselves. The existence of these types contributes to the power of PASCAL in two ways. First, a problem can be expressed more clearly and precisely if appropriate type definitions are employed, and this makes reading and writing programs easier. Secondly, type declarations enable us to give more information to the compiler about our problem, and the compiler can make use of this information to make more extensive error checks and to produce more efficient programs.

The new types are declared in a *type declaration section* which comes between the constant and variable declaration sections. Type declarations which appear within the body of a procedure are local to that procedure.

5.1 Scalars

The declaration of a scalar type is simply a list of the values that may be assumed by a variable of that type. The declaration

```
TYPE
    units = (inches,feet,furlongs,miles);
```

states that a variable to the type *units* may have any one of the four
values indicated, and no other values. The type *units* is used in a
variable declaration in the same way as one of the standard types.

```
VAR
    scale : units;
```

The two declarations may in fact be combined into one:

```
VAR
    scale : (inches,feet,furlongs,miles);
```

but in most cases it is preferable to keep the type declaration and
the variable declaration separate. Other examples of scalar type
declarations are:

```
TYPE
    day = (monday,tuesday,wednesday,thursday,
            friday,saturday,sunday);
    relationship = (parent,sibling,offspring,cousin);
    recordtype = (receivable,payable,invoice,creditnote);
    operator = (plus,minus,multiply,divide);
    trigfunction = (sine,cosine,tangent,
                    secant,cosecant,cotangent);
```

In the following variable declaration section we have declared some
variables with these types:

```
VAR
    holiday, workday : day;
    relative : relationship;
    inputrecord, outputrecord : recordtype;
    addingop, multop : operator;
```

A value may not belong to more than one type. The following declarations are incompatible because *tomato* appears in both value lists:

```
TYPE
    fruit = (apple,orange,lemon,pineapple,tomato);
    vegetable = (potato,carrot,tomato,pea,sprout);
```

The names of the values listed in the declaration of a scalar
type are constants of that type. Therefore we can write

```
holiday := sunday;
inputrecord := payable;
scale := miles;
addingop := minus;
```

Scalars

Mixed assignments are not permitted. You are not allowed to write

> *holiday := miles*

The only operators which can be used with scalar variables are the relational operators, and the resulting expressions have a boolean value. The ordering of scalar types is defined by the order in which they are enumerated in the type declaration. Consequently the following expressions are *true*:

> *monday < friday*
> *sibling > parent*
> *multiply > divide*

The standard type *boolean* is itself a scalar type, implicitly defined by the declaration

> *TYPE*
> *boolean = (false,true);*

Consequently, we have

> *false < true = true*

The functions *pred* and *succ* are defined for scalar arguments. The value returned is of the same type as the argument, and is the predecessor (or successor) of the argument in the definition list. We have for example

> *succ(monday) = tuesday*
> *pred(tangent) = cosine*

The first member of the list has no predecessor, and the last member has no successor.

The function *ord* has a scalar argument and returns an integer value which is the ordinal number of the scalar value in its definition list. The first value in the list has the ordinal number zero, and so

> *ord(payable) = 1*
> *ord(plus) = 0*
> *ord(cotangent) = 5*

Unfortunately, it is not possible in standard PASCAL to read or write a scalar value directly. If you wrote

> *relative := cousin;*
> *write(relative)*

you would not see 'cousin' in the output. In fact, you would probably not get any output at all, because the compiler would have reported an error. You could use

> *write(ord(relation))*

which would, when executed, print

> *3*

The *FOR* statement is often used in conjunction with scalar variables in constructions such as

> *FOR scale := inches TO miles DO*
> >   *convert*

Note that in this context, the *FOR* statement cannot be replaced by a *WHILE* statement. The statements

> *scale := inches;*
> *WHILE scale < miles DO*
> >   *BEGIN*
> > >   *convert;*
> > >   *scale := succ(scale)*
> >   *END*

will fail when the expression *succ(miles)* is evaluated.

5.2 Subranges

A *subrange type* is defined by two constants. For example

> *TYPE*
> >   *index = 1 .. 20;*

A variable of type *index* is an integer whose range is restricted. The constants in the declaration must be distinct and of the same type. The type of the constants may be *integer*, *char* or a scalar type. Subranges of *real* are not allowed. Here are some more examples of subrange types:

> *TYPE*
> >   *letter = 'a' .. 'z';*
> >   *digit = '0' .. '9';*
> >   *weekday = monday .. friday;*

Weekday is a subrange of the scalar type *day* defined in Section 5.1. The *associated scalar type* of a subrange type is the type of the

constants used to define it. For example the associated scalar type
of *weekday* is *day*. The constants are called the *lower bound* and *upper
bound* of the subrange type, and the declaration is only acceptable if

> *lowerbound* < *upperbound*

Subrange variables are declared in the usual way in the variable
declaration section.

```
VAR
    counter, entry : index;
    firstchar, lastchar : letter;
```

The two declarations necessary for a subrange variable can be combined
into one. We can write

```
VAR
    counter, entry : 1 .. 20;
    firstchar, lastchar : 'a' .. 'z';
```

In most cases, however, it is preferable to keep the type declaration
and the variable declaration separate.

Any operator which may be used with a variable of a particular
type may also be used with a subrange of that type. Furthermore,
different subranges of a type may be mixed in the same expression.
We could declare

```
VAR
    radix : 1 .. 10;
    smallnumber : 1 .. 100;
    result : integer;
```

and then write the expression

> *result + smallnumber DIV radix*

Subrange variables may also be used on both sides of assignment
statements. After the declarations above we would write

```
radix := smallnumber;
smallnumber := result
```

Attempting to assign a value to a subrange variable beyond its range
will, however, cause a run-time error.

All the functions defined for the associated scalar type may be
used with the subrange type. The value of a function is not necessarily a member of the subrange to which its argument belongs. For
example, the value of

sqr(smallnumber)

is not restricted to the range 0 .. 100.

The procedures *read* and *write* may be used with subranges of the types *integer* and *char*, and have the expected results.

Range-checking is an important, and often neglected, aspect of computer programming. Subranges take the burden of range-checking away from the programmer and pass it on to the compiler. You should use subranges, particularly subranges of integer, as frequently as possible. In fact, the type *integer* rarely appears in well-written PASCAL programs, because it is not often that the range of values of an integer variable is completely unpredictable. The use of subrange declarations also improves the readability of the program, because by telling the reader the range of values that a variable can take, you tell him something about its use.

5.3 Sets

A *set* is a collection of objects of the same type. If *S* is a set of objects of type *T*, then any object of type *T* is either a member of *S* or is not a member of *S*. Corresponding to any scalar type, we may define a set type. Values of the set type are sets of values of the scalar type. Declare the scalar type

```
TYPE
    ingredients = (apples,strawberries,bananas,
                   nuts,icecream,chocolatesauce,
                   cream,pastry,sugar,ice);
```

and the set type

```
TYPE
    dessert = SET OF ingredients;
```

Variables of the type *dessert* are declared in the variable declaration section in the usual way:

```
VAR
    sundae,applecrumble,feast : dessert;
```

The type *dessert* is the *associated set type* of the type *ingredients*. Conversely, *ingredients* is the *base type* of the type *dessert*.

The values of a constant or variable of the type *dessert* are subsets of the set of ingredients. A set is represented by a list of its members enclosed in square brackets, and these are constants of the type *dessert*:

>   [icecream,chocolatesauce]
>   [icecream,bananas,cream]
>   [icecream]

If the members of a set are consecutive values of the associated scalar type, only the first and last may be specified, and so

>   [apples,strawberries,bananas,nuts]

may be written

>   [apples .. nuts]

A set may have no members at all, ·in which case it is called the *empty set* and is written

>   [ ]

There are 2^{10} = 1024 possible values of dessert. In general, if the base type has n values, the associated set type has 2^n values.

The *union* of two sets is a set containing the members of both sets. The union operator is '+', and so we have

>   [apples] + [pastry,sugar] = [apples,pastry,sugar]

The *intersection* of two sets is a set containing only the objects which are members of both sets. The intersection operator is '*', and we have

>   [bananas,icecream,cream] * [icecream,nuts] = [icecream]

The *difference* of two sets is a set containing all the members of the first set which are not members of the second set, and it is denoted by the symbol '-'. We have

>   [apples,strawberries,bananas] - [strawberries,cream]
>   = [apples,bananas]

The relational operators may be used to compare sets.

>   = *denotes set equality*
>   ≠ *denotes set inequality*
>   ≤ *denotes 'is contained in'*
>   ≥ *denotes 'contains'*

A set *X contains* a set *Y* if every member of *Y* is also a member of *X*. The following expressions are *true*:

>   [icecream,chocolatesauce] = [chocolatesauce,icecream]
>   [icecream] ≠ [ice,cream]
>   [strawberries] ≤ [strawberries,cream]
>   [apples .. ice] ≥ [icecream .. cream]

The symbol *IN* (which is a reserved word of PASCAL) is used to test set membership. The left operand of *IN* is a scalar variable and the right operand is a variable of the associated set type. The expression

>   apples IN [apples,pastry,sugar]

is *true*, but the expression

>   apples IN [strawberries,cream]

is *false*.

The assignment statement may be used with set variables and set expressions in the usual way:

>   applecrumble := [apples,pastry,sugar];
>   feast := applecrumble + [icecream]

If you are familiar with set algebra, you will have noticed that the conventional symbols for set operations are not used in PASCAL. This is because the set operation symbols are not usually available on peripheral hardware. The following table shows the relationship between the conventional symbols and the PASCAL symbols.

Meaning	Conventional Symbol	PASCAL Symbol
Set	{ ... }	[...]
Union	∪	+
Intersection	∩	*
Contains	⊇	≥
Is Contained By	⊆	≤
Inclusion	∈	IN
Empty Set	∅	[ ]

Example: Tone Rows

If we represent the twelve tones of a chromatic octave by the type

>   TYPE
>   tonevalues = 1 .. 12;

then the tones in a *tone row* (which consists of several tones) can be

132

Sets

represented by the associated set type

```
TYPE
    row = SET OF tonevalues;
```

In serial music, each tone of the scale must be used exactly once
before it is repeated. Using the variables

```
VAR
    tone : tonevalues;
    sequence : row;
```

we can initialize a sequence by giving it no tones:

```
sequence := [ ]
```

and each time we add a new tone we can include it in the sequence
using the union operator:

```
sequence := sequence + [tone]
```

Furthermore, a tone is only permitted in the sequence if it has not
been used already, that is

```
IF NOT (tone IN sequence)
```

Finally, the sequence is complete when it contains each of the
twelve tones:

```
sequence = [1 .. 12]
```

These ideas, used in conjunction with the random number generator of
Chapter 4, lead to Program *tonerows* which generates a specified
number of random tone rows. The second parameter read by the program
is used to initialize the random number generator.

```
PROGRAM tonerows (input, output);
    CONST
        rowlength = 12;
    TYPE
        tonevalue = 1 .. rowlength;
        row = SET OF tonevalues;
    VAR
        seed, counter, cycles : integer;
        tone : tonevalues;
        sequence : row;

    FUNCTION randomtone (VAR randval : integer) : tonevalues;
        BEGIN
            randomtone := randval DIV (65535 DIV rowlength) + 1;
            randval := (25173 * randval + 13849) MOD 65536
```

```
      END; { randomtone }

  BEGIN
      read(cycles,seed);
      FOR counter := 1 TO cycles DO
          BEGIN
              sequence := [ ];
              REPEAT
                  tone := randomtone(seed);
                  IF NOT tone IN sequence
                      THEN
                          BEGIN
                              write(tone);
                              sequence := sequence + [tone]
                          END
                  UNTIL sequence = [1 .. rowlength];
                  writeln
          END { for }
  END. { tonerows }
```

Input:
```
   5     20000
```

Output:
```
   4    5    2   10    8   11    9    3    1    6   12    7
   8    2   12   10    7   11    6    1    4    5    9    3
   9    3    2    7    1   12    5   10    4   11    6    8
  10    3   12    7   11    4    9    1    6    2    8    5
   9    6    1    3    5   12    7    8    2   11   10    4
```

Example: A Combinatoric Problem

As another example of the use of sets, we will consider a simple combinatoric problem. Suppose that we have a bag containing r numbered balls, and that we are interested in possible ways of drawing k balls from it. The *number* of possible ways is of course easy to calculate using the appropriate binomial coefficient. A more interesting problem is to generate the selections one at a time. The bag may contain none, some, or all of the balls at any one time, and it may be appropriately represented by a set.

```
    CONST
        capacity = 20;
    TYPE
        object = 1 .. capacity;
        container = SET OF object;
    VAR
        bag : container;
        ball : object;
```

Now suppose that we have to select *total* balls from the bag, and that we have already selected *drawn* of them. Consider the problem of drawing the next one: either *drawn < total* and we have to look in the bag for another ball, or *drawn = total* and we have finished. This is done by the recursive procedure *select* in the program *selections*. As each ball is drawn, its number is printed. An entry in the third column, say, of the output listing indicates that the ball with that number was the third to be selected, and it also indicates the level of recursion.

```
PROGRAM selections (input, output);
    CONST
        capacity = 20;
    TYPE
        counter = 0 .. capacity;
        object = 1 .. capacity;
        container = SET OF object;
    VAR
        numballs, samplesize : counter;

    PROCEDURE select (bag : container;
                      sample, drawn : counter);
        VAR
            ball : object;
        BEGIN
            IF drawn < sample
                THEN
                    FOR ball := 1 TO capacity DO
                        IF ball IN bag
                            THEN
                                BEGIN
                                    writeln(ball : 3 * drawn);
                                    select(bag - [ball],sample,drawn + 1)
                                END
        END; { select }

    BEGIN
        read(numballs,samplesize);
        IF numballs ≥ samplesize
            THEN select([1 .. numballs],samplesize,0)
            ELSE writeln('Invalid data')
    END. { selections }
```

Input:
```
    4    3
```

Sets

Output:
```
1
    2
        3
        4
    3
        2
        4
    4
        2
        3
2
    1
        3
        4
    3
        1
        4
    4
        1
        3
....
```

It must be admitted that these two examples do not make a totally convincing case for the inclusion of sets in a programming language. Good applications of sets are hard to demonstrate, because they tend to be found in larger programs. Accordingly, we will conclude this section by describing some other uses of sets without giving complete examples.

Character sets have many uses. In simple cases, constant sets may be used. For example, the condition

('0' ≤ ch) AND (ch ≤ '9')

used in Programs *convert* (Chapter 3) and *calculator* (Chapter 4) can be written more succinctly as

ch IN ['0' .. '9']

If we declare

TYPE
    charset = SET OF char;

then we can write

PROCEDURE skipchars (VAR ch : char;
                     skipset : charset);

136

```
     BEGIN
        WHILE ch IN skipset DO
            read(ch)
     END;
```

The calls

```
     skipchars (ch,['a' .. 'z'])
```

and

```
     skipchars (ch,[',','.',';'])
```

will skip over letter and punctuation characters respectively.

It is often easier to work with symbols than with characters. In a PASCAL program, each of the following is regarded as a single symbol:

```
     BEGIN
     END
     varname
     1235.685
     :=
```

A procedure, usually called a *scanner*, is used to read characters from the input file and assemble them into symbols. The symbols are classified by a type declaration, and in a simple case, we might have

```
     TYPE
        symboltype = (reservedword,identifier,number,becomes);
        setofsymbol = SET OF symboltype;
```

Now we can write procedures *getsymbol*, which reads the next symbol and returns its type and value, and *skipsymbols* which skips over unwanted symbols in the same way as *skipchars* skips over characters.

During the execution of a large program, many kinds of errors may be detected. When an error is identified, an error code is printed, and at the end of the run explanations of the errors that occurred are printed. To implement this, we declare

```
     CONST
        maxerrorcode = 50;
     TYPE
        errorcode = 1 .. maxerrorcode;
        errorset = SET OF errorcode;
     VAR
        cumerror : errorset;
        error : errorcode;
```

During the initializations of the program, we set

  cumerror := [ ]

When an error is identified, we call the procedure *reporterror*:

```
PROCEDURE reporterror (error : errorcode);
   BEGIN
      writeln('Error', error : 3);
      cumerror := cumerror + [error]
   END;
```

At the end of the run, we execute this loop:

```
FOR error := 1 TO maxerrorcode DO
   IF error IN cumerror
      THEN write description of error
```

Syntax

The syntax for a simple type is defined by Fig. 5.1. A *type*

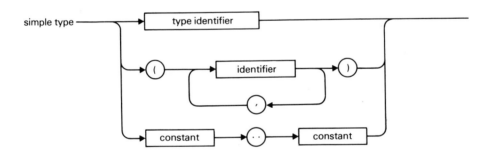

Fig. 5.1 *Simple Type* Syntax

identifier is either one of the standard identifiers *integer*, *real*, *boolean* or *char*, or it is an identifier defined in a previous type declaration. A *type* is either a *simple type* or the associated set type of a simple type, as shown in Fig. 5.2.

Note that two variables only have the same type if they are given the same type identifier. Following the declaration

```
VAR
   aset : SET OF 0 .. 25;
   bset : SET OF 0 .. 25;
```

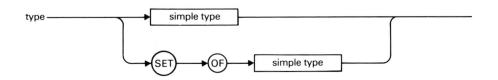

Fig. 5.2 *Type* Syntax

the variables *aset* and *bset* have different types, and could not be used in the same expression. After the declarations

        TYPE
            numset = SET OF 0 .. 25;
        VAR
            cset : numset;
            dset : numset;

the variables *cset* and *dset* have the same type.

5.4 The *CASE* Statement

The *IF* statement allows a process to select one of two possible choices of action according to the value of a boolean expression. The *CASE* is a generalization of the *IF* statement: it enables the process to execute one of several actions according to the value of a scalar or subrange variable.

As an introductory example, suppose that there is a toll-bridge at which the charges are:

        bicycles and motorcycles: free
        cars: 25¢
        cars with trailers: 50¢
        trucks: 25¢ per ton

We are required to write a program to calculate tolls. First, we make some declarations:

        CONST
            maxweight = 50;
            maxtoll = 1250;
        TYPE
            vehicletype = (cycle,car,carandtrailer,truck);

The CASE Statement

```
VAR
    weight : 1 .. maxweight;
    toll : 0 .. maxtoll;
    vehicle : vehicletype;
```

The section of the program that calculates the toll, using the CASE statement, looks like this:

```
CASE vehicle OF
    cycle :
        toll := 0;
    car :
        toll := 25;
    carandtrailer :
        toll := 50;
    truck :
        toll := 25 * weight
END
```

The variable *vehicle* in this statement is a *case selector*. The different values which the case selector can have appear in the CASE statement as *case labels*. After each label, there is a statement. The CASE construction allows us to write this program more tidily than if we had used the IF construction:

```
IF vehicle = cycle
    THEN toll := 0
ELSE IF vehicle = car
    THEN toll := 25
ELSE IF vehicle = carandtrailer
    THEN toll := 50
ELSE toll := 25 * weight
```

When the same action is required for several different values of the case selector, these values may be written in a list:

```
TYPE
    month = (jan,feb,mar,apr,may,jun,
             jul,aug,sep,oct,nov,dec);
    year + 1900 .. 2000;
    lenmonth = 28 .. 31;
VAR
    yy : year;
    mm : month;
    len : lenmonth;
....
    CASE mm OF
        jan,mar,may,jul,aug,oct,dec:
            len := 31;
        apr,jun,sep,nov :
            len := 30;
```

```
        feb :
           IF (yy MOD 4 = 0) AND (yy MOD 100 ≠ 0)
              THEN len := 29
              ELSE len := 28
     END { case }
```

Often, there are values of the case selector for which no action
is required, as for the value *sunday* in this example:

```
     VAR
        day : (sunday,monday,tuesday,wednesday,
              thursday,friday,saturday);
     ....
     CASE day OF
        sunday : ;
        monday,tuesday,wednesday,
        thursday,friday :
           BEGIN
              gotowork;
              work;
              comehome
           END;
        saturday :
           washcar
     END { case }
```

In situations where there is one action for which a long label list
is required, the *CASE* statement can be combined with an *IF* statement,
as in this example:

```
     VAR
        control : 1 .. 20;
     ....
     IF control IN [2,3,5,7,8,11,17,20]
        THEN
           CASE control OF
              2,5 :
                 action(1);
              3,7,11 :
                 action(2);
              8,17 :
                 action(3);
              20 :
                 action(4)
           END { case }
        ELSE writeln('illegal control value')
```

Program *calculator* revisited

Syntax

    Fig. 5.3 is a syntax diagram for the *CASE* statement.   The reserved
words *CASE* and *END* act as brackets around the statement.   The last
statement in the case list is not followed by a semicolon.   The complete syntax of PASCAL, given in Appendix B, allows a statement to be
empty.   Accordingly, there is no provision in Fig. 5.3 for a case
label without an action.

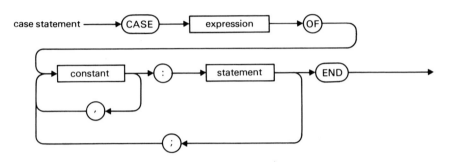

Fig. 5.3 *CASE Statement* Syntax

5.5 Program *calculator* revisited

    We conclude this chapter by presenting a second version of the
pocket calculator simulation featured in Chapter 4.   Two versions of
this program are given partly to illustrate the programming techniques
introduced in this chapter and partly to show how global identifiers
can be used at the expense of some program readability.   The changes
introduced in the second version of Program *calculator* are enumerated
below, and a discussion of their relative merits follows.

(1) All constants are declared in the constant declaration section of
    the main program, and so all constant identifiers are global.

(2) The variables *nextchar* and *nextcharpos* are altered directly by the
    procedures, rather than being passed as parameters.

(3) Procedure *readfactor* recognizes 'P'; the value of 'P' is the
    previous result, giving the 'calculator' a simple 'memory'.   The
    calculation

        *5,P*P,P*P*

    will yield

Program *calculator* revisited

> *5*
> *25*
> *625*

The global variable *prevresult* is accessed by the procedure *read-factor* to accomplish this.

(4) The global variable *nextcharpos* and the local variables *count* and *scale* have appropriate subrange types.

(5) The variables *digits*, *addingops*, *multops* and *terminators* are used as constant character sets to render the boolean expressions in the program more readable.

(6) Several *IF* statements are replaced by *CASE* statements.

Discussion

Since the two versions of Program *calculator* are functionally the same, except for the 'P' feature, we are interested primarily in the effect of the differences on the readability of the program. The first version of the program is written in such a way that the operation of any procedure can be deduced by reading that procedure only, provided that we know what the procedures it calls do. This is definitely advantageous in a long program. However, *calculator* is not a very long program, and the second version actually reveals its functional structure more clearly, because there is less repetition and because there are fewer variable names to remember. The fact that the procedure *readterm*, for example, returns the value of the term read as a parameter, but has side-effects on *nextchar* and *nextcharpos*, accurately represents its function in the program. Also, the single identifier *nextchar* replaces seven different identifiers in the original program, all referring to the same variable.

Observe that there is a general problem with respect to variables which act as constants in the program. We have declared *digits*, for example, as a global variable with the constant value

> *['0' .. '9']*

and accessed it from *readnumber* and *readfactor*. It is not possible to define a set constant in a constant declaration section, and so if *digits* was declared locally, the procedure would have to reset its value at every invocation, which is clearly inefficient. The value could be written as a literal wherever it was needed, but this makes the program harder to change to read, say, octal numbers, for which the appropriate value of *digits* is

> *['0' .. '7']*

Some of these considerations apply to constant declarations too.

Program *calculator* revisited

The use of global constants is often preferable for program maintenance. The second version of *calculator* is easily changed to use
square brackets rather than parentheses for nested expressions, for
instance.

Finally, we note that types must be non-local to a procedure if
parameters of that type are to be passed to the procedure. The type
position cannot be local to the procedure *readchar*, for instance.

We may conclude that decisions as to whether non-local identifiers
should be used must be made with reference to a particular problem.
The arguments presented here would not apply to a program of a hundred pages. Many teachers of programming take a harder line than we
have here, and state that the use of non-local identifiers is always
wrong. The fact is, however, that most non-trivial programs do have
some global identifiers, and they are more readable as a result.

```
PROGRAM calculator (input, output);
  CONST
    radix = 10;       maxscale = 20;     maxlinelen = 80;
    blank = ' ';      comma = ',';       semicolon = ';';
    point = '.';      plus = '+';        minus = '-';
    multiply = '*';   divide = '/';      marker = '↑';
    zero = '0';       nine = '9';        previous = 'P';
    leftparen = '(';  rightparen = ')';
  TYPE
    position = 0 .. maxlinelen;
    charset = SET OF char;
  VAR
    nextchar : char;
    nextcharpos : position;
    result, prevresult : real;
    digits, addingops, multops, terminators : charset;

  PROCEDURE readchar;
    BEGIN
      REPEAT
        IF eof
          THEN nextchar := semicolon
          ELSE IF eoln
            THEN
              BEGIN
                nextcharpos := 0;
                nextchar := comma;
                readln
              END
          ELSE
            BEGIN
              nextcharpos := nextcharpos + 1;
              read(nextchar)
```

```
            END
       UNTIL nextchar ≠ blank
     END; { readchar }

  PROCEDURE reporterror;
    BEGIN
       writeln(marker : nextcharpos);
       WHILE NOT (nextchar IN terminators) DO
          readchar
    END; { reporterror }

  PROCEDURE readnumber (VAR numvalue : real);
    TYPE
       scalefactor = 0 .. maxscale;
    VAR
       count, scale : scalefactor;
    BEGIN
       numvalue := 0;
       WHILE nextchar IN digits DO
         BEGIN
           numvalue := radix * numvalue + ord(nextchar)
                                       - ord(zero);
           readchar
         END; { while }
       IF nextchar = point
         THEN
           BEGIN
             readchar;
             scale := 0;
             WHILE nextchar IN digits DO
               BEGIN
                 numvalue := radix * numvalue + ord(nextchar)
                                             - ord(zero);
                 readchar;
                 scale := scale + 1
               END; { while }
             FOR count := 1 TO scale DO
                 numvalue := numvalue / radix
           END
    END; { readnumber }

  PROCEDURE readexpression (VAR exprvalue : real);
    VAR
       addop : char;
       nexttermval : real;

    PROCEDURE readterm (VAR termvalue : real);
      VAR
         mulop : char;
         nextfacval : real;
```

145

```
PROCEDURE readfactor (VAR factorvalue : real);
  BEGIN
    IF nextchar IN digits + [previous,leftparen]
      THEN
        CASE nextchar OF
          '0','1','2','3','4','5','6','7','8','9' :
            readnumber(factorvalue);
          'P' :
            BEGIN
              readchar;
              factorvalue := prevresult
            END;
          '(' :
            BEGIN
              readchar;
              readexpression(factorvalue);
              IF nextchar = rightparen
                THEN readchar
                ELSE reporterror
            END
        END { case }
      ELSE
        BEGIN
          reporterror;
          factorvalue := 0
        END
  END; { readfactor }

BEGIN { readterm }
  readfactor(termvalue);
  WHILE nextchar IN mulops DO
    BEGIN
      mulop := nextchar;
      readchar;
      readfactor(nextfacval);
      CASE mulop OF
        multiply :
          termvalue := termvalue * nextfacval;
        divide :
          IF nextfacval ≠ 0
            THEN termvalue := termvalue / nextfacval
            ELSE reporterror
      END { case }
    END { while }
  END; { readterm }

BEGIN { readexpression }
  readterm(exprvalue);
  WHILE nextchar IN addingops DO
    BEGIN
      addop := nextchar;
```

```
        readchar;
        readterm(nexttermval);
        CASE addop OF
          plus :
            exprvalue := exprvalue + nexttermval;
          minus :
            exprvalue := exprvalue - nexttermval
        END { case }
      END { while }
  END; { readexpression }

BEGIN { calculator }
  digits := [zero .. nine];
  addingops := [plus,minus];
  multops := [multiply,divide];
  terminators := [comma,semicolon];
  prevresult := 0;
  nextcharpos := 0;
  readchar;
  WHILE nextchar ≠ semicolon DO
    BEGIN
      readexpression(result);
      IF nextchar IN terminators
        THEN
          BEGIN
            writeln(result);
            prevresult := result
          END
        ELSE reporterror;
      readchar
    END { while }
END. { calculator }
```

Exercises

5.1 Show how a CASE statement may be used to print values of a
    scalar variable.

5.2 In the following program fragments, identify the statements which
    (1) will execute correctly, (2) may cause a run-time error, and
    (3) should cause a compile-time error. Assume that a statement
    which will necessarily fail if executed will cause a compile-time
    error. Assume also that variables not defined in these fragments
    have been assigned values elsewhere in the program.

Exercises

```
CONST
    min = -100;
    zero = 0;
    max = 100;
TYPE
    counter = 1 .. maxint;
    zeromin = min .. zero;
    zeromax =  zero .. max;
    coin = (penny,nickel,dime,quarter,halfdollar);
VAR
    count : counter;
    small : zeromin;
    big, value : zeromax;
    change : coin;
    flipflop : boolean;
    slot : SET OF coin;
BEGIN
    ....
    count := 0;
    small := big;
    change := penny;
REPEAT
    write(change : 10);
    change := succ(change)
UNTIL change > halfdollar;
dime := 2 * nickel;
count := count + ord(flipflop);
slot := slot + [halfdollar];
CASE coin OF
    penny :
        value := 1;
    nickel :
        value := 5;
    dime :
        value := 10;
    quarter :
        value := 25
END;
    ...
END
```

5.3 Given that

```
TYPE
    numberset = SET OF min .. max;
```

and min and max are integer constants, write a procedure *printset*
which prints the value of a variable of type *numberset*. For
example, the set whose members are 3, 7, 11 and 19 should be
printed as

148

Exercises

[3,7,11,19]

5.4 Write a program which reads a text counting words which contain at least four distinct vowels.

5.5 Determine experimentally the form of the function $p(k,N)$ defined as follows:

Declare

> *VAR*
> *x, y : SET OF 1 .. N;*

Generate random values of x and y such that each has k elements. Then

> $p(k,N)$ = probability that x and y are disjoint
> = $prob(x * y = [ ])$

5.6 Write a program which plays a game according to the following rules:

> The computer constructs a random set of digits. The player enters a set of digits using the keyboard of his terminal. The game ends when he enters a set identical to the one chosen by the computer. If his set is not identical to the computer's, the computer tells him how many digits the two sets have in common.

General Loader Functions

1) Binding
2) Allocation
3) Relocate
4) Loading

segment — a user program which
requires logical & sequential
allocation of memory

Passed to loader in object deck
1) text (includes transfer vector)
2) relocation bits,
3) length of transfer vector
4) length of program
5) define start pt. & name of segment.

BALR   12,0   do not zero then branch
                      to address in reg.
Using   *, 12

Structured Types

CHAPTER SIX

The variable types that we have encountered so far have all been simple types. The types that will be introduced in this chapter and the next are *structured types*. A structured type differs from a simple type in that the variables of a structured type have more than one *component*. Each component of a structured type is a variable which may have a simple or structured type. At the lowest level, the components of a structured variable have simple types, and these may be assigned values and used in expressions in the same way as simple variables. The important thing about a structured variable is the way in which its components are accessed. In this chapter we introduce variables of the type *ARRAY* and *RECORD*, which permit us to use the computer's memory in more flexible ways than we have seen hitherto. In the next chapter we introduce the type *FILE*, which enables information stored in media external to the memory to be accessed. We will use the terms *simple variable* and *structured variable* to denote variables whose types are simple and structured respectively.

6.1 Arrays

An *array* is an ordered collection of variables all of which have the same type. A line of text can be represented as an array of characters; a vector can be represented as an array of real numbers, and since a matrix consists of columns, each of which is a vector, a matrix can be represented as an array of vectors.

An array type is declared in terms of an *index type* and a *base type*.

```
TYPE
    direction = (x,y,z);
    vector = ARRAY [direction] OF real;
```

The index type of *vector* is *direction*, and the base type is *real*. We can declare variables of the type *direction* and *vector* in the usual way:

```
VAR
    s, t : direction;
    u, v : vector;
```

A variable of type *vector* has three components, one corresponding to each of the three values of the type *direction*. The three components of the vector *v* are

$$v[x], \ v[y], \ v[z]$$

The conventional mathematical notation for vectors uses subscripts to denote the components of a vector. The components of *v* are written in the form

$$v_x, \ v_y, \ v_z$$

For this reason, the values of an index type are often called *subscripts*.

Each of the components of *v* is a real variable, and may be used in any context where a real variable may be used. For example, the *norm* of a vector is the sum of the squares of its components. We could calculate the norm of *v* with either of the statements

```
    norm := sqr(v[x]) + sqr(v[y]) + sqr(v[z])
```

or

```
BEGIN
    norm := 0;
    FOR s := x TO z DO
        norm := norm + sqr(v[s])
END
```

The value of one array may be assigned to another array of the same type by a single assignment statement. The statement

152

```
        v := u
```

in which *u* and *v* are both vectors, is equivalent to the assignments

```
        v[x] := u[x];
        v[y] := u[y];
        v[z] := u[z]
```

An array may also be a value or variable parameter of a procedure or function. For example, the *inner product* of two vectors is computed by this function:

```
        FUNCTION innerproduct (u, v : vector) : real;
           VAR
              ip : real;
              s : direction;
           BEGIN
              ip := 0;
              FOR s := x TO z DO
                 ip := ip + u[s] * v[s];
              innerproduct := ip
           END;
```

The *outer product* of two vectors is itself a vector. The value of a function cannot be an array, and so it is not possible to write a function *outerproduct*. Instead, we can write *outerproduct* as a procedure which evaluates *w*, the outerproduct of *u* and *v*.

```
        PROCEDURE outerproduct (u, v : vector;
                                VAR w : vector);
           BEGIN
              w[x] := u[y] * v[z] - u[z] * v[y];
              w[y] := u[z] * v[x] - u[x] * v[z];
              w[z] := u[x] * v[y] - u[y] * v[x]
           END;
```

Syntax

The syntax of an *array declaration* is shown in Fig. 6.1 (a). The *index type* must be a scalar or subrange type. Remember that real is *not* a scalar type. The *base type* may be any type, even a structured type.

A *component* of an array has the same properties as a variable of the base type, and is therefore a variety of factor. The syntax of an *array component* is shown in Fig. 6.1 (b).

Example: Conversion of Numbers to Strings

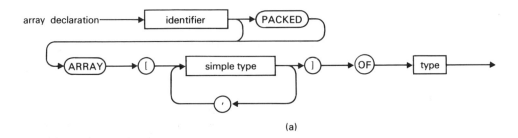

(a)

Fig. 6.1(a)   *Array Declaration* Syntax

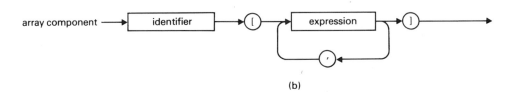

(b)

Fig. 6.1(b)   *Array Component* Syntax

Example: Conversion of Numbers to Strings

Program *convert* in Chapter 3 performed a conversion from a string
of digits to a number in the computer's internal form. We now consider the inverse problem, converting a variable to a string of digits.
The value of each digit in the string can be obtained easily enough by
repeated remaindering and division:

```
VAR
    datum, digit : integer;
 ....
    REPEAT
        digit := datum MOD 10;
        datum := datum DIV 10
    UNTIL datum = 0
```

Unfortunately, this simple program produces the numbers in the reverse
order to that in which we want to print them. For example, if *datum*
= 123, then, during the execution of the *REPEAT* statement, *digit* takes
the values 3, 2 and 1, in that order. We can get around this problem
by storing the successive values of *digit* in an array, and then writing them from the array in reverse order. Rather than storing the
integer values of *digit* in the array, we store their character
equivalents, so that when we have finished the number is ready for
printing. Declare

Example: Conversion of Numbers to Strings

```
CONST
    maxlen = 32;
    zero = '0';
    rad = 10;
VAR
    jp, kp : 0 .. maxlen;
    buffer : ARRAY [1 .. maxlen] OF char;
    num : integer;
```

The conversion loop now takes this form:

```
kp := 0;
REPEAT
    kp := kp + 1;
    buffer[kp] := chr(num MOD rad + ord(zero));
    num := num DIV rad
UNTIL num = 0
```

The digits can then be written in the correct sequence:

```
FOR jp := kp DOWNTO 1 DO
    write(buffer[jp])
```

We have chosen 10 as the divisor in the example because we are accustomed to using the decimal system. It is just as easy for the computer to use another divisor and print numbers in a different scale. Program *numberscales* reads a number using the standard procedure *read* (which performs a decimal conversion, of course) and then performs the inverse conversion for each of the scales 2 through 10 in turn.

```
PROGRAM numberscales (input, output);
    CONST
        maxradix = 10;
        maxlen = 32;
        minus = '-';
        zero = '0';
    TYPE
        radix = 2 .. maxradix;
    VAR
        datum : integer;
        scale : radix;

    PROCEDURE writenumber (num : integer; rad : radix);
        VAR
            jp, kp : 0 .. maxlen;
            buffer : ARRAY [1 .. maxlen] OF char;
        BEGIN
            IF num < 0
                THEN
                    BEGIN
```

Example: Sorting an Array

```
                    write(minus);
                    num := abs(num)
                END;
            kp := 0;
            REPEAT
                kp := kp + 1;
                buffer[kp] := chr(num MOD rad + ord(zero));
                num := num DIV rad
            UNTIL num = 0;
            FOR jp := kp DOWNTO 1 DO
                write(buffer[jp])
        END; { writenumber }

    BEGIN { numberscales }
        read(datum);
        FOR scale := 2 TO maxradix DO
            BEGIN
                writenumber(datum,scale);
                writeln
            END { for }
    END. { numberscales }
```

Input:
    100

Output:
    1100100
    10201
    1210
    400
    244
    202
    144
    121
    100

Example: Sorting an Array

The word *sorting* is used in Computer science to denote the process of arranging objects in the order of their size. This is possible if there is an ordering associated with the type of the objects. A collection of integers, such as

    4 1 -7 2 3 -4 4 9 0 2

can be sorted, because there is an ordering associated with the type integer. They may in fact be sorted in either ascending order or descending order:

Example: Sorting an Array

```
-7  -4  0  1  2  2  3  4  4  9
 9   4  4  3  2  2  1  0 -4 -7
```

More formally, we can declare an array *a* and an index *i*

```
VAR
   a : ARRAY [I] OF T;
   i, j : I;
```

and state that, if there is an ordering associated with the type *T*, then the array *a* is sorted in ascending order if

i > j   implies that a[i] ≥ a[j]

and that it is sorted in descending order if

i > j   implies that a[i] ≤ a[j]

The problem of sorting an unsorted array is one of the classical problems of computer science. The problem seems simple, and we have all performed some kind of mechanical sorting at one time or another— of playing cards, checks, library index cards, or bills. The simplicity is illusory. Although the first programs for sorting were written by von Neumann in 1945, the major advances in sorting theory did not occur until over twenty years later.

Sorting is still an important aspect of computer science, but its importance is diminishing. Increasingly, computer systems are designed to provide immediate access to stored information. A system which sorts the information once a day or once a week cannot provide immediate access efficiently. Modern systems are therefore designed in such a way that it is not necessary to sort large amounts of information.

The algorithm that we will use to sort an array was invented by Donald L. Shell in 1959. It is called the *Shell sort* or the *diminishing increment sort*. The program that we will construct reads numbers from an input file, stores them in an array, sorts the array, and then prints it. The Shell sort which it uses is an *interchange sort*, which means that sorting is accomplished by exchanging pairs of numbers in the array until the array is sorted. The efficiency of an interchange sort depends entirely on the choice of the numbers which are exchanged.

In any sort, an object has an initial position and a final position, and during the sorting process it moves from one to the other. In the simplest varieties of interchange sort, the objects only move one step at a time. The observation that led to Shell's sort is that the process could be speeded up by allowing the objects to take large jumps at first, and then smaller jumps as they approached their destination. Although the idea is very simple, the mathematical analysis of it turns out to be very complicated. It is not easy to decide how

Example: Sorting an Array

large the first jumps should be, and it is even harder to discover how
the jump size should diminish. We use a straightforward version of
the Shell sort, in which the initial jump size is half the array
length, and it is halved again at each step.

The sort consists of three nested loops. The outermost loop controls the jump size. Within this loop, the array is scanned repeatedly
until no more interchanges are possible with the current jump size.
The innermost loop actually does the scanning. These loops are shown
in the following schema. *Length* is the number of components in the
array to be sorted, which is called *row*.

```
jump := length;
WHILE jump > 1 DO
    BEGIN
        jump := jump DIV 2;
        REPEAT
            FOR m := 1 TO max DO
                BEGIN
                    n := m + jump;
                    IF row[m] > row[n]
                        THEN
                            interchange row[m] and row[n]
                END
        UNTIL no more interchanges possible
    END
```

The value of *max* in the *FOR* loop must be chosen so that the program
does not attempt to access components beyond the end of the array.
Accordingly, we must have

$$max + jump \leq length$$

and so a suitable value for *max* is

$$length - jump$$

Interchanging two values in a computer program always requires a
temporary variable. Introducing *temp*, we have for the interchange of
row[m] and *row[n]*

```
temp := row[m];
row[m] := row[n];
row[n] := temp
```

The *REPEAT* loop must continue scanning the array until a complete scan
without interchanges is performed. A boolean variable *alldone* is set
to *true* at the beginning of each cycle, and changed to *false* if an
interchange is performed. The loop is executed until *alldone* is found
to be true after a scan.

Example: Sorting an Array

The action of the sort is most easily understood from a diagram. The top row of numbers in Fig. 6.2 represents an unsorted array.

Original Sequence	9	8	1	7	6	3	4	5	4	1
Jump = 5	3	8	1	7	6	9	4	5	4	1
	3	4	1	7	6	9	8	5	4	1
	3	4	1	4	6	9	8	5	7	1
	3	4	1	4	1	9	8	5	7	6
Jump = 2	1	4	3	4	1	9	8	5	7	6
	1	4	1	4	3	9	8	5	7	6
	1	4	1	4	3	5	8	9	7	6
	1	4	1	4	3	5	7	9	8	6
	1	4	1	4	3	5	7	6	8	9
Jump = 1	1	1	4	4	3	5	7	6	8	9
	1	1	4	3	4	5	7	6	8	9
	1	1	4	3	4	5	6	7	8	9
	1	1	3	4	4	5	6	7	8	9
Final Sequence	1	1	3	4	4	5	6	7	8	9

Fig. 6.2 Action of a Shell Sort

The bottom row shows the same array after sorting. Each of the intermediate rows contains two underlined numbers: these are the numbers which are interchanged during the preceding step. The distance between the two underlined numbers is the value of *jump*, and it decreases during the sort, as shown by the column of numbers at the left.

The Shell sort demonstrates the way in which subscripts can be calculated and used to access the components of an array in a non-linear sequence. It also demonstrates two general properties of an interchange sort. First, the storage required consists of the array

159

Example: Sorting an Array

itself and one extra component (*temp*) used for interchanging. This is significant because faster methods of sorting usually require more storage: this is the price paid for increased speed. Secondly, the direction of the sort is determined solely by the expression

   row[m] > row[n]

In order to sort the numbers in descending order, it is only necessary to change this expression to

   row[m] < row[n]


```
PROGRAM shellsort (input, output);
  CONST
    maxlength = 1000;
  TYPE
    index = 1 .. maxlength;
    rowtype = ARRAY [index] OF integer;
  VAR
    inrow : rowtype;
    count : 0 .. maxlength;
    ix : index;

  PROCEDURE sort (VAR row : rowtype; length : index);
    VAR
      jump, m, n : index;
      temp : integer;
      alldone : boolean;
    BEGIN
      jump := length;
      WHILE jump > 1 DO
        BEGIN
          jump := jump DIV 2;
          REPEAT
            alldone := true;
            FOR m := 1 TO length - jump DO
              BEGIN
                n := m + jump;
                IF row[m] > row[n]
                  THEN
                    BEGIN
                      temp := row[m];
                      row[m] := row[n];
                      row[n] := temp;
                      alldone := false
                    END
              END { for }
          UNTIL alldone
        END { while }
    END; { sort }
```

```
BEGIN { shellsort }
  count := 0;
  read(inrow[count + 1]);
  WHILE NOT eof DO
    BEGIN
      count := count + 1;
      read(inrow[count + 1])
    END; { while }
  IF count > 0
    THEN
      BEGIN
        sort(inrow,count);
        FOR ix := 1 TO count DO
          write(inrow[ix])
      END
    ELSE write('no input')
END. { shellsort }
```

Input:
```
9  8  1  7  6  3  4  5  4  1
```

Output:
```
1  1  3  4  4  5  6  7  8  9
```

Multidimensional Arrays

The base type of an array may itself be an array. In these declarations, the base type of *matrix* is *column*.

```
CONST
  size = 10;
TYPE
  subscript = 1 .. size;
  column = ARRAY [subscript] OF real;
  matrix = ARRAY [subscript] OF column;
```

The declaration of *column* can be incorporated into the declaration of *matrix*:

```
TYPE
  matrix = ARRAY [subscript] OF
            ARRAY [subscript] OF real;
```

and this rather unwieldy expression can be further simplified to this more convenient form:

```
TYPE
  matrix = ARRAY [subscript,subscript] OF real;
```

161

Multidimensional Arrays

Now declare some variables:

```
VAR
    a,b,c : matrix;
    r,s,t : subscript;
```

Column s of matrix a is the component

```
a[s]
```

The component t of column s is a real variable which may be written

```
a[s][t]
```

By analogy with the abbreviated declaration, we can simplify this to

```
a[s,t]
```

The array a is called a two dimensional array because we can imagine that it is stored in this form:

```
a[1,1]  a[1,2]  a[1,3]  ...  a[1,10]
a[2,1]  a[2,2]  a[2,3]  ...  a[2,10]
a[3,1]  a[3,2]  a[3,3]  ...  a[3,10]

....

a[10,1] a[10,2] a[10,3] ...  a[10,10]
```

The two dimensional array is of course an abstraction, because the memory of the computer is one dimensional. The compiler has to perform a mapping from the abstract two dimensional array that we use to the actual one dimensional array which constitutes the computer's memory.

The *unit matrix* is defined by

```
a[s,t] = 1  if  s = t
a[s,t] = 0  if  s ≠ t
```

We can give a this value by executing the statement

```
FOR s := 1 TO size DO
    FOR t := 1 TO size DO
        IF s = t
            THEN a[s,t] := 1
            ELSE a[s,t] := 0
```

The product c of two matrices a and b is obtained by executing the statement

Example: Frequencies of Letter Pairs

```
FOR r := 1 TO size DO
    FOR s := 1 TO size DO
        BEGIN
            c[r,s] := 0;
            FOR t := 1 TO size DO
                c[r,s] := c[r,s] + a[r,t] * b[t,s]
        END
```

The component *c[r,s]* is accessed *2 * size* times within the innermost loop. If you use a good compiler, this will not matter, but if your compiler is simple-minded you could help it by referring to *c[r,s]* once only:

```
FOR r := 1 TO size DO
    FOR s := 1 TO size DO
        BEGIN
            sum := 0;
            FOR t := 1 TO size DO
                sum := sum + a[r,t] * b[t,s];
            c[r,s] := sum
        END
```

Example: Frequencies of Letter Pairs

As an example of the use of multidimensional arrays, we present a program that measures the frequencies of pairs of adjacent letters in words. It tells us, for example, whether 'EA' occurs more or less often than 'IE'. The program counts within-word pairs only, so that given 'THE CAT' it will count 'TH', 'HE', 'CA' and 'AT' but not 'EC'. The counters are stored in a two dimensional array whose index type is letter. We declare

```
TYPE
    letter = 'a' .. 'z';
VAR
    conmat : ARRAY [letter,letter] OF integer;
```

We need a 'window' two characters wide through which to look at the text. The window moves along one character at a time, and whenever both characters in the window are letters, the appropriate component of *conmat* is incremented. The central loop of the program has the form:

```
WHILE NOT eof DO
    BEGIN
        read(thischar);
        IF [thischar,prevchar] ≤ ['a' .. 'z']
            THEN
                conmat[thischar,prevchar] :=
```

163

Example: Frequencies of Letter Pairs

```
                           conmat[thischar,prevchar] + 1;
              prevchar := thischar
           END
```

Thischar and *prevchar* are the two characters visible through the window. Note, incidentally, that the use of sets considerably simplifies the boolean expression, which would otherwise be

```
        ('a' ≤ thischar) AND (thischar ≤ 'z')
   AND ('a' ≤ prevchar) AND (prevchar ≤ 'z')
```

```
PROGRAM contingencies (input, output);
  CONST
    numwidth = 4;
    blank = ' ';
    cha = 'a';
    chz = 'z';
  TYPE
    letter = cha .. chz;
  VAR
    conmat : ARRAY [letter,letter] OF integer;
    across, down : letter;
    thischar, prevchar : char;
  BEGIN
    FOR across := cha TO chz DO
      FOR down := cha TO chz DO
        conmat[across,down] := 0;
    prevchar := blank;
    WHILE NOT eof DO
      BEGIN
        read(thischar);
        IF [thischar,prevchar] ≤ [cha .. chz]
          THEN
            conmat[thischar,prevchar] :=
                conmat[thischar,prevchar] + 1;
        prevchar := thischar
      END;{ while }
    write(blank : 2);
    FOR down := cha TO chz DO
      write(blank : numwidth - 1, down);
    writeln; writeln;
    FOR across := cha TO chz DO
      BEGIN
        write(blank,across);
        FOR down := cha TO chz DO
          write(conmat[across,down] : numwidth);
        writeln
      END { for }
  END. { contingencies }
```

Packed Arrays

The components of an array are stored in consecutive words of the computer's memory. This is an efficient way of storing integer and real components, because on many computers they require a whole word of memory or more anyway. It is not always an efficient way of storing variables of other types, however, because space may be wasted. The amount of space wasted may be reduced by *packing* several components of an array into each word. The compiler will do this for you if you declare the array as *PACKED*. For example the array *longstring* declared as

```
VAR
    longstring : ARRAY [1 .. 1000] OF char;
```

occupies 1000 words of memory. The array declared as

```
VAR
    longstring : PACKED ARRAY [1 .. 1000] OF char;
```

occupies 100 words of memory on a CDC 6000 series computer (which stores 10 characters per word) and 250 words of memory on an IBM 360/370 computer (which stores 4 characters per word).

A packed array is used in a program in the same way as an unpacked array with one important exception: in many PASCAL implementations, a component of a packed array cannot be passed as a variable parameter to a procedure or function. A program using a packed array will execute somewhat more slowly than the same program using an unpacked array. This is because a component of an unpacked array can be accessed more efficiently than a component of a packed array. The decision as to whether to pack a particular array or not depends on many factors, including available memory size, processor speed, required response time and volume of data. A choice which is valid for one environment may be quite inappropriate to another.

In many cases, the extra time required for accessing packed arrays can be reduced by packing or unpacking all the components in a single operation rather than one at a time. This can be accomplished using the standard procedures *pack* and *unpack*. Suppose that we are reading text from a file and we want to store words of the text into the variable *word*, which is a *PACKED ARRAY* of 20 characters. Rather than copying characters from the file directly into *word*, we copy them into a temporary buffer, which is not packed. The declarations for these variables are

```
CONST
    wordsize = 20;
VAR
    buffer : ARRAY [1 .. wordsize] OF char;
```

Packed Arrays

```
word : PACKED ARRAY [1 .. wordsize] OF char;
```

When *buffer* contains a complete word, we use the procedure call

```
pack(buffer,1,word)
```

which packs all the characters in *buffer* into the packed array *word*.
The inverse operation is

```
unpack(word,buffer,1)
```

which transfers characters from the packed array *word* to the unpacked
array *buffer*.

In the general case, suppose that we have defined an array *A* of
type *T*, and a corresponding packed array *P*, also of type *T*.

```
VAR
   A : ARRAY [m .. n] OF T;
   P : PACKED ARRAY [i .. j] OF T;
```

i, *j*, *m* and *n* are scalar constants, and

$$n - m \geq j - i$$

The statement

```
FOR k := i TO j DO
   P[k] := A[k - i + m]
```

may be abbreviated to

```
pack(A,m,P)
```

and read as 'pack components $A[m]$ through $A[j - i + m]$ of *A* into
components $P[i]$ through $P[j]$ of *P*'.

The statement

```
FOR k := i TO j DO
   A[k - i + m] := P[i]
```

may be abbreviated to

```
unpack(P,A,m)
```

read as 'unpack components $P[i]$ through $P[j]$ of *P* to components $A[m]$
through $A[j - i + m]$ of *A*'.

Boolean Arrays

An array with base type *boolean* has the same properties as a set. Each component of the array corresponds to a potential member of the set, which may be absent (*false*) or present (*true*). If we declare

```
TYPE
    index = 1 .. 20;
VAR
    ix : index;
    xset : SET OF index;
    xarr : ARRAY [index] OF boolean;
```

then the operations

```
xarr[ix] := false
xarr[ix] := true
```

are equivalent to

```
xset := xset - [ix]
xset := xset + [ix]
```

and the boolean expression

```
xarr[ix]
```

is equivalent to

```
ix IN xset
```

The operators $\leq$ and $\geq$ for testing whether one set contains another cannot of course be applied to boolean arrays. The operations on a set will be faster than the corresponding operations on a boolean array, and so a set should be used in preference to a boolean array whenever possible. However, in many implementations of PASCAL, a boolean array can have more components than a set. When we need a very large set, say of 10,000 or 100,000 components, the program will probably be easier to write (and read) if a single boolean array is used rather than an array of sets. A considerable amount of space can be saved (at the expense of additional execution time) by packing the array.

The classical algorithm for enumerating prime numbers is the *sieve of Eratosthenes*. Suppose that we want to find the prime less than 10. We start by writing down the numbers from 2 to 10:

```
2  3  4  5  6  7  8  9  10
```

We then remove the lowest number, claim that it is prime, and remove its multiples. After the first step, we have 2 as a prime, and the sieve contains odd numbers only:

3   5   7   9

After the second step, we have 3 as a prime, and only 5 and 7 remain in the sieve. The process terminates when the sieve is empty.

We declare

```
CONST
    maximum = 100000;
VAR
    sieve : PACKED ARRAY [2 .. maximum] OF boolean;
```

Initially, we set each component of *sieve* to *true* indicating that all the numbers are present. As we remove numbers, we set the corresponding components to *false*. The program consists of two nested loops, one to find the lowest number still in the sieve, and the other to remove its multiples. The termination condition for the outer loop is that there are no numbers left in the sieve, and it can be expedited by maintaining a count of the numbers currently in the sieve.

```
PROGRAM primenumbers (input, output);
  CONST
    firstprime = 2;
    maximum = 100000;
  VAR
    sieve : PACKED ARRAY [firstprime .. maximum] OF boolean;
    leftin, range, factor, multiple : 0 .. maximum;
  BEGIN
    read(range);
    FOR factor := firstprime TO range DO
      sieve[factor] := true;
    leftin := range - firstprime + 1;
    factor := firstprime - 1;
    REPEAT
      factor := factor + 1;
      IF sieve[factor]
        THEN { factor is prime }
          BEGIN
            writeln(factor);
            multiple := 1;
            WHILE factor * multiple ≤ range DO
              BEGIN
                IF sieve[factor * multiple]
                  THEN { remove multiple }
                    BEGIN
                      sieve[factor * multiple] := false;
                      leftin := leftin - 1
                    END;
```

```
            multiple := multiple + 1
         END { while }
    END
UNTIL leftin = 0
END. { primenumbers }
```

Input:
    50

Output:
    2
    3
    5
    7
    11
    13
    17
    19
    23
    29
    31
    37
    41
    43
    47

Strings

We are already familiar with the use of characters or variables of type *char* in PASCAL programs. A string is merely a sequence of characters. These are strings:

> *cogito, ergo sum*
> *the wizard of oz*
> *men prize the thing ungain'd more than it is*

When a literal string is used in a PASCAL program, it must be enclosed in quotes. We can do this easily enough in the first two cases:

> *'cogito, ergo sum'*
> *'the wizard of oz'*

The third string presents a problem because it already contains a quote. We indicate to the compiler that the quote is actually a part of the string by writing another quote immediately after it:

> *'men prize the thing ungain''d more than it is'*

A constant string may be defined in a constant declaration, or used in a *write* statement:

```
CONST
    message = 'time to go home';
....
    write(message);
    write('time to go home')
```

The two *write* statements have exactly the same effect.

A constant string may not extend over more than one line. A
string may contain any character. The characters in a constant string
rperesent *themselves*, in contrast to other characters in a program
which represent numbers, identifiers, reserved words or other symbols.
Therefore,

```
'BEGIN'   has nothing to do with BEGIN
'123'     is not a number
'+'       is not an operator
```

A *string variable* is a packed array of characters. These are
string type declarations:

```
TYPE
    cardimage = PACKED ARRAY [1 .. 80] OF char;
    lineimage = PACKED ARRAY [1 .. 150] OF char;
    longstring = PACKED ARRAY [1 .. 1000] OF char;
```

The length of a string is determined by its type and is fixed. PASCAL
therefore offers less scope for string manipulation than do some other
programming languages which allow strings to vary in length during
execution.

Most of the properties of strings carry over from the usual prop-
erites of arrays. For example, strings of the same type may be copied
by assignment statements and compared with the operators '=' and '≠'.
Strings have the additional property that they are ordered. The
ordering is determined by comparing each character of the string in
turn, starting with the first, until unequal characters are found.
The unequal characters are then used to define the order. This is the
conventional 'dictionary' order if the strings contain letters only.
When the strings contain other characters, the order will depend on
the computer's representation of the characters. For example,

```
'perigee' > 'periapt'
```

because

```
'g' > 'a'
```

Strings must be read character by character, because the standard
procedures *read* and *write* do not automatically convert strings from
external to internal representation.

6.2 Records

A *record*, like an array, is a structured variable with several components. The components of a record may have different types, however, and they are accessed by name, not by subscript. Arrays and records are both abstractions of modes of data storage used at the machine language level.

A description of a planet might include the following information:

> *name*
> *visible with the naked eye (yes/no)*
> *diameter*
> *mean orbital radius*

We can use a string for the name; a boolean variable suffices for 'visible with the naked eye', and the other two quantities are real. We can declare the type *planet* as follows:

```
TYPE
    planet =
        RECORD
            name : PACKED ARRAY [1 .. 10] OF char;
            visible : boolean;
            diameter, orbitrad : real
        END;
```

Variables with this type can be declared in the usual way:

```
VAR
        inner, outer : planet;
```

A *component* of a record is selected by using both the name of the record variable and the name of the component, separated by a period:

> *inner . name*   *is the name of the planet inner*
>
> *outer . diameter* *is the diameter of the planet outer*

These names are called *record selectors*, and they are used in a program in exactly the same way as variables of the same type. We can write assignment statements such as these:

```
inner . name := 'venus     ';
inner . visible := true;
inner . diameter := 12104; { kilometers }
inner . orbitrad := 108.2; { gigameters }
```

```
    outer . name := 'neptune    ';
    outer . visible := false;
    outer . diameter := 49500;
    outer . orbitrad := 4496.6;
```

The structured types array and record can be combined. Using this
declaration of *planet*, we can further define:

```
    CONST
        furthest = 10;
    TYPE
        planet = (as above)
    VAR
        solarsystem : ARRAY [1 .. furthest] OF planet;
        numplan : 1 .. furthest;
```

We can then execute statements like these:

```
    FOR numplan := 1 TO furthest DO
        IF solarsystem[numplan] . orbitrad < 4000
            THEN solarsystem[numplan] . visible := true
            ELSE solarsystem[numplan] . visible := false
```

The names of the components must be unique within the record. We
could not use *name* again in the definition of *planet*, but we could use
it to denote a variable, or a component of another record. There are
no operators which may be used with records as operands. In particular, there is no ordering associated with records. The value of a
record can, however, be assigned to another record by an assignment
statement. Using the example above, the single statement

```
    inner := outer
```

is equivalent to the assignments

```
    inner . name := outer . name
    inner . visible := outer . visible
    inner . diameter := outer . diameter
    inner . orbitrad := outer . orbitrad
```

The *WITH* Statement

It is often necessary to access the same component of a record, or
different components of the same record, several times in a small
section of the program. The *FOR* statement above is an example : the
record *solarsystem[numplan]* is accessed three times on consecutive
lines. Using *WITH*, we can write this statement in the form:

```
        FOR numplan := 1 TO furthest DO
            WITH solarsystem[numplan] DO
                IF orbitrad < 4000
                    THEN visible := true
                    ELSE visible := false
```

The general form of the *WITH* statement is

```
        WITH record identifier DO
            statement
```

Within the *statement*, components of a record may be referred to by field name only: the compiler supplies the record name. In addition to saving some writing, the *WITH* statement may be helpful to the compiler because the record need only be located once, instead of several times.

Despite its usefulness, the *WITH* statement should be used with discretion. Indiscriminate use of *WITH* statements can lead to programs which are confusing and even ambiguous. In an ambiguous situation, the compiler may not interpret the program in the same way that you do.

Records with Variants

Records of the same type do not necessarily contain the same components. We will illustrate this with an example from coordinate geometry. Suppose that we need a program that will perform calculations with points, lines and circles. We start with the declaration

```
        TYPE
            coordinate =
                RECORD
                    xcoor, ycoor : real
                END;
```

A point is easily represented by its coordinates:

```
        TYPE
            point =
                RECORD
                    position : coordinate
                END;
```

A line is best represented by the coefficients in its equation

$$A.x + B.y + C = 0$$

Records

```
TYPE
    line =
        RECORD
            xcoeff, ycoeff, con : real
        END;
```

A circle may also be represented in terms of its equation

$$(x - p)^2 + (y - q)^2 = r^2$$

and in this case we have the simple interpretation that the circle has its center at the point (p,q) and radius r.

```
TYPE
    circle =
        RECORD
            center : coordinate;
            radius : real
        END;
```

The record types *point*, *line* and *circle* can be condensed into a single declaration of a record type which we call *figure*.

A record with *variants* such as *figure*, has two parts. The first part is called the *fixed part*, and the second part is called the *variant part*. In this example, the fixed part of the record type *figure* is simply a *tag* which tells us what kind of figure the record represents, and the variant part contains the declarations of *point*, *line* and *circle* which we have already used. The complete declaration for *figure* follows:

```
TYPE
    coordinate =
        RECORD
            xcoor, ycoor : real
        END;
    shape = (point, line, circle);
    figure =
        RECORD
            tag : shape;
            CASE shape OF
                point :
                    (position : coordinate);
                line :
                    (xcoeff, ycoeff, con : real);
                circle :
                    (center : coordinate;
                     radius : real)
        END;
```

This declaration contains several points of interest. The use of

174

CASE is superficially similar to the *CASE* statement of Chapter 5, and indeed the *CASE* statement is very useful for manipulating record variants, as we shall see. There are important differences between the two uses of *CASE*, however. First, the case selector in a record declaration is a *type*, not a variable. In this example, the *CASE* selector is the type *shape*. Secondly, the *CASE* does not require a matching *END*, because the *END* required by the *RECORD* declaration suffices to terminate the *CASE* also. Since the variant part of the record declaration must follow the fixed part, there can never be any further fields after the *CASE* clause in a record declaration. The identifiers used in different variants must be unique within the record: a field identifier cannot be used in two variants of the same record, nor can it be used in both the fixed and the variant parts of the same record. The same field identifier may be used in another declaration of a record of a different type, however.

Although in principle it is possible to eliminate the tag field (which contains the shape of the figure in this example), it is clear that in most cases we are going to need a tag field in a record with variants. Accordingly, the declaration above may be abbreviated to the following equivalent form:

```
TYPE
    figure =
        RECORD
            CASE tag : shape OF
                point :
                    (position : coordinate);
                line :
                    (xcoeff, ycoeff, con : real);
                circle :
                    (center : coordinate;
                     radius : real)
        END;
```

The tag must be a scalar type. It is not necessary to define a record variant for every possible value of the tag, although in the interests of program security it is obviously desirable.

The *CASE* clause used in the declaration of a record with variants is often paralleled by a *CASE* statement in the body of the program. The following procedure has a record of type *figure* as its formal parameter, and it prints values associated with the figure:

```
PROCEDURE printfigure (pic : figure);
    BEGIN
        WITH pic DO
            CASE tag OF
                point :
                    WITH position DO
                        write('Point: (',xcoor,',',ycoor,')');
```

```
            line :
              write('Line:'xcoeff,' * X +',ycoor,
                    ' * Y +'con,' = 0');
            circle :
              WITH center DO
                write('Circle: center (',xcoor,',',ycoor,
                      ') Radius:',radius)
        END; { case }
      writeln
    END; { printfigure }
```

The technical term for a record with variants is *union type*. A union
is *discriminated* if it has a tag field, and *free* if it does not. This
term is used because a record with variants is in fact a union of two
or more types. Declare

```
    TYPE
      thingtype = (int,re,bool);
      thing =
        RECORD
          CASE thingtype OF
            int :
              (intval : integer);
            re :
              (reval : real);
            bool :
              (boolval : boolean)
          END;
    VAR
      something : thing;
```

Thing is now a free union. *Something* is an object with three different names: *something . intval, something . reval* and *something . bool-
val.* According to the name that we use, this object will be treated
as an *integer, real* or *boolean* variable. There are a few situations
in which free unions are appropriate, but they are rare. In most
cases, you should discriminate your unions by providing a tag-field,
and take care that the value of the tag and the contents of the
record are compatible at all times.

Syntax for Records

    The syntax for *record declaration* is shown in Fig. 6.3. Records,
like arrays, may be packed to conserve space at the expense of access
time. In some implementations, a component of a packed record may not
be passed as a parameter to a procedure or function. The syntax for
field list shows that a record may contain a *fixed part*, a *variant
part*, or both, but that if it contains both, the fixed part must come
first. The syntax for *variant part* contains *field list*, and so
variant records may be nested. The following record declaration

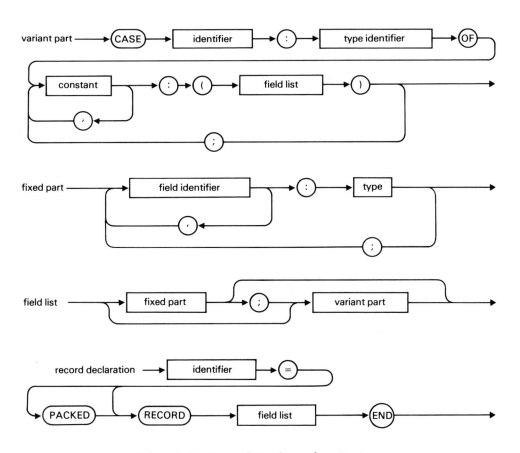

Fig. 6.3 *Record Declaration* Syntax

contains three levels of nesting.

```
TYPE
    mediumtype = (string,wind);
    methodtype = (struck,bowed);
    materialtype = (brass,wood);
    instrument =
        RECORD
            CASE medium : mediumtype OF
                string :
                    (
                        CASE method : methodtype OF
                            struck :
                                (
                                    CASE keyboard : boolean OF
                                        false :
```

```
                                    (range : real);
                              true :
                                    (numberofkeys : 1 .. 100)
                        );
                  bowed :
                        (size : (bass,cello,viola,violin))
            );
      wind :
            (
                  CASE material : materialtype OF
                        brass :
                              (technique : (keyed,slide));
                        wood :
                              (reed : (single,double))
            )
      END;
```

A variable of type *instrument* has either three or four simple components.

```
      VAR
            piano : instrument;
      ....
            piano . medium := string;
            piano . method := struck;

            piano . keyboard := true;
            piano . numberofkeys := 88
```

Fig. 6.4 shows the syntax for a *record component*. When a component of a record is itself a record, the notation is extended in the

Fig. 6.4 *Record Component* Syntax

obvious way. If *roundthing* is a *circle*, then

    roundthing . center

is the coordinate of its center, and

    roundthing . center . xcoor := 0

assigns zero to the *x* coordinate of its center.

Example: Constructing the Circumcircle

Fig. 6.5 shows the syntax of the *WITH* statement. Note that
several record identifiers may appear within a single *WITH* clause.

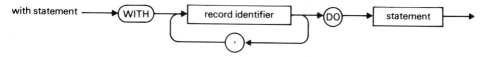

Fig. 6.5 *WITH Statement* Syntax

The statement above can be written in any of the alternative forms

> *WITH roundthing DO*
> *WITH center DO*
> *xcoor := 0*

or

> *WITH roundthing, center DO*
> *xcoor := 0*

or

> *WITH roundthing . center DO*
> *xcoor := 0*

Example: Constructing the Circumcircle

We will use the declaration of the record type *figure* as a starting point for a program which constructs the circumcircle of a
triangle, or equivalently, the circle which passes through three
given points. The algorithm we use follows:

> *Let the given points be p_1, p_2 and p_3. Draw three circles c_1, c_2
> and c_3 with the same radius and centers p_1, p_2 and p_3. (The
> radius is arbitrary but should be large enough to ensure that the
> circles intersect.) Draw the line s_1 through the points of
> intersection of c_1 and c_2, and the line s_2 through the points of
> intersection of c_2 and c_3. Then s_1 and s_2 meet at the circum-
> center of the three points, and the radius of the circumcircle
> is the distance from this point to any of the given points.*

We can express this algorithm as a program schema:

> *choose a radius, r;*
> *drawcircle(p_1, r, c_1);*
> *drawcircle(p_2, r, c_2);*
> *drawcircle(p_3, r, c_3);*

Example: Constructing the Circumcircle

```
        intersect(c₁, c₂, s₁);
        intersect(c₂, c₃, s₂);
        meet(s₁, s₂, circumcenter);
        circumradius := distance(p₁, circumcenter);
        drawcircle(circumcenter, circumradius, circumcircle)
```

Sometimes the construction will not work. Some or all of the points may coincide, in which case the construction is impossible, or the points may be collinear, in which case the lines s_1 and s_2 will be coincident. Since we do not expect exact results from our computations, we should test for 'very close' rather than 'coincident', and 'almost parallel' rather than 'parallel'. This will avoid potential problems of overflow and underflow, and will prevent the construction from being performed when it might be inaccurate. We add the additional value *empty* to the type *shape*. A procedure can then communicate failure by returning an empty figure. The new declarations are

```
    TYPE
        shape = (empty, point, line, circle);
        figure =
            RECORD
                CASE tag : shape OF
                    empty :
                        ( );
                    point :
                        (position : coordinate);
                    line :
                        (xcoeff, ycoeff, con : real);
                    circle :
                        (center : coordinate;
                         radius : real)
            END;
```

The procedure *drawcircle* offers no particular difficulties:

```
    PROCEDURE drawcircle (cen : figure;
                          rad : real;
                          VAR circ : figure);
        BEGIN
            WITH circ DO
                IF (cen . tag = point) AND (rad > 0)
                    THEN
                        BEGIN
                            tag := circle;
                            center := cen . position;
                            radius := rad
                        END
                    ELSE tag := empty
        END;
```

The procedure *meet* finds the point of intersection of two lines,

Example: Constructing the Circumcircle

provided they are not parallel. Suppose that the lines are *aline* and *bline*:

> aline : A.x + B.y + C = 0
> bline : D.x + E.y + F = 0

Then if A.E - B.D = 0 the lines are parallel or coincident, otherwise they meet at the point

> x = - (C.E - B.F)/(A.E - B.D)
> y =   (C.D - A.F)/(A.E - B.D)

The procedure *intersect* finds the line of intersection of two circles. Suppose that the circles are *acirc* and *bcirc*:

> acirc : $(x - A)^2 + (y - B)^2 = C^2$
> bcirc : $(x - D)^2 + (y - E)^2 = F^2$

then by subtraction we have

$$-2.A.x + A^2 + 2.D.x - D^2 - 2.B.y - B^2 + 2.E.y - E^2 = C^2 - F^2$$

and so the equation of their line of intersection is

$$x(A - D) + y(B - E) + ((C^2 - A^2 - B^2) - (F^2 - D^2 - E^2))/2 = 0$$

This is actually the equation of the locus of a point equidistant from the centers of the circles, and so for our application it will be the correct line even if the circles do not in fact meet.

```
PROGRAM circles (input, output);
  CONST
    delta = 1E-6;
  TYPE
    shape = (empty,point,line,circle);
    coordinate =
      RECORD
        xcoor,ycoor : real
      END; { coordinate }
    figure =
      RECORD
        CASE tag : shape OF
          empty :
            ( );
          point :
            (position : coordinate);
          line :
            (xcoeff,ycoeff,con : real);
          circle :
            (center : coordinate;
             radius : real)
```

```
    END; { figure }
VAR
  p1,p2,p3,c1,c2,c3,s1,s2,
  circumcenter,circumcircle : figure;
  r,circumradius : real;

PROCEDURE printfigure (pic : figure);
  BEGIN
    WITH pic DO
      CASE tag OF
        empty :
          write('Null figure');
        point :
          WITH position DO
            write('Point: (', xcoor, ',', ycoor, ')');
        line :
          write('Line:', xcoeff, ' * X +', xcoeff,
                ' * Y +', con, ' = 0');
        circle :
          WITH center DO
            write('Circle: center (', xcoor, ',', ycoor,
                  ') Radius:', radius)
      END; { case }
      writeln
  END; { printfigure }

PROCEDURE readpoint (VAR pnt : figure);
  BEGIN
    WITH pnt, position DO
      BEGIN
        tag := point;
        read(xcoor,ycoor)
      END { with }
  END; { readpoint }

FUNCTION distance (afig,bfig : figure) : real;
  BEGIN
    IF (afig.tag = point) AND (bfig.tag = point)
      THEN distance := sqrt(sqr(afig.position.xcoor
                              - bfig.position.xcoor)
                          + sqr(afig.position.ycoor
                              - bfig.position.ycoor))
      ELSE distance := 0
  END; { distance }

FUNCTION veryclose (afig,bfig : figure) : boolean;
  BEGIN
    veryclose := distance(afig,bfig) < delta
  END; { veryclose }
```

Example: Constructing the Circumcircle

```
PROCEDURE drawcircle (cen : figure; rad : real;
                      VAR circ : figure);
   BEGIN
     WITH circ DO
       IF (cen.tag = point) AND ( rad > 0)
          THEN
            BEGIN
              tag := circle;
              center := cen.position;
              radius := rad
            END
          ELSE tag := empty
   END; { drawcircle }

PROCEDURE meet (aline,bline : figure;
               VAR pnt : figure);
   VAR
     den : real;
   BEGIN
     IF (aline.tag = line) AND (bline.tag = line)
       THEN
         BEGIN
           den := aline.xcoeff * bline.ycoeff
                - aline.ycoeff * bline.xcoeff;
           IF abs(den) < delta
             THEN pnt.tag := empty { parallel lines }
             ELSE
               WITH pnt DO
                 BEGIN
                   tag := point;
                   WITH position DO
                     BEGIN
                       xcoor := - (aline.con * bline.ycoeff
                                 - aline.ycoeff * bline.con)/den;
                       ycoor :=   (aline.con * bline.xcoeff
                                 - aline.xcoeff * bline.con)/den
                     END { with position }
                 END { with pnt }
         END
       ELSE pnt.tag := empty
   END; { meet }
PROCEDURE intersect (acirc,bcirc : figure;
                     VAR intline : figure);
   BEGIN
     IF (acirc.tag = circle) AND (bcirc.tag = circle)
       THEN
         WITH intline DO
           BEGIN
             tag := line;
             xcoeff := acirc.center.xcoor - bcirc.center.xcoor;
             ycoeff := acirc.center.ycoor - bcirc.center.ycoor;
```

Example: Constructing the Circumcircle

```
                con := ((  sqr(acirc.radius)
                        - sqr(acirc.center.xcoor)
                        - sqr(acirc.center.ycoor)
                    - (  sqr(bcirc.radius)
                        - sqr(bcirc.center.xcoor)
                        - sqr(bcirc.center.ycoor))))/2
            END { with }
        ELSE intline.tag := empty
    END; { intersect }

  BEGIN { circles }
    readpoint(p1);
    readpoint(p2);
    readpoint(p3);
    IF    veryclose(p1,p2)
      OR veryclose(p2,p3)
      OR veryclose(p3,p1)
      THEN writeln('The points are not distinct')
      ELSE
        BEGIN
          r := distance(p1,p2) + distance(p2,p3);
          drawcircle(p1,r,c1);
          drawcircle(p2,r,c2);
          drawcircle(p3,r,c3);
          intersect(c1,c2,s1);
          intersect(c2,c3,s2);
          meet(s1,s2,circumcenter);
          circumradius := distance(p1,circumcenter);
          drawcircle(circumcenter,circumradius,circumcircle);
          printfigure(circumcircle)
        END
    END. { circles }


Input:
    -1000    0
     1000    0
        0    1

Output:
    Circle: center (0,-499999.5)  radius: 500000.5
```

Example: Text Concordance

The final example of this chapter uses an array whose components
are records, and also illustrates the use of packed arrays. The
program reads a text and then prints a list of the words which occur
in the text, together with the number of times each word was found.
A list of this kind is called a *concordance* of the text. The form of
the output required suggests that the program should maintain a table,
each entry of which contains a word and a counter. We can start by
declaring:

```
CONST
    tablesize = 1000;
TYPE
    tableindex = 1 .. tablesize;
    entrytype =
        RECORD
            word : wordtype;
            count : counttype
        END;
    tabletype = ARRAY [tableindex] OF entrytype;
```

We can represent a word by a packed array, and a counter by a positive
integer.

```
CONST
    maxwordlen = 20;
TYPE
    charindex = 1 .. maxwordlen;
    wordtype = PACKED ARRAY [charindex] OF char;
    counttype = 1 .. maxint;
```

The program will have three sections. First, the table is initialized; secondly, the text is read and entries are made in the table;
and finally, the contents of the table are printed. When the program
has read a word from the text, either the word has been encountered
before, in which case its counter is incremented, or it is a new word
which must be entered into the table. Clearly, the efficiency of the
program will depend heavily on the technique we use to look for the
word in the table. In this program we use a simple *linear search*, in
which the word read is compared with each table entry in turn. We use
a variable *nextentry*, which is the index of the next free space in the
table at the time when there are already *nextentry - 1* words in the
table. We read a word and put it into this free space. The linear
search then takes the form

```
entry := 1;
WHILE table[entry] . word ≠ table[nextentry] . word DO
    entry := entry + 1
```

Example: Text Concordance

The loop will always terminate provided that *nextentry* ≥ *1*, which we can ensure by initializing it to 1 (meaning that there are 0 entries in the table), and always increasing it. The loop will terminate with

> *entry < entrycount*

if the word is already in the table, or

> *entry = entrycount*

if it is a new word. In the latter case, the word is already in the correct place (the next free space), and so all we have to do is increment *nextentry*, and initialize the counter.

The program uses two procedures: *readword* assembles a word of the text into a buffer and then packs it; and *printword* unpacks a word and prints it.

```
PROGRAM concordance (input, output);
  CONST
    tablesize = 1000;
    maxwordlen = 20;
  TYPE
    charindex = 1 .. maxwordlen;
    counttype = 1 .. maxint;
    tableindex = 1 .. tablesize;
    wordtype = PACKED ARRAY [charindex] OF char;
    entrytype =
      RECORD
        word : wordtype;
        count : counttype
      END;
    tabletype = ARRAY [tableindex] OF entrytype;
  VAR
    table : tabletype;
    entry, nextentry : tableindex;
    tablefull : boolean;
    letters : SET OF char;

  PROCEDURE readword (VAR packedword : wordtype);
    CONST
      blank = ' ';
    VAR
      buffer : ARRAY [charindex] OF char;
      charcount : 0 .. maxwordlen;
      ch : char;
    BEGIN
      IF NOT eof
        THEN
          REPEAT
            read(ch)
```

Example: Text Concordance

```
          UNTIL eof OR (ch IN letters);
     IF NOT eof
        THEN
          BEGIN
            charcount := 0;
            WHILE ch IN letters DO
              BEGIN
                IF charcount < maxwordlen
                  THEN
                    BEGIN
                      charcount := charcount + 1;
                      buffer[charcount] := ch
                    END;
                IF eof
                  THEN ch := blank
                  ELSE read(ch)
              END; { while }
            FOR charcount := charcount + 1 TO maxwordlen DO
              buffer[charcount] := blank;
            pack(buffer,1,packedword)
          END
   END; { readword }

PROCEDURE printword (packedword : wordtype);
  CONST
    blank = ' ';
  VAR
    buffer : ARRAY [charindex] OF char;
    charpos : 1 .. maxwordlen;
  BEGIN
    unpack(packedword,buffer,1);
    FOR charpos := 1 TO maxwordlen DO
      write(buffer[charpos])
  END; { printword }

BEGIN { concordance }
  letters := ['a' .. 'z'];
  tablefull := false;
  nextentry := 1;
  WHILE NOT (eof OR tablefull) DO
    BEGIN
      readword(table[nextentry] . word);
      IF NOT eof
        THEN
          BEGIN
            entry := 1;
            WHILE table[entry].word ≠ table[nextentry].word DO
              entry := entry + 1;
            IF entry < nextentry
              THEN table[entry].count := table[entry].count + 1
            ELSE IF nextentry < tablesize
```

187

```
                THEN
                   BEGIN
                      nextentry := nextentry + 1;
                      table[entry].count := 1
                   END
                ELSE tablefull := true
             END
      END; { while }
   IF tablefull
      THEN writeln('The table is not large enough')
      ELSE
         FOR entry := 1 TO nextentry -1 DO
            WITH table[entry] DO
               BEGIN
                  printword(word);
                  writeln(count)
               END { with }
   END. { concordance }
```

Exercises

6.1 An array is used to store descriptions of people. Each component
of the array is a record with fields containing information about
height, weight, hair color, eye color, and sex. Write appropriate
declarations and use them in a program which can read a description or print a list of stored descriptions. Extend the program so
that when a new description is added, the closest description
already filed is located and printed.

6.2 This book may be defined by the following declarations:

```
      CONST
         linelen = 70;
         pagesize = 55;
         thickness = 330;
      TYPE
         line = ARRAY [1 .. linelen] OF char;
         page = ARRAY [1 .. pagesize] OF line;
         volume = ARRAY [1 .. thickness] OF page;
      VAR
         book : volume;
```

Identify the type and value of each of the following expressions:

```
      book[25]
      book[187] [50]
      book[46][7][10]
```

Write a program to print the contents of book in an appropriate
format.

Exercises

6.3 Write a program that reads a text and prints a frequency distribution of word lengths. (How many words had one letter, how many had two letters, etc.) The program should also print the mean and standard deviation of word lengths.

6.4 Write a program that prints a list of the numbers which are palindromes in both binary and decimal notation. (A palindromic number is unchanged if its digits are reversed: 79488497 is a decimal palindrome.)

6.5 If an array is already sorted, the linear search is not the best method of locating an entry in it. A better method is the *binary search*. Assume that the array *arr* is sorted in ascending order, and contains a component whose value is *key*. *Lower* and *upper* are the bounds of a range of subscripts. After executing the statements

> *middle := (lower + upper) DIV 2;*
> *IF key > arr[middle]*
> *   THEN lower := middle + 1*
> *   ELSE upper := middle - 1*

either *arr[middle] = key*, and we have found the component we want, or the bounds are set for a search over a smaller range. Write a recursive procedure and an iterative procedure to perform a binary search. What happens if the array does not contain the component sought? Modify your procedures to take this into account.

6.6 Extend Program *concordance* so that it prints two lists. In the first list, the words are in alphabetical order, and in the second they are in order of frequency of occurrence, with the most frequent first. The program should contain a sorting procedure based on procedure *sort* of Program *shellsort*, and one of the parameters of this procedure should specify which sort is to be performed.

6.7 A text contains words of 10 characters or less. Write a program that reads a text of up to 1000 words and then prints the same words arranged in a random order.

6.8 The expression

> *factor * multiple*

is evaluated three times in the inner loop of Program *prime-numbers*. Modify the program to eliminate this inefficiency.

6.9 Write a procedure that reads and writes hexadecimal (scale of sixteen) numbers, using the 16 characters

> *0 1 2 3 4 5 6 7 8 9 A B C D E F*

Exercises

6.10 Write a program that converts integers from one scale to another. The symbols '<' and '>', followed by a decimal integer between 2 and 10 set the input and output scales. For example, the input string

        <8 >2

instructs the program to read octal numbers and print their binary equivalents.

6.11 *Clock patience* is played with a standard deck of 52 playing cards. The cards are dealt in piles of four cards arranged in a clocklike pattern with the thirteenth pile at the center. A *move* consists of taking the top card from a pile and placing it under the pile where it belongs (Jack = 11, Queen = 12, King at center), and this pile provides the card for the next move. The game terminates when the four Kings have been placed on the center pile, and is deemed successful if all the other cards are correctly placed. Write a program that simulates clock patience, using a pseudo-random number generator to 'deal' the cards.

6.12 One way of overcoming PASCAL'S limited ability to handle strings of different lengths is to use a *string table*.

        CONST
            tablesize = 10000;
            maxstringlen = 100;
        TYPE
            charindex = 1 .. tablesize;
            string =
                RECORD
                    first, last : charindex
                END;
        VAR
            stringtable : PACKED ARRAY [charindex] OF char;
            buffer : ARRAY [1 .. maxstringlen] OF char;

If the string table contains

        'TOOTHEATERRIBLE ... '

then the strings 'TOO', 'TOOTH', 'THEATER' and 'TERRIBLE' are represented by records (1,3), (1,5), (4,10), (8,15). Devise procedures for determining whether the table contains a given string, adding a new string to the table, comparing strings, generating substrings, and concatenating strings. Assume that no individual string, or the result of a concatenation, may have more than *maxstringlen* characters.

6.13 The game of *Life*, invented by John Horton Conway of Cambridge university, takes place on a rectangular array of cells, each of

190

which may contain an organism. Each cell has eight neighbors, and we will denote by *occ(k)* the number of cells adjacent to cell *k* which are occupied by an organism. The configuration of a new generation of organisms is obtained from the previous generation by applying two simple rules:

(1) An organism in cell *k* survives to the next generation if $2 \leq occ(k) \leq 3$, otherwise it dies.

(2) An organism is born in an empty cell *k* if *occ(k)* = 3

Write a program to (1) read an initial configuration of occupied cells, (2) calculate a series of generations according to the rules and (3) print each configuration. Note that all changes occur *simultaneously*, and so the program must maintain two copies of the configuration. Test your program with a seven cell U-shaped pattern, the first six generations of which are shown below

6.14 An undirected graph with *maxvert* vertices can be represented by an array

$$graph : ARRAY [1 .. maxvert, 1 .. maxvert] \ OF \ boolean;$$

in which *graph[u,v]* is *true* if vertices *u* and *v* are joined by an edge, and *false* otherwise.

(a) Describe an equivalent representation of an undirected graph using an array of sets.

(b) A vertex *v* can be reached from a vertex *u* by traversing at most *n* edges if

$$graph^{n}[u,v] = true$$

where $graph^{n}$ is calculated by matrix 'multiplication' in which the boolean operators *OR* and *AND* replace addition and multiplication.

Can $graph^{n}$ be computed easily using the set representation?

(c) Write a program which reads edge descriptors, each consisting of two numbers, and prints $graph^{n}$ for

$$n = 1,2,...,5$$

Exercises

    (d) Can you find a way of terminating the program when *n* is the length of the longest path, rather than arbitrarily after 5 cycles?

6.15 If you did exercise 4.11, you have a program that will evaluate complex expressions. You can now write it more elegantly using the declaration

```
TYPE
   complex =
      RECORD
         realpart, imagpart : real
      END;
```

Files

The programs that we have studied so far have all produced some *output*, and in most cases they have also accepted some *input*. This they have done by means of the files whose names are the standard identifiers *input* and *output*. In this chapter, we will consider these and other files in a more detailed way.

Files are important for three reasons. First, a process can only communicate with its environment by means of files. Secondly, a process is usually short-lived: a program is loaded into memory and executed, and as soon as it terminates the memory is used by another program. If the program does not alter a file during its execution, there will be no evidence that it ran at all. The third reason for the importance of files is that much larger amounts of data may be stored in a file than in the memory.

In PASCAL, a file is a variable. We can see from the above, however, that it is a somewhat anomalous sort of variable, because it may exist both before and after the program is executed, and because it may be larger than the program itself. For these reasons, the actions that a PASCAL program can perform with a file are restricted in certain ways, and the program can only access one component of a file at a time.

Since PASCAL files are an abstraction of actual files, the program does not contain information about the physical nature of a file. For example, although you know that the effect of a call to the standard procedure *read* will be to transfer data from a file to a variable in your program, you do not have to state (or even to know) whether the data will be obtained from a deck of cards, a disk file, or the keyboard of a terminal. It is a function of the operating system to assign actual files to your program at run time. This it does according to directions which are not part of your PASCAL program.

The relationship between the formal files declared and referenced within the program, and the actual files provided by the operating system at run time is loosely analogous to the relationship between the formal parameters of a procedure and the actual parameters provided by the calling program when the procedure is executed. This analogy is reflected in the syntax of a PASCAL program heading (Fig. 2.11) which is rather like a procedure heading (Fig. 4.3).

7.1 Sequential Files

A *FILE* type is declared in a PASCAL program by writing an appropriate type description.

```
CONST
    maxcol = 80;
TYPE
    colindex = 1 .. maxcol;
    card = PACKED ARRAY [colindex] OF char;
    cardfile = FILE OF card;
```

The file itself is declared as a variable:

```
VAR
    deck : cardfile;
```

The name of the file must also be included in the program heading:

```
PROGRAM cardshuffler (input, output, deck);
```

The standard files *input* and *output* must not be declared in the variable declaration section. However, *input* must appear in the program heading if *read*, *eof* or *eoln* are used without a file name, and *output* must appear in the program heading if *write* is used without a file name parameter. Some systems insist that *output* is mentioned in the program heading even if the program contains no calls to *write*, so that there is a destination for error messages.

The *base type* of the file *deck* is *card*. A *component* of the file is a variable of the base type. At any one time exactly one component of the file is accessible to the program. The component of *deck* to which we have access is a variable of type *card* and is written

deck↑

It is customary to refer to a component of a file as a *record* of the
file. The PASCAL word *RECORD* does not cause confusion in this
context, because in many cases each record of a file is in fact a
RECORD variable.

The file is structured as a *sequence*. We can represent a sequence
diagrammatically as a row of boxes, as is done in Fig. 7.1.

Fig. 7.1 A Sequential File

Writing to a File

A file is created or extended by *writing* to it. Each write operation adds a new component to the file. Components can only be added
to the end of a sequential file. We can imagine a *marker* associated
with the file which tells us where the next component will be placed.
In Fig. 7.2 the marker is represented by an arrow. Fig. 7.2 (a) shows

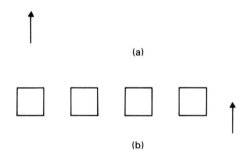

(a)

(b)

Fig. 7.2 Writing to a File

an empty file, with the marker indicating the position in which the
first record will be placed, and Fig. 7.2 (b) shows a file to which
four records have been written, with the marker indicating where the
fifth will be placed.

The operation of setting the marker to the beginning of the file
and preparing it for writing is performed by the procedure call

> *rewrite(deck)*

This operation will also destroy any existing information in the file
deck. After it has been executed, the situation is as shown in Fig.
7.2 (a). In order to write a component to the file, we assemble the
data into *deck↑* and call the procedure *put*:

> *put(deck↑)*

which has the effect of creating a new component of the file in the
position indicated by the marker, and moving the marker one place to
the right.

Suppose that we have declared

> *VAR*
>   *buffer : card;*

and that *buffer* contains information to be written to the file. Then
the statements

> *deck↑ := buffer;*
> *put(deck↑)*

may be abbreviated to

> *write(deck,buffer)*

Reading from a File

Having created the file, we can read from it. Before starting to
read the file *deck*, we execute

> *reset(deck)*

which moves the marker to the beginning of the file as shown in Fig.
7.3 (a). The procedure *reset* also transfers information from the first
component of the file into the variable *deck↑*. In order to read the
next component of the file we call the procedure

> *get(deck↑)*

which advances the pointer and copies information from the next component into *deck↑*. There comes a time when we move the pointer to the
right and there is no information there, as in Fig. 7.3 (c). In this
case, *deck↑* is undefined, and the boolean function *eof(deck)* returns
the value *true*. After calling *get*, then, we have one of two
situations:

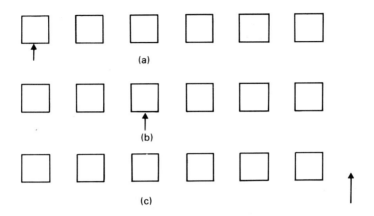

Fig. 7.3   Reading from a File

  eof(deck) = false and *deck↑* contains the next component

or

  eof(deck) = true and *deck↑* is undefined

If the file happens to be empty at the time when we read the first record, as in Fig. 7.2 (a), then *eof(deck)* will be *true* immediately after *reset* has been called. For this reason, it is best to test *eof* before calling *get*. The procedure *read* may also be used:

  read(deck,buffer)

is equivalent to

  buffer := deck↑;
  get(deck↑)

  Originally, *get* and *put* were the only file access procedures provided in PASCAL. Later, *read* and *write* were added for more convenient control of text files (text files are the subject of the next section), and according to the PASCAL Report they can *only* be used for text files. We have assumed here that *read* and *write* may be used with files of any type, because this is true for several recent implementations. The procedures *readln* and *writeln* are of course meaningless for files other than textfiles.

Restrictions on Reading and Writing

The PASCAL type *FILE* is an abstraction of a magnetic tape. The operators *reset* and *rewrite* correspond to rewinding the tape and preparing to read from it or write to it respectively. A *write* operation must not be followed by a *read*, and a *read* operation must not be followed by a *write*. Therefore, if a file is going to be used for both input and output, it must be rewound, written, rewound again, and read. The physical nature of the actual file may impose further restrictions. We can only read from a deck of cards or a keyboard, and we can only write to a printer or a display-screen. For this reason, PASCAL forbids writing to the file *input* or reading from the file *output*.

Example: Card Copying

Files, unlike variables of other types, cannot be copied by an assignment statement. Rather, they must be copied one component at a time. The function of Program *copydeck* is to copy a deck of cards, reading from the file *indeck* and writing to the file *outdeck*. Blank cards in *indeck* are not copied to *outdeck*.

```
PROGRAM copydeck (indeck, outdeck, output);
    CONST
        maxcol = 80;
        blank = ' ';
    TYPE
        colindex = 1 .. maxcol;
        card = PACKED ARRAY [colindex] OF char;
        cardfile = FILE OF card;
    VAR
        indeck, outdeck : cardfile;
        buffer, blankcard : card;
        column : colindex;
    BEGIN
        FOR column := 1 TO maxcol DO
            blankcard[column] := blank;
        reset(indeck);
        rewrite(outdeck);
        WHILE NOT eof(indeck) DO
            BEGIN
                read(indeck,buffer);
                IF buffer ≠ blankcard
                    THEN write(outdeck,buffer)
            END { while }
    END. { copydeck }
```

7.2   Text Files

When we used the procedures *read* and *write* without a filename
parameter in the preceding chapters, we were implicitly using the
files *input* and *output*. These files must be declared in the program
heading, but they need not be declared in the program. The implicit
declarations are

```
TYPE
    text = PACKED FILE OF char;
VAR
    input, output : text;
```

The identifiers *input* and *output* are default parameters of the
procedures *read*, *write* and *eof*. The type *text* is a standard type,
and so you can declare your own files to be of type *text*.

Automatic Conversion

Text files are the most commonly used variety of file, and so
PASCAL provides many special facilities to make text files easy to
use. The most important of these is the implicit conversion performed
by *read* and *write*. According to the definition of *read* and *write*
given in Section 7.1, the statements

read(x) and *write(x)*

are only valid if the type of *x* is *char*. However, as we saw in
Chapter 2, the type of *x* may also be *integer* or *real* (or *boolean* in
the case of *write*), and the procedures will provide automatic
conversion. Automatic conversion is also provided for files of type
text other than *input* and *output*.

Suppose that we have a text file containing statistical data.
The data is in groups, and each group contains ten real numbers. The
file is large, containing perhaps several thousand such groups, and it
must be processed many times. It is inefficient to keep such a file
in text form, because thousands of conversions must be performed every
time it is read. It is more efficient to convert the numbers once
only and store them in another file in binary form for subsequent
processing. Program *convertgroups* reads the text from file *datafile*
and writes the data in binary form in file *binaryfile*. A component of
binaryfile consists of an array of ten real values. The conversion is
done implicitly by the call

read(datafile,binaryfile↑[ix])

which reads one number in character form, converts it to internal
real form, and stores the result directly in the component *binary-file↑*.

```
PROGRAM convertgroups (datafile, binaryfile, output);
    CONST
        groupsize = 10;
    TYPE
        index = 1 .. groupsize;
        group = ARRAY [index] OF real;
    VAR
        datafile : text;
        binaryfile : FILE OF group;
        ix : index;
        groupcount : integer;
    BEGIN
        reset(datafile);
        rewrite(binaryfile);
        groupcount := 0;
        REPEAT
            ix := 1;
            read(datafile,binaryfile↑[ix]);
            IF NOT eof(datafile)
                THEN
                    BEGIN
                        REPEAT
                            ix := ix + 1;
                            read(datafile,binaryfile↑[ix])
                        UNTIL (ix = groupsize) OR eof(datafile);
                        IF eof(datafile)
                            THEN writeln('File ends with short group')
                            ELSE
                                BEGIN
                                    put(binaryfile);
                                    groupcount := groupcount + 1
                                END
                    END
        UNTIL eof(datafile);
        writeln(groupcount, 'Groups converted')
    END. { convertgroups }
```

Parameters for *Read* and *Write*

The procedures *read* and *write* may have several parameters when
they are used with text files. Each parameter may be of the type
integer, real or *char*. The procedure *write* will also accept a parameter which is *boolean* or a packed array of characters. In these
examples, *fn* is the name of a text file, and $p_1, p_2, \ldots, p_n$ are
parameters.

Text Files

$$read(fn, p_1, p_2, \ldots, p_n)$$

is equivalent to

```
read(fn,p₁);
read(fn,p₂);
....
read(fn,pₙ)
```

$$read(fn, p_1);$$
$$read(fn, p_2);$$
$$\ldots$$
$$read(fn, p_n)$$

and

$$write(fn, p_1, p_2, \ldots, p_n)$$

is equivalent to

$$write(fn, p_1);$$
$$write(fn, p_2);$$
$$\ldots$$
$$write(fn, p_n)$$

The filename *fn* may be omitted. If it is omitted, *input* is assumed for *read* and *output* is assumed for *write*.

Line Structure

Text files in the real world, such as programs, data and prose, are not merely streams of characters. They are structured in various ways, conventionally by lines and pages. There are standard procedures and functions in PASCAL which enable programs to generate files with this structure, and also to recognize such structure in an input text file.

Lines are represented in different ways by different computers and operating systems. PASCAL therefore provides a boolean standard function, *eoln*, that is *true* at the end of a line and *false* everywhere else, independently of the actual representation of line terminators. When *eoln* is *true*, the current character is a blank. The standard procedure *readln* skips over characters until the end of the current line. The call

$$readln(fn)$$

in which *fn* is the name of a text file, is equivalent to the statements

```
WHILE NOT eoln(fn) DO
    get(fn);
get(fn)
```

The next call to *read* will obtain the first character of the next line unless the end of the file has been reached. The filename may be omitted, in which case *input* is assumed. *Readln* may also be used with parameters:

$$readln(fn,p_1,p_2,\ldots,p_n)$$

is equivalent to

```
read(fn,p1);
read(fn,p2);
....
read(fn,pn);
readln(fn)
```

Readln can be used to skip over redundant information, such as comments or units, in the input. Be careful not to skip over things that you intended to read, however.

The procedure *writeln* is used to terminate the current output line and start a new one. The call

$$writeln(fn,p_1,p_2,\ldots,p_n)$$

is equivalent to

```
write(fn,p1);
write(fn,p2);
....
write(fn,pn);
writeln(fn)
```

The filename *fn* may be omitted, in which case it is assumed to be *output*.

7.3 Input and Output

In real computer programs, as opposed to the examples in this book, the input and output sections are often the largest. For a program to be generally useful, all input must be fully validated, and invalid data must be displayed with accurate and specific diagnostic messages. Printed output must be neatly organized so that the significant results are immediately apparent to the reader. Moreover, a careful balance must be struck between too little output, with useful or important results absent, and too much output, in which potentially useful results are lost in a morass of useless detail. The programs in this book are skeleton programs, bereft of the flesh of good input and output. This is for reasons of space: most of them would be two or three times as long as they are at present if full input validation, good diagnostics and neat output layout was included, and the additional code would be repetitive and irrelevant to the points being made. It is the purpose of this section to give some guidelines for designing the input and output sections of programs.

The conventions used for input and output should be chosen according to the mode in which the program is to be run. In general, programs intended to be run in batch mode should produce more output than programs intended to be run in interactive mode. In particular, a batch program should copy all or most of its input file to the output file, along with suitable annotation. This is what the PASCAL compiler does, for example. The input file for the PASCAL compiler is your PASCAL program, and its output is also your PASCAL program, together with headings, line numbers and perhaps error messages. The PASCAL compiler also generates another file, containing the machine language translation of your program. The program listing is an important part of the compiler's output: without it, you would have to obtain a listing of your program using a separate copy utility, and it would be harder to relate the error messages to the program. Similar considerations apply to other programs; if your program prints only answers, you may find yourself wondering in six months time what the questions were.

Input

A program that does not read data is useless because it will do exactly the same things each time it is run. It is sometimes tempting, especially if you are using a system with good interactive editing facilities, to incorporate data into the program itself, in the form of constant declarations, and then to alter these declarations before each run. This is bad programming practice. Constant declarations are intended to be used for defining values which are applicable to many different runs of the program. Any value which is changed every time the program is run is input data, and belongs in the input file.

Input data may be in *free format* or *fixed format*. PASCAL is more suited to reading data in free format, by virtue of its ability to read one character at a time from the input file. Program *calculator* of Chapter 4 reads data in free format. When you are designing a program to read free format data you will find it helpful to draw syntax diagrams for the permitted input data structures. These will simplify the design of the program and will also aid other users when they are preparing data for it. Fixed format input is the older method, dating from the time when decks of cards were used extensively in data processing. The card (or input record) is divided into *fields* of fixed length, and each item of data is assigned a field. Fig. 7.4 shows a simple fixed field card layout. Fixed field records are most

field	column		format
	from	to	
name	1	30	alphabetic
address	31	70	alphanumeric
ref number	71	80	numeric

Fig. 7.4   Fixed Field Layout

easily handled in PASCAL by reading the entire record into an array and then validating and converting each field in turn.

Suppose that a program is to read 80 column cards with several unsigned numeric fields, and we have declared:

```
CONST
    maxcol = 80;
TYPE
    colindex = 1 .. maxcol;
    cardimage = PACKED ARRAY [colindex] OF char;
VAR
    data : FILE OF cardimage;
    inputcard : cardimage;
```

Then we could use the following procedure to validate and convert selected fields:

```
PROCEDURE convertnumericfield (card : cardimage;
                              first,last : colindex;
                              VAR value : integer;
                              VAR error : boolean);
    CONST
        blank = ' ';
        radix = 10;
    VAR
        col : colindex;
        leadingblanks : boolean;
    BEGIN
        leadingblanks := true;
        value := 0;
        error := false;
        FOR col := first TO last DO
            IF (card[col] = blank)
                    AND NOT leadingblanks
                THEN error := true
            ELSE IF card[col] IN ['0' .. '9']
```

```
                        THEN
                            BEGIN
                                leadingblanks := false;
                                value := radix * value + ord(card[col])
                                                        - ord('0')
                            END
                        ELSE error := true
            END;
```

A problem which arises when an input file is processed character
by character is that responses and error messages are generated while
a line of input is being read. If the program is running in batch
mode, and copying its input stream to the output file, the output file
will get very confused. This can be avoided by reading and printing
the input file a line at a time, but only passing one character at a
time back to the calling program. This requires a *line buffer*. Declare in the main program:

```
        CONST
            maxlinelen = 100;
        TYPE
            buffer =
                RECORD
                    line : ARRAY [1 .. maxlinelen] OF char;
                    index, length : 0 .. maxlinelen
                END;
        VAR
            inputbuffer : buffer;
            infile, outfile : text;
```

Perform the following initialization:

```
        reset(infile);
        rewrite(outfile);
        inbuf . index := 0
```

In order to read a character from the input file, call this procedure:

```
PROCEDURE readchar (VAR ch : char;
                    VAR inbuf : buffer;
                    VAR infile, outfile : text);
  BEGIN
    WITH inbuf DO
        IF NOT eof(infile)
            THEN
                BEGIN
                    IF index = 0
                        THEN
                            BEGIN
                                length := 0;
                                WHILE NOT eoln(infile) DO
```

```
                    BEGIN
                      read(infile,ch);
                      write(outfile,ch);
                      IF length < maxlinelen
                        THEN
                          BEGIN
                            length := length + 1;
                            line[length] := ch
                          END
                      END; { while }
                      readln(infile);
                      writeln(outfile)
                    END;
            ch := line[index + 1];
            IF index < length - 1
              THEN index := index + 1
              ELSE index := 0
        END
  END; { readchar }
```

Output

All programs should write something to the output file, even if the bulk of the data written by the program goes to some other file. A program which merges two files, for example, should write a report of its activities, such as

```
14371  records read from file 'MASTER'
 7320  records read from file 'TRANSACTIONS'
   11  records occurred in both files
21680  records written to file 'NEW MASTER'
```

A program which produces more than one page of output should always display its results with page divisions and page numbers. A procedure can conveniently be used to generate page throws when necessary. The standard procedure *page(fn)* will generate a skip to the next page of the file *fn*. If the parameter *fn* is omitted, the file *output* is understood. Declare in the main program:

```
CONST
    pagesize = 60;
    maxpages = 1000;
TYPE
    linecounter = 1 .. pagesize;
    pagecounter = 1 .. maxpages;
VAR
    linesonpage : linecounter;
    pagenumber : pagecounter;
```

Input and Output

and assign these initial values:

```
linesonpage := pagesize;
pagecounter := 1
```

Subsequently in the program, whenever a line of output has been assembled by *write* statements, use this procedure call to signal the end of the line, not *writeln*:

```
newline(linesonpage,pagenumber)
```

The definition of *newline* follows.

```
PROCEDURE newline (VAR line : linecounter;
                   VAR page : pagecounter);
   CONST
      heading = ' My Results';
   BEGIN
      IF line ≥ pagesize
         THEN
            BEGIN
               page;
               writeln(heading,' ':60,'Page',page:5);
               writeln; writeln;
               page := page + 1;
               line := 3
            END
         ELSE
            BEGIN
               writeln;
               line := line + 1
            END
   END;
```

Interactive Programs

Interactive programs and batch programs use different conventions for input and output. The first and most obvious difference is that output from an interactive program should be minimal. The user does not want to sit and watch the program type or display long and pre-dictable messages. In particular, an interactive program should not copy data from the input file to the output file, because the user can already see what his input is.

An interactive program should report errors as soon as they are recognized. Users do not appreciate being told when they have typed ten lines that there was an error in the first line. Nor should interactive programs collapse when they encounter invalid data. The call

Example: Table Processing

      read(value)

where *value* is an integer or real variable will cause the program to
halt if the input file does not contain a syntactically correct
number. This means that a useful interactive program cannot use
automatic conversion, and therefore it must do its own conversion.
Program *calculator* of Chapter 4 is intended for interactive use, and
does not use automatic conversion. When this program reads an
incorrect expression, it marks the offending character and sets the
value of the expression to zero.

7.4 Examples

It is difficult to work in the field of computing theory for long
without becoming acquainted with the fact that there are two schools
of programming methodology and two kinds of programmers. One school
is concerned with what has come to be known as *computer science*, and
the other with *commercial data processing*. Programmers who work for
the most part on one side of the divide tend to think that the problems of the other side are uninteresting, trivial or useless. This
schism is so deep that there are many languages, and even computers,
designed to solve either commercial or scientific problems, but not
both. There is some justification for this. The commercial programmer requires efficient access to large amounts of data, but does not
indulge in 'number crunching', whereas the scientific programmer is
often involved with smaller amounts of data but more intensive
calculation. Requirements differ even at the very basic level of
number representation, because commercial programs require a small
range of values but sufficient precision to ensure that they do not
lose pennies, whereas scientific programs require a wider range of
values at lower precision.

These dichotomies tend to mask the fact that the basic programming
problems are actually rather similar. Although more recent programming languages have attempted to bridge the gap, they have done this
by providing 'scientific features' amd 'commercial features.' The
object of the examples in this section is to show that PASCAL, with a
relatively small number of basic constructs, can nevertheless be used
effectively to solve problems outside the domain of academic programming.

Example: Table Processing

Suppose that there is a company which uses a computer for accounting purposes, and has a receivables file defined as follows:

Example: Table Processing

```
TYPE
   receivable =
      RECORD
         customerid, invoiceid : ident;
         invoicedate : date;
         balance : real
      END;
VAR
   recfile : FILE OF receivables;
```

Fig. 7.5 shows a portion of this receivables file, displayed in read-able form. The file is maintained in ascending sequence by *customerid*

Today's Date: May 1

customerid	invoiceid	invoicedate	amount
CR1046	P1123	Apr 21	66-35
CR1046	P1127	Apr 23	78-00
CR1046	P1145	Apr 29	15-50
CU1214	P1009	Feb 16	216-95
CU1214	P1114	Apr 18	78-00
CU1214	S851	Jan 2	7-41
CY1249	P1110	Apr 18	23-90
CY1249	P1149	Apr 30	78-00

Fig. 7.5   Extract from Receivables File

and *invoiceid*. The company has several branch offices and so the dates
are not in the same sequence as the invoice numbers; consequently, the
records are not sequenced chronologically. The problem is this: we
have to write a program that will list all the transactions for a
customer who has had *any* invoice outstanding for more than 90 days,
for all the customers in the file.

There are several ways of writing a program to do this. One way
is to sort the file maintaining the ordering by *customerid*, but arranging the records chronologically for each customer. We will suppose
however, that the ordering by *invoiceid* is preferred for accounting
purposes, and that the file is too large to sort economically.
Another approach would be to read the entire file, creating a list of
delinquent customers, and then to read it again, printing every transaction of a customer who was recorded in the list. There is a third

Example: Table Processing

way, which we shall adopt here: process the file by customers rather
than by individual records. (Remember that for each customer there is
a *group* of records.) In order to do this, we will need a data structure in memory large enough to hold all the records relating to any one
customer. An array is a suitable structure. An array of records is
often called a *table*.

   We consider next a general algorithm for constructing and processing tables. We associate a key with each table. When we read a
record from the file, we look at its key: if it is the same as the
current table key, the new record is added to the table. If it is
different, we process the current table and start a new one. Here is
a schema, in which we are using *customerid* as the key and *entrycount*
to record the number of entries in the table.

```
WHILE NOT eof(recfile) DO
    BEGIN
        read(recfile,nextrec);
        IF nextrec . customerid ≠ key
            THEN
                BEGIN
                    processtable(table,entrycount);
                    key := nextrec . customerid;
                    entrycount := 0
                END;
        IF entrycount < tablesize
            THEN
                BEGIN
                    entrycount := entrycount + 1;
                    table[entrycount] := nextrec
                END
            ELSE table is full
    END
```

This schema works well enough in the middle of the file, but it is
unsatisfactory at the beginning and the end of the file. To start
the program off on the right track, we set the first table key from
the first record. The *WHILE* loop above is preceded by the statements

```
entrycount := 1;
read(recfile,table[entrycount]);
key := table[entrycount] . customerid
```

At the end of the file, there will be an unprocessed table in the
memory, and so we conclude the schema with the statement

```
processtable(table,entrycount)
```

   In the program which follows, this schema is used to build tables
of records which all have the same *customerid*, and the procedure
processtable prints all of these records if any one of them is more

Example: Table Processing

than 90 days old. The program calls a procedure *readdate* which
returns the date of the day of processing: this is a request to the
operating system whose form will vary with the implementation, and so
the definition of *readdate* is not given here.

```
PROGRAM tableprocessor (recfile, input, output);
  CONST
    tablesize = 100;
    idenlen = 10;
    maxage = 90;
    longestmonth = 31;
    feblen = 29;
    firstyear = 70;
    lastyear = 99;
    lenyear = 365;
    leap = 4;
  TYPE
    month = (jan,feb,mar,apr,may,jun,
                jul,aug,sep,oct,nov,dec);
    day = 1 .. longestmonth;
    idenindex = 1 .. idenlen;
    tableindex = 0 .. tablesize;
    ident = PACKED ARRAY [idenindex] OF char;
    date =
      RECORD
        yy : firstyear .. lastyear;
        mm : month;
        dd : day
      END;
    receivable =
      RECORD
        customerid, invoiceid : ident;
        invoicedate : date;
        balance : real
      END;
    rectable = ARRAY [tableindex] OF receivable;
  VAR
    recfile : FILE OF receivable;
    table : rectable;
    entrycount : tableindex;
    nextrec : receivable;
    key : ident;
    today : date;
    lenmonth : ARRAY [month] OF day;

  PROCEDURE processtable (tab : rectable;
                          size : tableindex;
                          procdate : date);
    VAR
      index : tableindex;
      oldtran : boolean;
```

```
FUNCTION age (dt : date) : integer;
  VAR
    mth : month;
    dys : integer;
  BEGIN
    WITH dt DO
      BEGIN
        dys := dd - 1;
        IF mm > jan
          THEN
            FOR mth := jan TO pred(mm) DO
              dys := dys + lenmOnth[mth];
          IF (mth > feb) AND (yy MOD leap = 0)
            THEN dys := dys + 1;
          dys := dys + lenyear * (yy - firstyear)
      END; { with }
    age := dys
  END; { age }


PROCEDURE printrec (rec : receivable);

  PROCEDURE printident (id : ident);
    VAR
      ix : 1 .. idenlen;
    BEGIN
      FOR ix := 1 TO idenlen DO
        write(id[ix]);
      write(' ')
    END; { printiden }

  BEGIN { printrec }
    WITH rec DO
      BEGIN
        printident(customerid);
        printident(invoiceid);
        WITH invoicedate DO
          BEGIN
            write(dd : 2, '/');
            write(ord(mm)+1 : 2, '/');
            write(yy : 2, ' ')
          END; { with invoicedate }
        writeln(amount : 12 : 2)
      END { with rec }
  END; { printrec }

BEGIN { processtable }
  oldtran := false;
  index := 0;
  WHILE (index < size) AND NOT oldtran DO
    BEGIN
      index := index + 1;
```

212

Example: Sequential Update

```
            IF age(procdate)-age(table[index].invoicedate) > maxage
                THEN oldtran := true
        END; { while }
    IF oldtran
        THEN
            FOR index := 1 TO size DO
                printrec(table[index])
    END; { processtable }

BEGIN { tableprocessor }
  lenmonth[jan] := 31; lenmonth[feb] := 28; lenmonth[mar] := 31;
  lenmonth[apr] := 30; lenmonth[may] := 31; lenmonth[jun] := 30;
  lenmonth[jul] := 31; lenmonth[aug] := 31; lenmonth[sep] := 30;
  lenmonth[oct] := 31; lenmonth[nov] := 30; lenmonth[dec] := 31;
  reset(recfile);
  readdate(today);
  entrycount := 1;
  read(recfile,table[entrycount]);
  key := table[entrycount] . customerid;
  WHILE NOT eof(recfile) DO
    BEGIN
      read(recfile,nextrec);
      IF nextrec . customerid ≠ key
        THEN
          BEGIN
            processtable(table,entrycount,today);
            key := nextrec . customerid;
            entrycount := 0
          END;
      IF entrycount < tablesize
        THEN
          BEGIN
            entrycount := entrycount + 1;
            table[entrycount] := nextrec
          END
        ELSE writeln('Table overflow')
    END; { while }
  processtable(table,entrycount,today)
END. { tableprocessor }
```

Example: Sequential Update

The second example of file processing that we will consider is
that of updating a sequential file. We suppose that there is a
master file, containing many records, and a *transaction file* containing relatively few records. The sequential update program reads from
an old master file *oldfile*, and a transaction file, *transfile*, and

213

creates an updated master file *newfile*. Each step in the execution
of the program consists either of copying a record from *oldfile* to
newfile, or applying a transaction to an *oldfile* record to create a
newfile record. There are three kinds of transaction: *change*, *delete*
and *insert*. A *change* alters the value of a master record, a *delete*
deletes a master record, and an *insert* creates a new master record.
The information required for *change* and *insert* is contained in the
transaction file. The *change* transaction is actually redundant,
since it can be accomplished by a deletion and an insertion, but we
include it for completeness.

Some way of identifying the records to be affected is clearly
necessary. We will assume that both master records and transaction
records contain a *key*, and moreover that both have been sorted into
ascending sequence on this key. As a simple example, suppose that the
master file contains descriptions of cars, and that each record has an
integer key. Here is a portion of the master file:

    2   Chevrolet   red   76
    3   Pontiac   green   69
    4   Buick   blue   74
    6   Oldsmobile   brown   75
    7   Cadillac   black   76

The following transactions are to be applied to this master file:

    3   change   Pontiac   green   70
    5   insert   Mercury   grey   74
    7   delete

After these transactions have been applied, the new master file
contains:

    2   Chevrolet   red   76
    3   Pontiac   green   70
    4   Buick   blue   74
    5   Mercury   grey   74
    6   Oldsmobile   brown   75

If our program is to be useful, we must allow more than one transaction to affect a single master record. We should allow the following transactions for example:

    4   change   Buick   grey   74
    4   change   Volkswagen   grey   74

We must also check the validity of transactions. A master record can
only be changed or deleted if it already exists, and conversely we
cannot insert a record if the master file already contains a record
with that key. Therefore, the following transactions cannot be
applied to our original master file:

Example: Sequential Update

```
3  insert  Dodge  white  75
5  delete
```

The program will consist of a loop in which a new record is read
and processed. The new record may come from either the master file
or from the transaction file, and processing it may or may not result
in writing a record to the new master file. The loop will have two
parts: in the first part we decide from which file to read a record,
and in the second part we process the record that we have. We can
write:

```
WHILE NOT (eof(oldfile) AND (eof(transfile)) DO
    BEGIN
        selectrecord;
        processrecord
    END
```

We can refine *selectrecord* by considering key values. It is clearly
essential to keep the two input files in step so that when we have a
transaction to apply, *oldfile* is positioned at the record which the
transaction is going to affect. Let us introduce file buffers for
each file called *oldbuf*, *newbuf* and *transbuf*, and consider the schema:

```
IF oldbuf . key ≤ transbuf . key
    THEN
        BEGIN
            newbuf := oldbuf;
            readfile(oldfile,oldbuf)
        END
    ELSE
        BEGIN
            newbuf := transbuf;
            readfile(transfile,transbuf)
        END
```

When this statement has been executed, we will need to effect a
transaction if

```
newbuf . key = transbuf . key
```

otherwise we merely copy some more records from *oldfile* to *newfile*.

Since this statement will fail if either *oldbuf.key* or *transbuf.key*
is undefined, we must ensure that these values are always defined.
We can ensure that they are initially correct by reading one record
from each input file before we enter the processing loop. It will
simplify the further development of the program if we assume that
each file ends with a dummy record with a very large key value which
we call *highkey*. We will also need an indicator telling us from
which file *newbuf* came, and we introduce the boolean variable
readtrans for this purpose. We can now write:

Example: Sequential Update

```
read(oldfile,oldbuf);
read(transfile,transbuf);
WHILE     (oldbuf . key < highkey)
      AND (transbuf . key < highkey) DO
   BEGIN
      IF oldbuf . key ≤ transbuf . key
         THEN
            BEGIN
               newbuf := oldbuf;
               read(oldfile,oldbuf);
               readtrans := false
            END
         ELSE
            BEGIN
               newbuf := transbuf;
               read(transfile,transbuf);
               readtrans := true
            END;
         processrecord
   END
```

We now continue with the development of *processrecord*. We have already noticed that there is a transaction to perform if the keys of *transbuf* and *newbuf* are equal, and in fact there may be several transactions to perform, so we write

```
WHILE transbuf . key = newbuf . key DO
```

The next step is to examine the transaction and decide what to do about it; this is most conveniently done with a *CASE* statement. When a transaction is effected, *newbuf* contains the current *oldfile* record, and *transbuf* contains the current transaction. If the transaction is a change, we copy *transbuf* to *newbuf*. If the transaction is a deletion, we inhibit the writing of *newbuf* to *newfile*. Finally, if there is an insertion to be made, the record to be inserted is already in *newbuf*, because the record to be inserted has a key which does not exist in *oldfile*. We can expand *processrecord* in this way:

```
WHILE transbuf . key = newbuf . key DO
   BEGIN
      WITH transbuf DO
         CASE transaction OF
            change :
               newbuf := transbuf;
            delete :
               newbuf . key := highkey;
            insert :
         END;
      read(transfile,transbuf)
   END;
IF newbuf . key ≠ highkey
   THEN write(newfile,newbuf)
```

Example: Sequential Update

We now have to consider the possible errors for each transaction type. It turns out that *change* and *delete* are valid only if *select-record* chose an *oldfile* record, and *insert* is valid only if *select-record* did not choose an *oldfile* record. We can therefore elaborate the *CASE* statement from the above in this way:

```
CASE transaction OF
    change :
        IF readtrans
            THEN error
            ELSE newbuf := transbuf;
    delete :
        IF readtrans
            THEN error
            ELSE newbuf . key := highkey;
    insert :
        IF NOT readtrans
            THEN error
END
```

We can now write the complete program.

```
PROGRAM update (output,oldfile,transfile,newfile);
  CONST
    desclen = 30;
    highkey = maxint;
  TYPE
    transtype = (change,delete,insert);
    description = PACKED ARRAY [1 .. desclen] OF char;
    filerec =
      RECORD
        transaction : transtype;
        key : integer;
        model, color : description;
        year : 0 .. 99
      END;
    editfile = FILE OF filerec;
  VAR
    oldfile, transfile, newfile : editfile;
    oldbuf, transbuf, newbuf : filerec;
    readtrans : boolean;

  PROCEDURE readrecord (VAR filename : editfile;
                        VAR buffer : filerec);
    BEGIN
      IF eof(filename)
        THEN buffer . key := highkey
        ELSE read(filename,buffer)
    END; { readrecord }
```

Example: Sequential Update

```
PROCEDURE error (err : transtype;
                 errorkey : integer);
  BEGIN
    CASE err OF
      change :
        write('Change ');
      delete :
        write('Delete ');
      insert :
        write('Insert ')
    END; { case }
    writeln('error at key', errorkey)
  END; { error }

BEGIN { update }
  reset(oldfile);
  reset(transfile);
  rewrite(newfile);
  readrecord(oldfile,oldbuf);
  readrecord(transfile,transbuf);
  WHILE (oldbuf . key < highkey) OR (transbuf . key < highkey) DO
    BEGIN
      IF oldbuf . key ≤ transbuf . key
        THEN
          BEGIN
            newbuf := oldbuf;
            readrecord(oldfile,oldbuf);
            readtrans := false
          END
        ELSE
          BEGIN
            newbuf := transbuf;
            readrecord(transfile,transbuf);
            readtrans := true
          END;
      WHILE transbuf . key = newbuf . key DO
        BEGIN
          WITH transbuf DO
            CASE transaction OF
              change :
                IF readtrans
                  THEN error(change,key)
                  ELSE newbuf := transbuf;
              delete :
                IF readtrans
                  THEN error(delete,key)
                  ELSE newbuf . key := highkey;
              insert :
                IF NOT readtrans
                  THEN error(insert,key)
          END; { with and case }
```

```
            readrecord(transfile,transbuf)
        END; { while }
      IF newbuf . key < highkey
        THEN write(newfile, newbuf)
    END { while }
  END. { update }
```

7.5   Subfile Structure

A backing-store device, such as a tape or a disk, has a large
capacity. It would be wasteful to store one file only on a tape or
disk unless the file was unusually large. A disk is a random access
device which cannot be represented accurately in a PASCAL program.
A multi-file tape, on the other hand, is simpler in structure and can
be represented by standard PASCAL types.

It is possible to write a special character on a tape, called a
tape-mark, which is distinguishable from ordinary data. Several files,
separated by tape-marks, may be written on a tape. These files are
usually called *subfiles* of the tape. In order to read the *n*'th subfile, we execute

```
      reset(tape);
      FOR m := 1 TO n - 1 DO
        skip to tape-mark
```

The tape unit is able to recognize tape-marks without transferring
information in the intervening subfiles into the computer's memory,
and so skipping to a tape-mark is a more efficient operation than
reading a subfile. The subfile structure may be represented in
PASCAL by declaring a file in this way:

```
      VAR
        tape : FILE OF FILE OF t;
```

in which *t* is the type of a component of a subfile. Note that all
subfiles must be of the *same* type. The variable *tape↑* is a subfile.
The operation *get(tape)* is equivalent to the operation *skip to tape-
mark* used in the example above. The function *eof(tape)* becomes *true*
at the end of the tape. The variable *tape↑↑* is of type *t* and is one
record of the subfile. The operation *get(tape↑)* reads one item from
the subfile, and the function *eof(tape↑)* becomes *true* at the end of a
subfile. The operation *put(tape↑)* writes one record to a subfile,
and the operation *put(tape)* terminates a subfile by writing a tape-
mark.

Although files with a subfile structure are not strictly

sequential files, since subfiles may be skipped, they do not enable us
to employ the much more powerful facilities of true random access
devices such as disks. Most modern computer systems use disks to
provide immediate access storage, and only use magnetic tape for
archiving, storing very large amounts of data, and for sending data to
other installations. In view of the widespread and increasing use of
random access techniques, the lack of random access facilities in
standard PASCAL is something of an anachronism.

Exercises

7.1 Write programs to generate test data for Programs *update* and *processtable* and use them to test these programs.

7.2 Modify Program *processtable* so that it calculates the age of each
record as it is read, and does not execute *processtable* at all if
no item is over 90 days old.

7.3 Write a program that generates an *aged receivables report*. Assume
that the input file contains records of the type *receivable* used
in Program *processtable*. The report lists the customer number,
invoice number and date in fixed columns at the left of the page.
The amount is printed in one of four columns according to the age
of the receivable item: current (less than 30 days old), 31 to 60
days old, 61 to 90 days old, and over 90 days old. At the end of
the report, the total amount for each column is printed, together
with the grand total (total of all columns).

7.4 Two files of the same type contain records sorted by a key. Write
a program that reads the two files and *merges* them, producing a
single output file also sorted by the key. Write a program that
generates test data for this program.

7.5 You have a computer with three tape units and a small memory, and
a tape which has to be sorted. The records on the tape are so
large that only two of them will fit in the memory at the same
time. Write a program which sorts the input tape and leaves the
sorted file on one of the other two tapes.

7.6 Write a program which reads text consisting of words separated by
blanks, and writes the same text formatted for a specified page
size. For example, the page size might be given as 40 lines of at
most 50 characters each. Words longer than the specified line
length may be rejected. The program should print a page heading
and number at the top of each page.

7.7 Write a line oriented *text editor*. This program reads text from

an *input file* and an *edit file*. It writes to an *output file* which
is a copy of the input file except where directives on the edit
file were encountered. The edit file contains directives of the
form

R m n
     lines of text

which means 'replace lines *m* through *n* of the input file by the
following text', and

I m
     lines of text

which means 'insert the following text after line *m* of the input
file'. Give a full specification of your program, including
restrictions on the sequencing of commands, and the contents of
textual insertions.

7.8 Extend Program *update* so that it prints a report showing the
number of changes, deletions and insertions made, and the number
of records in *oldfile* and *newfile*. Provide an option so that the
user can, if he wants to, obtain a list of the records inserted
or changed during the run.

Process

A — P_1 ... P_2 (diagram with markers b, w)

B — P_2 ... P_1 (diagram with markers b, w, B)

C — P_1 (diagram with marker p)

D — P_2 ... P_2 (diagram with markers p, p)

Legend:

├── P_i ──┤ Running (on control process i)

├─ ─ ─┤ Blocked

╰╱╲╱╲╯ Ready

⋏ (p) preemption occurs

⋏ (b) call to block to wait for an event

⋏ (w) event occurs (call wakeup by another process)

Critical section of a program is a set of instruction in which the result of the execution may vary unpredictably if variables ~~available~~ referenced in the section & are available to other parallel processes, are changed during execution

- We can not be in two critical sections at one ~~same~~ time

Def - Synchronization of process means to ensure that it not proceed past a given pt. without an explicit signal that it cannot generate itself.

Dynamic
Data Structures

CHAPTER EIGHT

A static data structure is a data structure that remains fixed in size throughout its lifetime. The PASCAL types *ARRAY* and *RECORD* allow us to define static structures. We can always determine the size of a static structure by examining the declarations in the program. *Dynamic data structures*, on the other hand, change in size during the execution of the program. In this chapter we will discuss how dynamic data structures can be defined and used.

In order to see why dynamic data structures might be useful, we will consider the problem of maintaining a list. Each component of the list can be represented by a variable of the type *object*. The type *object* may be a simple type such as *char* or *real*, or a structured type such as *ARRAY* or *RECORD*. We could represent the list by an array:

```
VAR
    list: ARRAY [1 .. listsize] OF object;
```

but there are several problems with this representation. In the first place, we have to decide how many components the list will eventually contain before we start, because we have to declare the value of *listsize*. The next problem is that we can only add a component at the end of the list. Deleting a component is inconvenient because it leaves a 'hole' in the array which must be marked in some way. Finally, it is difficult to keep the components of the list sorted, unless we are prepared to sort the array after every insertion.

In order to solve these problems elegantly and efficiently, we need a data structure that will permit us to insert and delete components without having to worry about where new components fit or what happens to the empty space left by a deletion. The tool which we need to create such a data structure is called a *pointer*.

8.1 Pointers

Pointer is a simple type, like *integer*, *real* and *boolean*. *Pointer* is not, however, a standard identifier. Instead, pointers are declared like this:

> *TYPE*
>   *link = ↑object;*

This declaration is read:

   'The type *link* is a pointer to an *object*'

and it is the arrow (↑) which tells us that *link* is a pointer type. A variable of the type *object* may be associated with a pointer of the type *link*, and this situation is represented diagrammatically in Fig. 8.1 (a). The variable ℓ in this diagram is of type *link*, and the

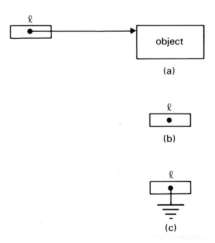

Fig. 8.1 Links and Objects

object with which it is associated is designated *ℓ↑*. Sometimes we
have a pointer for which there is no variable of type *object* to
associate, and in this case we write

    ℓ := NIL

A pointer with the value *NIL* is represented diagrammatically in Fig.
8.1 (b), which establishes the convention for drawing *NIL* pointers in
this book. You may see the electrical 'ground' symbol used to represent *NIL* pointers, as in Fig. 8.1 (c), in some books. The symbol Λ
(capital lambda) is often used in theoretical discussions of data
structures to denote a *NIL* pointer. The symbol *NIL* is a reserved word
in PASCAL.

It is important to understand the distinction between pointers and
the things to which they point. Fig. 8.2 (a) shows two variables *p*

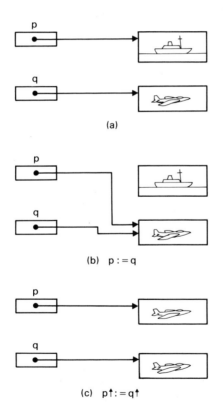

(a)

(b) p := q

(c) p↑ := q↑

Fig. 8.2 Pointer and Record Assignment

and *q*, of type *link*, pointing to different objects. The assignment

$p := q$

has the effect of assigning the value of the pointer q to the pointer p. After this assignment, the situation is as shown in Fig. 8.2 (b). Both pointers point to the airplane, and the ship has been lost (unless there was another pointer to it — two pointers can point to the same thing). The statement

$p\uparrow := q\uparrow$

has a quite different effect. We are now copying the *value* of the object $q\uparrow$ to the object $p\uparrow$ and the result is shown in Fig. 8.2 (c). The pointers are unchanged, but the value of $p\uparrow$ has been altered.

In order to define a dynamic data structure, we need an object that contains a pointer. There are three candidates for the type of such an object: *pointer*, *ARRAY* and *RECORD*. We can rule out the type pointer because it cannot contain any information apart from the value of the pointer. The components of an array must all be of the same type, which is rather a serious restriction, so we are left with the type *RECORD*. We can define an object containing a pointer and some other information like this:

```
TYPE
    object =
        RECORD
            next : link;
            data : datatype
        END;
```

Now we are confronted by a chicken-and-egg problem: do we declare *link* or *object* first? Fortunately the designers of PASCAL anticipated this problem, and we are allowed to define a pointer to an object before we have defined the object itself. We can therefore write

```
TYPE
    link = ↑object;
    object =
        RECORD
            next : link;
            data : datatype
        END;
```

In the next section, we will see how these declarations can be used to solve the list maintenance problem with which we introduced this chapter. Before proceeding with this, however, we must make one further point about pointer declarations. A pointer is *bound* to the variables of the type for which it was declared. Following the declarations

Linked Lists

```
TYPE
    P = ↑A;
    Q = ↑B;
VAR
    p : P;
    q : Q;
```

in which *A* and *B* are different types, the assignments

    p := q

and

    q := p

are not permitted. The first one, for example, would require that *p*, which is a pointer to an object of type *A*, would point to an object of type *B*, and this is not allowed in PASCAL.

8.2 Linked Lists

The *linked list* is the simplest type of dynamic data structure. It provides a solution to the problem of maintaining a list to which components may be added or deleted at random.

Fig. 8.3 shows a data structure built from a single pointer variable *base*, and three components of type *object*. This data structure is a *linked list*. We will now demonstrate how the structure of Fig. 8.3 can be assembled by a program.

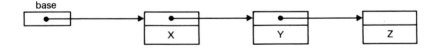

base

| X | | Y | | Z |

Fig. 8.3 A Linked List

Suppose that we want to use the pointer variable *base* as an anchor for the list, as in Fig. 8.3. Initially we want the list to be empty, and so we write

    base := NIL

We now need a component to insert into the list. Components are created dynamically by the standard procedure *new*, whose argument is a pointer. Let us declare

Linked Lists

VAR
   p : link;

and call

   new(p)

This will create a component of type *object* whose name is *p↑*. We now have the situation of Fig. 8.4 (a).

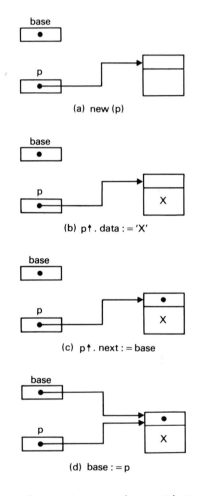

(a) new (p)

(b) p↑ . data : = 'X'

(c) p↑ . next : = base

(d) base : = p

Fig. 8.4   Creating a List

The next step is to assign some information to the new component.

228

Since *p*↑ is a record, the field *data* of *p* is designated *p*↑.*data*, and assuming that a single character can be stored in *data*, we write

> *p*↑.*data* := *'X'*

The result of this assignment is shown in Fig. 8.4 (b). The next step, for which the reason will shortly become apparent, is the assignment

> *p*↑.*next* := *base*

The current value of *base* is *NIL*, and so the effect of this statement is to set *p*↑.*next* to *NIL*, as shown by Fig. 8.4 (c). Finally, we assign

> *base* := *p*

obtaining the desired result shown in Fig. 8.4 (d). We have constructed a list containing one component. The sequence

> *p*↑.*next* := *base;*
> *base* := *p*

which was used to create the first component is in fact a general algorithm for inserting a component at the beginning of the list. Figs. 8.5 (a) and 8.5 (b) show how a second component containing the information 'Y' is inserted using the same two statements.

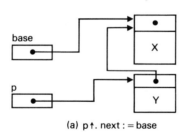

(a) p↑. next : = base

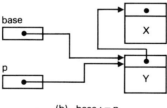

(b) base : = p

Fig. 8.5 Extending a List

Linked Lists

Linked List Traversal

We can now turn to the problem of accessing the components of a list. Consider again the list of Fig. 8.3. It is easy to access the first component, because its name is *base↑*, and so we have

$$base↑.data = 'X'$$

We can access the second component using the pointer *next* of the first component. The name of the second component is *base↑.next* and we have

$$base↑.next↑.data = 'Y'$$

We could continue in this way, but the method is clearly unsuitable for accessing the components of a long list. To do this, we need a dynamic algorithm. The key to this algorithm lies in the fact that, if *p* points to a component of the list, then, after the assignment

$$p := p↑.next$$

p points to the component's successor in the list. The assignment can be repeated until *p* becomes *NIL*, which indicates that we are at the end of the list. Accordingly, the algorithm for *traversing* a list is:

```
p := base;
REPEAT
    p := p↑.next
UNTIL p = NIL
```

Actually, we can improve on this slightly. If we write instead:

```
p := base;
WHILE p ≠ NIL DO
    p := p↑.next
```

we have an algorithm which will not fail if the list happens to be empty. The process of scanning the components of the list in this way is called *traversing the list*. Program *reverselist* uses the list insertion and traversal techniques which we have discussed to read a string of characters, store them in a list, and print them in reverse order.

```
PROGRAM reverselist (input, output);
   TYPE
      link = ↑object;
      object =
         RECORD
            next : link;
            data : char
         END;
   VAR
      base, p : link;
   BEGIN
      base := NIL;
      WHILE NOT eof DO
         BEGIN
            new(p);
            read(p↑.data);
            p↑.next := base;
            base := p
         END; { while }
      WHILE p ≠ NIL DO
         BEGIN
            write(p↑.data);
            p := p↑.next
         END { while }
   END. { reverselist }
```

We can see from this example that a simple linked list is a
last-in, first-out (LIFO) structure. A structure with this property
is called a *stack*, or if there is a risk of ambiguity, a *LIFO stack*.

Queues

The simple linked list is useful in some applications, but it
suffers from the disadvantage that only the first component of the
list is readily accessible. It is not difficult to arrange a list
so that it can be used as a *queue*. A queue is a structure in which
components are stored, and only the component which has been in the
queue for the longest time can be retrieved. The term 'queue' is
used by analogy to a queue of people in which newcomers join the rear
of the queue, and the person currently at the front of the queue is
served. The data structure is a list of the kind we have used
already, with an additional pointer to its rear component, as shown
in Fig. 8.6. We can declare, as before:

```
TYPE
   link =  object;
   object =
      RECORD
         next : link;
```

```
        data : datatype
    END;
VAR
  front, rear : link;
```

The procedure *retrieve* removes the first component from the queue and sets the pointer *first* pointing to it. Special action is needed when the last component of the queue is removed and the queue becomes empty.

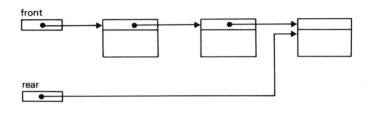

Fig. 8.6   A Queue

```
PROCEDURE retrieve (VAR first, front, rear : link);
    BEGIN
        first := front;
        IF front ≠ NIL
            THEN
                BEGIN
                    front := front↑.next;
                    IF front = NIL
                        THEN rear := NIL
                END
    END;
```

If the queue is empty when *retrieve* is called, it will return *first = NIL*, indicating that there is nothing to retrieve. When the queue becomes empty as a result of a *retrieve*, both *front* and *rear* become *NIL*. The procedure *enterqueue* places a new component at the rear of the queue. *Arrival* is a pointer to the new component provided by the calling of the program. Once again it is necessary to take special action when the queue is empty.

```
PROCEDURE enterqueue (arrival : link;
                      VAR front, rear : link);
    BEGIN
        IF front = NIL
            THEN front := arrival
            ELSE rear↑.next := arrival;
        rear := arrival
    END;
```

Linked Lists

General Insertion and Deletion

We now consider the problem of inserting and deleting components
which may be in the middle of a list. It is not difficult to insert
a component into the middle of a list if we have a pointer to the
component which is to precede the new component in the restructured
list. Suppose that we have a list containing the component *tom*↑ and
we want to insert *dick*↑ after *tom*↑. The procedure *insertafter* will do
this:

```
PROCEDURE insertafter (tom, dick : link);
    BEGIN
        dick↑.next := tom↑.next;
        tom↑.next := dick
    END;
```

The effect of *insertafter* is illustrated in Fig. 8.7. The situation
prior to the execution of the procedure is shown in Fig. 8.7 (a), and
the situation afterwards in Fig. 8.7 (b). *Insertafter* will work if
tom↑ is the last component of the list, but it will fail if *tom* = *NIL*.
If *dick*↑ is already in the list, then *insertafter* will have the
serious consequence of creating a loop in the list, which will cause
any subsequent attempt to traverse the list to fail.

The procedure *insertbefore* which is used when we have a pointer to
the component which is to follow the new component in the new list is
more difficult to realize because we do not have immediate access to
the pointer which must be altered in order to restructure the list.
The situation that we hope to reach after executing the procedure call
insertbefore(tom,dick) is shown in Fig. 8.7 (c). (The initial conditions are the same as before, Fig. 8.7 (a).) We first have to traverse
the list in this way:

```
VAR
    here : link;
....
WHILE here↑.next ≠ tom DO
    here := here↑.next
```

If we assume that *tom* ≠ *NIL* then the list cannot be empty. *Tom*↑ might,
however, be the first component of the list, and in this case the
traversal suggested above would not find him. Therefore we have to
check for the special case in which *tom*↑ is the first component of the
list. The procedure *insertbefore* may be written as follows:

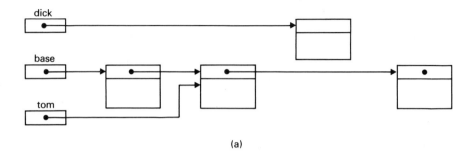

(a)

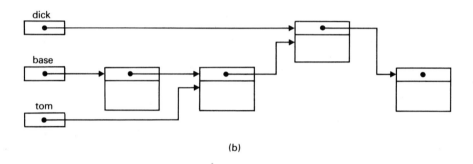

(b)

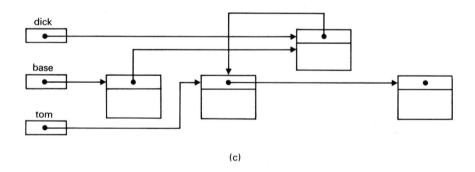

(c)

Fig. 8.7 List Insertion

```
      PROCEDURE insertbefore (tom, dick : link;
                                VAR base : link);
         VAR
            here : link;
         BEGIN
            IF tom = base
               THEN
                  BEGIN
                     dick↑.next := tom;
                     base := dick
                  END
               ELSE
                  BEGIN
                     here := base;
                     WHILE here↑.next ≠ tom DO
                        here := here↑.next;
                     here↑.next := dick;
                     dick↑.next := tom
                  END
         END;
```

There is another way of implementing *insertbefore* which can be used when the amount of information in each component is not large. We can use the procedure *insertafter* to insert the new component in the wrong place in the list, and then interchange the contents of *tom↑* and *dick↑*.

```
      PROCEDURE insertbefore (tom, dick : link);
         VAR
            tempstore : datatype;
         BEGIN
            dick↑.next := tom↑.next;
            tom↑.next := dick;
            tempstore := tom↑.data;
            tom↑.data := dick↑.data;
            dick↑.data := tempstore
         END;
```

This version of *insertbefore* is better if the list may be very long, because it is not necessary to traverse the list. The earlier version of *insertbefore* may be preferable if the list is short, but each component is large.

When we want to delete a component of a list, we encounter a similar problem. The deletion is simple enough if we have a pointer to the component preceding the component to be deleted, called, say, *predecessor*:

```
      predecessor↑.next := predecessor↑.next↑.next
```

It is more likely, however, that we will have a pointer to the

component itself, and in this case we have to traverse the list in
order to find its predecessor. The case when the first component of
the list has to be deleted has to be treated specially.

```
PROCEDURE  delete (tom : link;
                      VAR base : link);
    VAR
       here : link;
    BEGIN
       IF tom = base
          THEN base := tom↑.next
       ELSE
          BEGIN
             here := base;
             WHILE here↑.next ≠ tom DO
                here := here↑.next;
             here↑.next := tom↑.next
          END
    END;
```

Recursive List Processing

    We can define a list recursively as follows:

    A list is either empty, or consists of a node
    containing a pointer to a list.

We can write recursive procedures to process lists. The structure of
the procedure corresponds to the definition in that the procedure will
contain an *IF* statement; one branch of the *IF* statement performs the
actions appropriate for an empty list, and the other branch performs
the necessary actions to a single node, and then calls the procedure
recursively to process the remainder of the list. Two recursive
procedures are used in the program below to read a string of characters and print them in the order in which they were read. There are
of course much simpler ways to copy a list of characters: the purpose
of this program is to illustrate recursive list processing.

```
PROGRAM copylist (input, output);
    TYPE
       link = ↑object;
       object =
          RECORD
             next : link;
             data : char
          END;
    VAR
       base : link;
```

```
PROCEDURE append (VAR ptr : link);
   BEGIN
      IF ptr = NIL
         THEN
            BEGIN
               new(ptr);
               ptr↑.next := NIL;
               read(ptr↑.data)
            END
         ELSE append(ptr↑.next)
   END; { append }

PROCEDURE writelist (ptr : link);
   BEGIN
      IF ptr ≠ NIL
         THEN
            BEGIN
               write(ptr↑.data);
               writelist(ptr↑.next)
            END
   END; { writelist }

BEGIN { copylist }
   base := NIL;
   WHILE NOT eof DO
      append(base);
   writelist(base)
END. { copylist }
```

Doubly Linked Rings

We can eliminate the inconvenience of having to check for special cases by elaborating the structure of the list. We can use two pointers in each component, one pointing to the preceding component and one to the following component. The declaration becomes

```
TYPE
   link =  object;
   object =
      RECORD
         fptr, bptr : link;
         data : datatype
      END;
```

Fptr is the pointer to the following component and is called the *forward pointer*. Bptr is the pointer to the preceding component and is called the *backward pointer*. We can complete the symmetry of the structure by linking the first and last components together. The result, illustrated in Fig. 8.8 (a), is called a *doubly linked ring*.

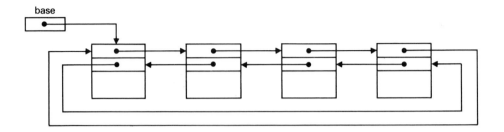

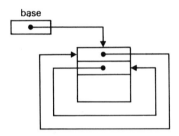

Fig. 8.8   A Doubly Linked Ring

The procedures for manipulating rings are simplified if we define the empty ring to be a ring with a single dummy component linked to itself, as shown in Fig. 8.8 (b). Procedures for inserting and deleting components from rings follow.

```
{  insert dick↑after tom↑  }
PROCEDURE insertafter (tom, dick : link);
   BEGIN
      dick↑.fptr := tom↑.fptr;
      dick↑.bptr := tom;
      tom↑.fptr↑.bptr := dick;
      tom↑.fptr := dick
   END;

{  insert dick↑before tom↑  }
PROCEDURE insertbefore (tom, dick : link);
   BEGIN
      dick↑.fptr := tom;
      dick↑.bptr := tom↑.bptr;
      tom↑.bptr↑.fptr := dick;
      tom↑.bptr := dick
   END;

{  delete tom↑   }
```

```
PROCEDURE delete (tom : link);
    BEGIN
        tom↑.fptr↑.bptr := tom↑.bptr;
        tom↑.bptr↑.fptr := tom↑.fptr
    END;
```

These procedures work in all cases, and it is interesting to note that they do not need to know the value of *base*, the 'anchor' of the ring. There is naturally a price to pay for this convenience: the components of the ring are larger, because they contain two pointers instead of just one, and the procedures are slower in some cases because there are more pointers to update. As a whole, however, the doubly linked ring is a more elegant structure because no traversals are necessary for simple operations, and there is no need to consider special cases.

Traversing a ring is not quite the same as traversing a list, because we cannot look for a *NIL* pointer. Instead, we have to remember the place from which we started. In the example below, *start* and *round* are pointers:

```
round := start↑.fptr;
WHILE round ≠ start DO
    BEGIN
        S;
        round := round↑.fptr
    END
```

The statement *S* will be executed once for each component of the ring. At the time of execution of *S*, *round* points to the current component. If the ring is empty in the sense defined by Fig. 8.8 (b), then *S* will not be executed at all. The ring can be traversed in the opposite direction using *bptr* instead of *fptr*.

Operations on Pointers

PASCAL does not permit you to do anything with a pointer variable except use it to point at something (or point at nothing, if it is *NIL*). This is reasonable because most operations on pointers are either meaningless or heavily machine dependent. Occasionally, however, we would like to be able to write the value of a pointer, for example in a post-mortem dump procedure. In many implementations, the value of a pointer is a memory address, and it can be regarded as an integer. If this is the case, we can use the following procedure to write a pointer value:

```
    PROCEDURE writepointer (pnt : pointer);
      TYPE
        rep = (pointerrep,integerrep);
        aliastype =
          RECORD
            CASE rep OF
              pointerrep :
                (pointerval : pointer);
              integerrep :
                (integerval : integer)
            END;
      VAR
        alias : aliastype;
      BEGIN
        alias . pointerval := pnt;
        write(alias . integerval)
      END;
```

You will recall from Chapter 6 that *aliastype* is a free union. This
is a programming trick. It contravenes the spirit of PASCAL; it is a
programming device that may not work on all implementations; that may
fail in certain cases (if pointer = *NIL*, for example); and is entirely
machine dependent. We mention it because there are situations where
printing a pointer value is useful, particularly in program development. Do not allow procedures like this to remain in finished
programs, and do not under any circumstances use them in a program
which may be run at another installation.

8.3 Example: Discrete Event Simulation

Computers are frequently used to simulate natural phenomena.
Provided that the underlying theoretical model is adequate, useful
results can be obtained from simulations in circumstances where
experiments would be expensive or impossible. Simulation programs
are classified by the type of process being simulated, and for the
purpose of simulation, many processes can be considered as a success-
ion of discrete events. In this example we construct a program which
simulates a bus service. Although in reality a bus service is a
continuous process, we can design an abstract model of it using parameters which change only at discrete points in time. For example,
we assume that a bus is travelling or stationary, and that a passenger
is waiting for a bus, boarding a bus, or sitting in a bus.

The bus company provides a service that consists of *bustot* buses
travelling around a circular route consisting of *stoptot* bus stops.
The bus company has done its utmost to ensure regularity of service
by guaranteeing that the time required for a bus to travel from one

240

Example: Discrete Event Simulation

stop to the next, and the time required for a passenger to board a
bus, are both constants. The service would be entirely regular but
for the fact that passengers arrive at bus stops at random intervals.
In the simulation we consider three kinds of event:

(a) A person arrives in the queue at a bus stop;

(b) A bus arrives at a bus stop;

(c) A person boards the bus.

The problem ignores disembarking passengers, assuming that they get
out at the back faster than boarding passengers get in at the front.
For each of the events above, we can specify another event which must
follow:

(a) After a random interval of time, another person arrives in the
    queue;

(b) If there is no one in the queue, the bus proceeds to the next stop
    and its arrival there is the next event; otherwise, the next event
    is the first person in the queue boarding the bus;

(c) The length of the queue diminishes by 1. If there the queue is
    now empty, the bus proceeds to the next stop, otherwise the next
    passenger boards the bus.

We will represent one of these events by a record. We can
declare:

```
TYPE
    eventkind = (person,arrival,boarder);
    event =
        RECORD
            kind : eventkind
        END;
VAR
    currentevent : event;
```

We can write a provisional schema for the program as follows:

```
REPEAT
    get the current event;
    CASE currentevent . kind OF
        person :
            BEGIN
                queuelength := queuelength + 1;
                genevent(person)
            END;
        arrival :
            IF queuelength = 0
```

241

```
                    THEN genevent(arrival)
                    ELSE genevent(boarder);
          boarder :
             BEGIN
                queuelength := queuelength - 1;
                IF queuelength = 0
                    THEN genevent(arrival)
                    ELSE genevent(boarder)
             END
       END
    UNTIL end of simulation
```

In this schema we have assumed the existence of a procedure *genevent* which will schedule an event which is to occur at some time in the future. We have also written the statement *get the current event*. This suggests that we will need a data structure to store events in chronological order, so that the 'next' event is immediately accessible. Note, however, that events are not generated in chronological order, and so a queue is not an adequate structure. A more appropriate structure is a ring in which each component is an event. The parameters of an event are its *eventkind*, the time at which it will occur, and the numbers of the bus stop and bus to which it applies. We can write the following more detailed declarations for the event record and the event ring:

```
    TYPE
       link = ↑event;
       event =
          RECORD
             fptr, bptr : link;
             kind : eventkind;
             stopnum : stopnumber;
             busnum : busnumber
          END;
    VAR
       base : link;
       currentevent : link;
```

Fig. 8.9 (a) identifies the various fields of an event record, and Fig. 8.9 (b) shows the form of the ring during the simulation. Note that the events are ordered chronologically. In accordance with the conventions of Section 8.2, we include a dummy event in the ring, and consider the ring to be empty when it contains no components other than the dummy component. The current event is

```
    currentevent := base↑.fptr
```

and so the current time is

```
    currentevent↑.time
```

Example: Discrete Event Simulation

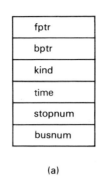

(a)

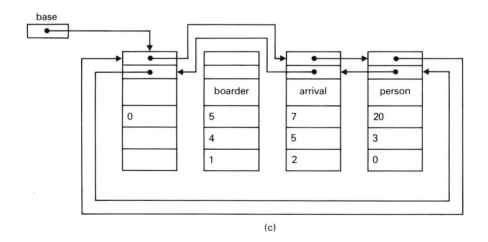

Fig. 8.9   The Data Structure for Program *buses*

Example: Discrete Event Simulation

When we have processed the current event, we delete it, so that the
next event becomes the current event. These assignments suffice to
delete the current event, and their effect is depicted in Fig. 8.9(c):

    base↑.fptr := currentevent↑.fptr;
    currentevent↑.fptr↑.bptr := base

The number of people waiting at a bus stop can be represented by an
integer, because we need to know only how many people there are in the
queue, not who they are. The lengths of all the queues can be summarized in an array:

    queue : ARRAY [stopnumber] OF integer;

Using these declarations, we can write a refined version of the main
program.

```
REPEAT
    currentevent := base↑.fptr;
    WITH currentevent↑ DO
        CASE kind OF
            person :
                BEGIN
                    queue[stopnum] := queue[stopnum] + 1;
                    genevent(person,time,stopnum,0)
                END;
            arrival :
                IF queue[stopnum] = 0
                    THEN genevent(arrival,time,nextstop,busnum)
                    ELSE genevent(boarder,time,stopnum,busnum);
            boarder :
                BEGIN
                    queue[stopnum] := queue[stopnum] - 1;
                    IF queue[stopnum] > 0
                        THEN genevent(boarder,time,stopnum,busnum)
                        ELSE genevent(arrival,time,nextstop,busnum)
                END
        END;
    base↑.fptr := currentevent↑.fptr;
    currentevent↑.fptr↑.bptr := base
UNTIL currentevent↑.time > maxtime
```

When a bus departs from a bus stop, we call

    genevent(arrival,time,nextstop,busnum)

to generate an event representing the arrival of the bus at the next
stop. If we suppose that the stoptot bus stops are numbered 1 through
stoptot, we have

    nextstop = (stopnum MOD stoptot) + 1

Example: Discrete Event Simulation

The procedure *genevent* has to calculate the time at which the new event will occur, construct the event, and insert it into the event ring. The time for which the new event is scheduled depends on what kind of event it is. We have three kinds of events, and so there are three different times, which we can store in an array:

```
VAR
     evtime : ARRAY [eventkind] OF real;
```

Evtime[arrival] and *evtime[boarder]* are constants, but the arrival of a person at a bus stop is a random event, and so *evtime[person]* must be multiplied by a random variable each time it is used. The new event is inserted into the ring by first searching the ring backwards until the event immediately preceding the new event in time is found. This will always work provided that we assign time zero to the dummy event. The procedure *genevent* looks like this:

```
PROCEDURE genevent (evkind : eventkind;
                    newtime : real;
                    stop : stopnumber;
                    bus : busnumber);
VAR
   ev, newev : link;
   delay : real;
BEGIN
   IF evkind = person
      THEN delay := evtime[evkind] * random
      ELSE delay := evtime[evkind];
   new(newev);
   WITH newev↑ DO
      BEGIN
         kind := evkind;
         time := newtime + delay;
         stopnum := stop;
         busnum := bus
      END;
   ev := base;
   REPEAT
      ev := ev↑.bptr
   UNTIL newev↑.time ≥ ev↑.time;
   newev↑.fptr := ev↑.fptr;
   newev↑.bptr := ev;
   ev↑.fptr↑.bptr := newev;
   ev↑.fptr := newev
END;
```

The initial conditions of a simulation must be considered carefully if the simulation is to give useful results. The bus simulation starts with the buses distributed uniformly over the route, and no one waiting at a bus stop. The purpose of the simulation is to discover whether the uniform spacing between buses is maintained or not. The simulation confirms what commuters already know — buses tend to bunch together. This is intuitively reasonable, because as a bus gets closer to the bus in front, the queues at the bus stops get shorter, and so the bus moves faster. Conversely, a bus which is a long way behind the bus in front will move slowly because it will encounter long queues. In the version of the simulation described above, the bunching effect is so strong that the buses rapidly form a convoy and never split up. The program given below eliminates convoys by a simple mechanism which, for some reason, is prohibited by many bus companies.

```
PROGRAM buses (input,output);
  CONST
    stopmax = 100;
    busmax = 100;
    queuemax = 100;
  TYPE
    stopnumber = 0 .. stopmax;
    busnumber = 0 .. busmax;
    queuelength = 0 .. queuemax;
    eventkind = (person,arrival,boarder);
    link = ↑event;
    event =
      RECORD
        fptr,bptr : link;
        kind : eventkind;
        time : real;
        stopnum : stopnumber;
        busnum : busnumber
      END;
  VAR
    queue : ARRAY [stopnumber] OF queuelength;
    atstop : ARRAY [stopnumber] OF boolean;
    evtime : ARRAY [eventkind] OF real;
    gap,stop,stoptot : stopnumber;
    bus,bustot : busnumber;
    maxtime : real;
    currentevent,base : link;
    randomseed : integer;
    evindex : eventkind;

  FUNCTION random (VAR seed : integer) : real;
    BEGIN
      random := - ln((seed + 1) / 65536);
      seed := (25173 * seed + 13849) MOD 65536
    END; { random }

  PROCEDURE genevent (evkind : eventkind;
                      newtime : real;
                      stop : stopnumber;
                      bus : busnumber);
```

246

Example: Discrete Event Simulation

```
  VAR
    ev,newev : link;
    delay : real;
  BEGIN
    IF evkind = person
      THEN delay := evtime[evkind] * random(randomseed)
      ELSE delay := evtime[evkind];
    new(newev);
    WITH newev↑ DO
      BEGIN
        kind := evkind;
        time := newtime + delay;
        stopnum := stop;
        busnum := bus
      END; { with }
    ev := base;
    REPEAT
      ev := ev↑.bptr
    UNTIL newev↑.time ≥ ev↑.time;
    newev↑.fptr := ev↑.fptr;
    newev↑.bptr := ev;
    ev↑.fptr↑.bptr := newev;
    ev↑.fptr := newev
  END; { genevent }

BEGIN { buses }

{ read simulation parameters }

  read(stoptot,bustot);
  FOR evindex := person TO boarder DO
    read(evtime[evindex]);
  read(maxtime);

{ create an empty event ring }
  new(base);
  WITH base↑ DO
    BEGIN
      fptr := base;
      bptr := base;
      time := 0
    END; { with }

{ distribute buses evenly along the route }

  IF stoptot < bustot
    THEN gap := 1
    ELSE gap := stoptot DIV bustot;
  stop := 1;
  FOR bus := 1 TO bustot DO
    BEGIN
```

Example: Discrete Event Simulation

```
        genevent(arrival,0,stop,bus);
        IF stop + gap > stoptot
           THEN stop := stop + gap
           ELSE stop := 1
      END; { for }

 { create a queue at each bus stop }
   FOR stop := 1 TO stoptot DO
      BEGIN
         queue[stop] := 0;
         genevent(person,0,stop,0);
         atstop[stop] := false
      END; { for }

 { simulate }
   REPEAT
      currentevent := base↑.fptr;
      WITH currentevent↑ DO
         CASE kind OF
            person :
               BEGIN
                  queue[stopnum] := queue[stopnum] + 1;
                  genevent(person,time,stopnum,0)
               END;
            arrival :
               IF atstop[stopnum] OR (queue[stopnum] = 0)
                  THEN genevent(arrival,time,
                               (stopnum MOD stoptot)+1,busnum)
                  ELSE
                     BEGIN
                        atstop[stopnum] := true;
                        genevent(boarder,time,stopnum,busnum);
                        write(time : 8 : 3);
                        write(' ' : 3 * stopnum);
                        writeln(busnum : 1)
                     END;
            boarder :
               BEGIN
                  queue[stopnum] := queue[stopnum] - 1;
                  IF queue[stopnum] > 0
                     THEN genevent(boarder,time,stopnum,busnum)
                     ELSE
                        BEGIN
                           atstop[stopnum] := false;
                           genevent(arrival,time,
                                   (stopnum MOD stoptot)+1,busnum
                        END
               END
      END; { with and case }
      base↑.fptr := currentevent↑.fptr;
      currentevent↑.fptr↑.bptr := base
```

UNTIL base↑.fptr↑.time ≥ maxtime
END. { buses }

The event ring is a useful data structure because it permits us to simulate concurrent events using a single processor. Program *buses* is a single sequential process when it is executing, but it accurately models the behavior of an arbitrary number of buses and queues. We can generalize the requirements of a simulation of concurrent processes in the following way:

(1) For each process being simulated, there must be a record of the current status of that process.

(2) The single processor must serve each process in turn. When a process has been served, either its updated process record is returned to the event ring, or (as in Program *buses*) a new process record is created.

(3) There must be a means of scheduling processes. In Program *buses* the scheduling is controlled by event times.

8.4   Trees

Pointers can be used in representations of structures more general than lists and rings. Suppose that we have a structure consisting of records linked by pointers in which each record may contain pointers to several other records. This is a representation of a *directed graph*. The *vertices*, or *nodes*, of the graph are represented by records, and the *edges* of the graph are represented by pointers. A *tree* is a particular kind of graph with the following properties: the substructures linked to any node are disjoint, and there is a node called the *root* from which every node in the tree can be reached by traversing a finite number of edges. Fig. 8.10 is a diagrammatic representation of a tree of which *A* is the root. The nodes *D, E, F, I, J* and *K* are *terminal nodes* or *leaves* of the tree.

You may feel that Fig. 8.10 is upside-down, since the root *A* is at the top. However, there is a tradition in computer science that trees are drawn upside-down. We are accustomed to starting a drawing at the top of the page and drawing downwards, and it is easier to draw the root of the tree before its leaves.

A tree is a recursive structure. We can in fact define a tree by saying: *a tree is either empty or it consists of a node containing pointers to disjoint trees*. This definition is very similar to the recursive definition of a list. Whereas lists may be manipulated easily by either recursive or iterative algorithms, trees are

249

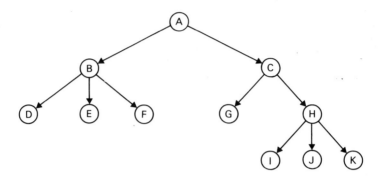

Fig. 8.10   A Tree

manipulated much more easily by recursive algorithms, as we shall see.

Binary Trees

    In a binary tree, each node has at most two offspring. If both
offspring are present, they are called the *left* and *right* offspring.
In a binary tree, the offspring are not interchangeable. Fig. 8.11
shows three different binary trees: Fig. 8.11 (b) and Fig. 8.11 (c)
do not represent the same tree. We use a PASCAL record to represent
a node of a binary tree:

```
TYPE
    link = ↑node;
    node =
        RECORD
            left, right : link;
            data : datatype
        END;
```

    Binary tree traversal can be defined recursively: at each node
there are three things to do. The term 'visit' is used to denote an
operation which is to be applied to each node of the tree.

        Visit the node
        Traverse the left subtree
        Traverse the right subtree

There are six different ways in which these three steps can be
arranged, and so there are six different ways of traversing the tree.
These six ways are conventionally reduced to three by specifying that
the left subtree is always traversed before the right subtree. The
three remaining traversals are given names: a *preorder* traversal

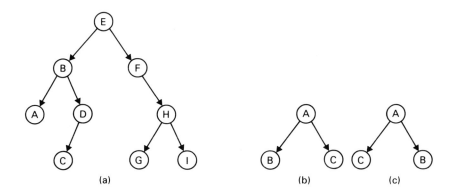

Fig. 8.11   Binary Trees

visits the node first, and then the subtrees; an *inorder* traversal
visits the left subtree, the node and then the right subtree; and a
postorder traversal visits the subtrees and then the node. We can
easily write a recursive procedure to traverse a binary tree:

```
PROCEDURE traverse (tree : link);
    BEGIN
        IF tree ≠ NIL
            THEN
                BEGIN
                    visit(tree);
                    traverse(tree↑.left);
                    traverse(tree↑.right)
                END
    END;
```

This version of traverse performs a preorder traversal. The other
orderings are obtained by permuting the three statements of the
clause. Traversals of the tree of Fig. 8.11 (a) visit the nodes in
these sequences:

```
Preorder:    E  B  A  D  C  F  H  G  I
Inorder:     A  B  C  D  E  F  G  H  I
Postorder:   A  C  D  B  G  I  H  F  E
```

The inorder traversal produces an ordered sequence. This is not
a coincidence, because Fig. 8.11 (a) was drawn so that this would
occur. The tree of Fig. 8.11 (a) is called a *binary search tree*, and
the binary search tree is a very useful structure, as we shall see
from the procedures which follow. Procedure *insert* adds a node to a
binary search tree, preserving the ordering.

```
        PROCEDURE insert (VAR tree : link;
                          newdata : datatype);
      BEGIN
        IF tree = NIL
          THEN
            BEGIN
              new(tree);
              WITH tree↑ DO
                BEGIN
                  left := NIL;
                  right := NIL;
                  data := newdata
                END { with }
            END
          ELSE
            WITH tree↑ DO
              IF newdata < data
                THEN insert(left,newdata)
              ELSE IF newdata > data
                THEN insert(right,newdata)
              ELSE { duplicate entry }
      END;
```

The following function returns a pointer to a node in the tree containing the given data, or NIL if there is no such node.

```
        FUNCTION find (tree : link;
                       key : datatype) : link;
      BEGIN
        IF tree = NIL
          THEN find := NIL
        ELSE
          WITH tree↑ DO
            IF key < data
              THEN find := find(left,key)
            ELSE IF key > data
              THEN find := find(right,key)
            ELSE find := tree
      END;
```

We can also write find without using recursion:

```
        FUNCTION find (tree : link;
                       key : datatype) : link;
      VAR
        finished : boolean;
      BEGIN
        finished := false;
        REPEAT
          IF tree = NIL
            THEN finished := true
```

Example: Word Concordance

```
            ELSE
                WITH tree↑ DO
                    IF key < data
                        THEN tree := left
                    ELSE IF key > data
                        THEN tree := right
                    ELSE finished := true
            UNTIL finished;
            find := tree
        END;
```

Finally, we note that the entries in a binary search tree can be listed in sequence by an inorder traversal. The only operation which is not easy to perform on a binary tree is the deletion of a node which is not a leaf. The binary search tree is a more efficient structure for storing and retrieving data than an array. We must be careful to ensure that the new entries do not arrive in ascending or descending order, because in this case the tree will degenerate into a linear list. In many practical cases, however, entries arrive in an essentially random order, and a reasonably efficient search tree will be constructed. In a random binary search tree with N nodes, the time required to insert or delete a node is proportional to $log(N)$, whereas the corresponding time for an array, using linear search, is proportional to N.

Example: Word Concordance

Program *concordance* of Chapter 6 reads a text and prints a list of the words in the text together with their frequencies. The following program does the same thing but uses a binary search tree to store the words rather than an array. The new program has two advantages over the earlier version: it will be faster because a tree search is more efficient than a binary search, and it prints the words in alphabetical order without having to sort them. On the other hand, this version of the program will require more memory for a given table size, because each entry now contains two pointers as well as the word and its counter.

```
PROGRAM concordance (input, output);
  CONST
    maxwordlen = 20;
  TYPE
    charindex = 1 .. maxwordlen;
    counttype = 1 .. maxint;
    wordtype = PACKED ARRAY [charindex] OF char;
    pointer = ↑entrytype;
    entrytype =
      RECORD
        left, right : pointer;
```

Example: Word Concordance

```
          word : wordtype;
          count : counttype
      END;
VAR
  wordtree : pointer;
  nextword : wordtype;
  letters : SET OF char;

PROCEDURE readword (packedword : wordtype);
  { see page 185 }

PROCEDURE
  { see page 186 }

PROCEDURE makentry (VAR tree : pointer; entry : wordtype);
  BEGIN
    IF tree = NIL
      THEN
        BEGIN
          new(tree);
          WITH tree↑ DO
            BEGIN
              word := entry;
              count := 1;
              left := NIL;
              right := NIL
            END; { with }
        END
      ELSE
        WITH tree↑ DO
          IF entry < word
            THEN makentry(left,entry)
          ELSE IF entry > word
            THEN makentry(right,entry)
          ELSE count := count + 1
  END; { makentry }

PROCEDURE printtree (tree : pointer);
  BEGIN
    IF tree ≠ NIL
      THEN
        WITH tree↑ DO
          BEGIN
            printtree(left);
            printword(word);
            writeln(count);
            printtree(right)
          END { with }
  END; { printtree }
```

```
BEGIN { concordance }
  letters := ['a' .. 'z'];
  wordtree := NIL;
  WHILE NOT eof DO
    BEGIN
      readword(nextword);
      IF NOT eof
        THEN makentry(wordtree,nextword)
    END; { while }
  printtree(wordtree)
END. { concordance }
```

General Trees

We now consider the problem of representing a tree in which a node may contain pointers to more than two subtrees. If the largest number of subtrees is limited to some reasonably small value, then it may be practical to use an array of pointers to point to subtrees. In this case, we could declare the data structure in this way:

```
CONST
  maxnodes = 6;
TYPE
  link = ↑node;
  node =
    RECORD
      subnode : ARRAY [1 .. maxnodes] OF link;
      data : datatype
    END;
```

Having to preset the value of maxnodes is a serious limitation. If we make maxnodes too small, we will sooner or later encounter a tree that we cannot represent, and if we make maxnodes too large, the unused pointers will waste memory space. An alternative solution is to attach to each node of the tree a linked list of its offspring. Fig. 8.12 shows the tree of Fig. 8.10 transformed in this way. This representation requires that each node contains two pointers (either of which may be NIL): one to the eldest descendant of the node, and one to the next sibling. In Fig. 8.12 parent-offspring links are drawn vertically and sibling links are drawn horizontally. We have in fact transformed the tree into a binary tree.

255

Exercises

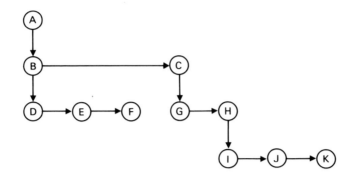

Fig. 8.12   The Transformed Tree

Exercises

8.1 Draw diagrams to illustrate the operations of insertion and
deletion on a doubly linked ring. What is the effect of *delete*
on an empty ring?

8.2 Show that in any binary tree, more than half of the pointer
values are *NIL*. (This is rather wasteful, and advanced programs
using binary tree often use vacant fields to store pointers back
to nodes at higher levels.)

8.3
(a) Draw diagrams of some of the possible forms a binary tree can
assume. In particular, show the best and worst possible forms
of a tree used for symbol storage and retrieval.

(b) Devise an algorithm for deleting a non-terminal node from a
binary search tree without destroying the ordering.

8.4 The *level* of the root of a tree is defined to be 0. The level of
any other node is defined to be one greater than the level of its
parent. The *depth* of the tree is the level of the node whose
level is the largest. The *internal path length* of a tree is the
total number of edges within the tree. Write procedures to:
(a) find the level of a specified node in the tree;
(b) find the depth of a given tree;
(c) find the internal path length of a given tree.

8.5 There are several ways of representing binary trees on paper,
other than the topological form of Fig. 8.11. For example, Fig.
8.11 (a) can be described in either of these two ways:

Exercises

(a) E(B(A(,),D(C,)),F(,H(G,I)))
(b)   E
         B
           A
           D
               C
         F
           H
             G
             I

Write a program that reads a binary tree in format (a) and then prints the same tree in format (b).

8.6 Algebraic expressions may be represented by binary trees. Each node of the tree contains an operator (+, -, * or /) and pointers to two subexpressions. Fig. 8.13 is the tree corresponding to the expression

        (a * b) + c - a * (b + c)

Using Program *calculator* as a starting point, write a program that reads an expression and constructs the corresponding tree.

8.7 Program *buses* is run with 15 bus stops and 5 buses. Draw a graph showing approximately the size of the event ring as a function of time.

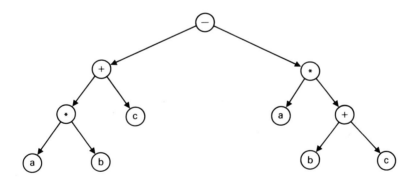

Fig. 8.13   An Expression Tree

8.8 Describe the mechanism used by Program *buses* to prevent buses from forming convoys, and explain its effect on a real bus service.

8.9 Write a procedure that takes a 'snapshot' of the current situation in Program *buses*. The procedure should be activated

257

once during initialization and should subsequently reactivate itself at regular intervals. Use this to plot the positions of buses as a function of time.

8.10 Modify Program *buses* to allow for disembarking passengers under one of the following assumptions:

(a) Passengers disembark at the same rate as they join queues.
(b) The journey length for any passenger is a random variable with a negative exponential distribution.

8.11 Design a data structure that models family relationships. Each person is represented by a record which contains his or her name, and pointers to parents, spouse and children. Write a procedure to insert a new person into the structure, and write procedures to establish the relationships of the new person to existing members of the family, such as:

```
offspring(parent,child)
marry(wife,husband)
```

Write a boolean function *cousin* which is *true* if its two arguments are pointers to cousins.

8.12 Write an interactive coordinate geometry program. The user of the program should be able to write simple commands to create figures of various shapes, to which he may give names. For example, he might write

```
A = point 0 0
B = point 2 3
L = line  A B
```

8.13 Jobs arrive in the input queue of a computer system at a mean rate of λ and are serviced at a mean rate of μ. Write a simulation program to investigate the average queue length as a function of λ and μ. Modify the system so that there are two queues, one for high priority jobs which arrive at a rate λ_H and another for low priority jobs which arrive at a rate of λ_L. No jobs are interrupted during processing, but a low priority job is only started if there are no jobs in the high priority queue. Investigate the queue lengths for various values of λ_H and λ_L.

Note: If events occur at a mean rate R, then the time between any two consecutive events is a random variable

$$t = -\ln(x)/R$$

where x is uniformly distributed between 0 and 1.

Advanced Topics

CHAPTER NINE

This is the last chapter in which we describe features of PASCAL. Many programs, even complicated ones, can be written without the constructions used in this chapter, and you should be reasonably fluent in PASCAL before you attempt to use them.

9.1 The *GOTO* Statement

The *GOTO* statement is the only PASCAL statement that we have not used previously in this book. This is no accident, because programs can be written without it. In fact, some versions of PASCAL do not even recognize the *GOTO* statement.

The *GOTO* statement permits direct transfer of control from one part of the program to another, with certain restrictions which we will consider later. One common use of *GOTO* is to exit from a loop. The following loop is taken from Program *tableprocessor* of Chapter 9.

```
oldtran := false;
index := 0;
WHILE (index < size) AND NOT oldtran DO
    BEGIN
        index := index + 1;
        IF age(procdate) - age(table[index].invoicedate) > maxage
            THEN oldtran := true
    END;
IF oldtran
    THEN
        FOR index := 1 TO size DO
            printrec(table[index])
```

Examination of the *WHILE* loop reveals that it is actually a *FOR* loop in disguise. We could write:

```
oldtran := true;
FOR index := 1 TO size DO
    IF age(procdate) - age(table[index].invoicedate) > maxage
        THEN oldtran := true;
IF oldtran
    THEN
        FOR index := 1 TO size DO
            printrec(table[index])
```

The only difference between these program fragments is that the loop in the first will terminate as soon as an entry satisfying the condition is found, whereas the second will examine all the components of the table whether there is an entry satisfying the condition or not. We see that the *WHILE* construction was used solely so that we could terminate the loop in the middle of the table. Moreover, we had to introduce a spurious variable, *oldtran*, in order to trip the *WHILE* statement. We can achieve the same effect in this way:

```
FOR index := 1 TO size DO
    IF age(procdate) - age(table[index].invoicedate) > maxage
        THEN GOTO 1;
GOTO 2;
1 :
    FOR index := 1 TO size DO
        printrec(table[index]);
2 :
```

The statement *GOTO 1* causes a direct transfer of control to the statement labeled *1*.

GOTO may also be used to solve the problem that we encountered in Chapter 4: how does a function, which may be called from anywhere in the program, signal an error in a useful way? One solution is to assign a label, such as *99*, at the end of the main program, to which any function detecting an error can jump. We could then write the function *squareroot* of Chapter 4 in this way:

```
FUNCTION squareroot (value : real) : real;
   CONST
      epsilon = 1E-6;
   VAR
      root : real;
   BEGIN
      IF value < 0
         THEN
            BEGIN
               writeln('squareroot argument =',value);
               GOTO 99
            END
      ELSE IF value = 0
         THEN
            ....
```

At the end of the main program, we write:

```
   99 : writeln('execution terminate')
END.
```

The label used in a *GOTO* statement must be declared. The *label declaration section* is placed before the other declaration sections in a block, and its syntax is shown in Fig. 9.1. Note that a label must be a positive integer constant.

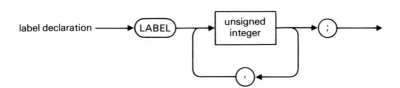

Fig. 9.1 *Label Declaration* Syntax

There are some important restrictions on the use of the *GOTO* statement. A *GOTO* statement can be used to jump within a level, or from an inner level to an outer level, but it cannot be used to jump from an outer level to an inner level. In particular, although you can jump out of a procedure, you cannot jump into one. These are *valid* uses of *GOTO*.

The *GOTO* Statement

```
LABEL 2;
....
    PROCEDURE jumpabout;
        LABEL 1;
        BEGIN
            ....
            GOTO 1;
            ....
            GOTO 2;
            ....
            1 : S1
        END;
    BEGIN
        ....
        IF p
            THEN GOTO 2;
        ....
        2 : S2
    END
```

These are *invalid* uses of the *GOTO* statement:

```
GOTO 3;
....
IF p
    THEN S1
    ELSE 3 : S2
....
WHILE q DO
    BEGIN
        S3;
        4 : S4
    END;
....
GOTO 4;
....
    PROCEDURE donut;
        LABEL 5;
        BEGIN
            ....
            5 : S5;
            ....
        END;
    BEGIN
        ....
        GOTO 5;
        ....
```

A label and its colon constitute a statement even if no action follows the colon. Accordingly, the semi-colon after *writeln* in the following example is required to separate the statement *writeln* from the label *99*:

    BEGIN
       ....
       GOTO 99;
       ....
       writeln;
       99 :
    END

9.2   Procedures and Functions as Parameters

We have seen that a procedure or function may invoke another. Indeed, it would be hard to write non-trivial programs if this were not so. We sometimes encounter circumstances in which we wish to write a procedure or function which invokes another procedure or function whose effect is not determined until the program is executed. For example, we might want a function *integrate* such that when we called

    integrate(f,a,b)

we obtained the value of

$$\int_a^b f(x)\ dx$$

so that we could write statements such as

    integrate(sin,0,t)

It is possible to write such functions in PASCAL. We will illustrate the technique by designing a function *solve* which estimates a solution of the equation

    $f(x) = 0$

in which f is a function passed to *solve* as a parameter.

Any estimation process requires at least one initial approximation to the solution because the function f may have several zeros. The method we use to find the zero is the *secant method*, which in fact requires two approximations to start it off. The concept is illustrated in Fig. 9.2. The approximations to the true root ξ are x_1 and x_2. The points $A_1 = (x_1, f(x_1))$ and $A_2 = (x_2, f(x_2))$ are on the curve

    $y = f(x)$

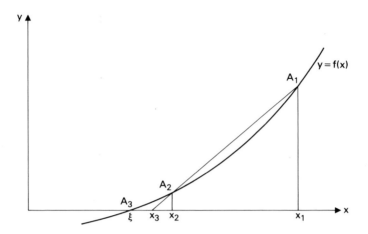

Fig. 9.2   Approximating a Root of $f(x) = 0$

We calculate a third approximation x_3 which is the x-coordinate of the point of intersection of the line A_1A_2 and the abscissa.   If (x,y) is a point on A_1A_2 we have

$$\frac{y - y_2}{x - x_2} = \frac{y_2 - y_1}{x_2 - x_1}$$

in which we have written y_1 for $f(x_1)$ and y_2 for $f(x_2)$.   We know that the point $(x_3,0)$ is on this line, and therefore that

$$x_3 = x_2 - y_2 \cdot \frac{x_2 - x_1}{y_2 - y_1}$$

and from this we can derive the recurrence relation

$$x_{n+2} = x_{n+1} - f(x_{n+1}) \cdot \frac{x_{n+1} - x_n}{f(x_{n+1}) - f(x_n)}$$

which provides a new approximation x_{n+2} in terms of two preceding approximations x_n and x_{n+1} provided that

$$f(x_{n+1}) \neq f(x_n)$$

It can be shown that $x_n \to \xi$ as $n \to \infty$ provided that the initial approximations are good enough, $f'(\xi) \neq 0$, and $f''(x)$ is continuous within the interval we are considering.   Of these, the most important in practice is $f'(\xi) \neq 0$, which prevents us from using this technique to find repeated roots. We could not, for example, find the zero of the function graphed in Fig. 9.3 A mathematical demonstration of convergence does not necessarily mean that a program based on the method will always work, because rounding errors in the computation may invalidate the mathematical results. The secant method works quite well with reasonable functions.

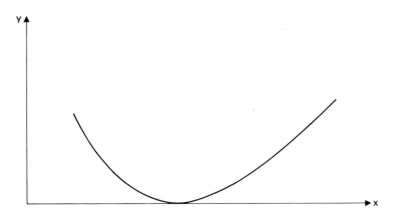

Fig. 9.3 A Repeated Root

Since we possess computers with finite speed, we require a termination condition for the calculation. An iteration changes the amount of the current approximation by an amount

$$\delta = -f(x_{n+1}) \cdot \frac{x_{n+1} - x_n}{f(x_{n+1}) - f(x_n)}$$

and we will terminate the calculation when

$$\left| \delta / x_{n+1} \right| < \varepsilon$$

The function *solve* requires four parameters: two approximations to the root, a value for ξ, and the function $f(x)$. We write the heading for *solve* in this way:

```
FUNCTION solve(x1,x2,epsilon : real;
          FUNCTION f : real) : real;
```

Note that we write only the name and they type of f, we do not specify its parameters. This is a loophole in the security of PASCAL, because the compiler cannot check, without great difficulty, that the use of

265

the formal function *f* within the body of *solve* corresponds to the functions which we subsequently use as actual parameters.

Program *equations* uses the function *solve* to find the smallest positive roots of the equations

$$cos(x).cosh(x) - 1 = 0 \qquad\qquad (9.2.1)$$
$$cos(x).cosh(x) + 1 = 0 \qquad\qquad (9.2.2)$$

which arise in elementary vibration theory.   Fig. 9.4 shows graphs of

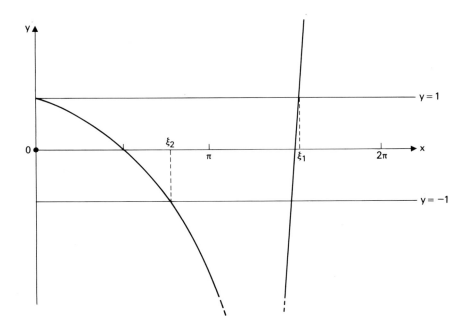

Fig. 9.4   Solutions of *cos(x).cosh(x)* $\pm$ *1 = 0*

the functions

$$y = cos(x).cosh(x)$$
$$y = -1$$
$$y = 1$$

from which we can see that the first root ξ_1 of 9.2.1 satisfies $\pi < \xi_1 < 2\pi$ and the first root ξ_2 of 9.2.2 satisfies $0 < \xi_2 < \pi$.   In Program *equations* we define the functions

$$ccp = cos(x).cosh(x) - 1$$
$$ccm = cos(x).cosh(x) + 1$$

and call *solve* twice.

```
PROGRAM equations (input,output);
  CONST
    tolerance = 1E-6;
  VAR
    approx1, approx2 : real;

  FUNCTION solve (x1,x2,epsilon : real;
                  FUNCTION f : real) : real;
    VAR
      x3,y1,y2,delta : real;
      solved : boolean;
    BEGIN
      solved := false;
      y1 := f(x1);
      y2 := f(x2);
      REPEAT
        delta := - y2 * (x2 - x1) / (y2 - y1);
        x3 := x2 + delta;
        IF abs(delta) < epsilon
          THEN solved := true
          ELSE
            BEGIN
              x1 := x2;
              x2 := x3;
              y1 := y2;
              y2 := f(x2)
            END
      UNTIL solved;
      solve := x3
    END; { solve }

  FUNCTION ccp (x : real) : real;
    VAR
      expx : real;
    BEGIN
      expx := exp(x);
      ccp := cos(x) * (expx + 1/expx) / 2 + 1
    END; { ccp }

  FUNCTION ccm (x : real) : real;
    VAR
      expx : real;
    BEGIN
      expx := exp(x);
      ccm := cos(x) * (expx + 1/expx) / 2 - 1
    END; { ccm }

  BEGIN  { equations }
    read(approx1,approx2);
```

```
    writeln(solve(approx1,approx2,tolerance,ccp));
    writeln(solve(approx1,approx2,tolerance,ccm))
  END. { equations }
```

Input:
    5   7

Output:
    4.694092
    4.730040

The secant method on based on the more familiar Newton-Raphson method which uses the formula

$$x_{n+1} = x_n - \frac{f(x_n)}{f'(x_n)}$$

What we have done is to approximate $f'(x_n)$ by the expression

$$\frac{f(x_n) - f(x_{n-1})}{x_n - x_{n-1}}$$

We need two initial approximations in order to estimate the first value of $f'(x)$. Newton-Raphson's method can be used if an analytic expression for $f'(x)$ is available, but it does not necessarily yield a faster algorithm. If we apply Newton-Raphson's method to equation 9.2.1 we must evaluate

$$\frac{cos(x).cosh(x) - 1}{cos(x).sinh(x) - sin(x).cosh(x)}$$

during each iteration.

Not all procedures and functions can be passed as parameters. The parameters of the procedure or function which is passed as a parameter must be value parameters. To make this clearer, suppose that we have declared the following procedures:

```
    PROCEDURE a (PROCEDURE p);
    PROCEDURE b (m,n : integer);
    PROCEDURE c (VAR x,y : real);
    PROCEDURE d (FUNCTION f : real);
```

In the program following these definitions, we could write

> *a(b)*

meaning 'execute procedure *a* using procedure *b* as an actual parameter'
but we could not write

> *a(c)*

or

> *a(d)*

because *c* has variable parameters, and *d* has a function parameter.

9.3 Memory Allocation

We have seen in Chapter 8 how to use the standard procedure *new*
to create a new record dynamically and set the value of a pointer
pointing to it. In reality, of course, the procedure *new* does not
'create' a record, it simply finds an unused area of memory of the
appropriate size and sets the pointer accordingly. The area of
memory reserved for dynamic variables is often called the *heap*, in
contrast to the area used for static variables (global variables and
local variables of procedures) which is called the *stack*.

If the program continues to call *new*, there will come a time when
all the memory allocated to the heap has been used up, and the program
will fail. In many cases, however, the program will be able to
release dynamic variables which it no longer requires. Program *buses*
of Chapter 8, for example, has no further use for an event record
after the event has been processed. Since the procedure *new* has no
way of knowing which areas of memory are still in use, the released
records cannot be re-used unless they are marked explicitly by the
program. There is a standard procedure *dispose* which releases the
record to which its argument is a pointer. *New* and *dispose* are
complementary:

> *new(p);*
> *{ use record p↑ }*
> *dispose(p)*

The precise effect of *dispose* is not specified in the PASCAL Report,
and so its implementation is left to the compiler writer. The
simplest version of *dispose* will do nothing at all. More sophisticated versions will enable some or all of the memory to be re-used. You
can obtain some idea of how effective *dispose* is on your implementation
by running Program *testdispose*. Very few computers are able to
allocate 1,000,000 words of memory, and so if this program runs to

completion, some kind of memory recycling is going on.

```
PROGRAM testdispose (output);
   CONST
      size = 1000;
      numberofnodes = 1000;
   TYPE
      link = node;
      node = ARRAY [1 .. size] OF integer;
   VAR
      p : link;
      n : 1 .. numberofnodes;
   BEGIN
      FOR n := 1 TO numberofnodes DO
         BEGIN
            new(p);
            dispose(p)
         END { for }
   END. { testdispose }
```

It is bad programming practice to write a program to test a property of a language: you should always refer to the specification of the language. In this case, we are testing an *implementation* property, not specified in the PASCAL Report. Of course, if you have a Reference Manual for the implementation that you are using, you should use this rather than Program *testdispose*.

If the procedure *dispose* does not enable memory to be re-used then you will have to keep track of available memory yourself. The simplest way to do this is to maintain a linked list of unused records, called the *free list*. Whenever a new record is required, it is taken from the free list, unless the free list is empty, in which case the procedure *new* is used. When the program finishes using a record, the record is returned to the free list. All records which are on the free list are variants of the type *free*, and a pointer variable is used as the base of the free list. In these declarations we show the *free* variant only:

```
TYPE
   kind = (free,...);
   link = ↑cell;
   cell =
      RECORD
         CASE tag : kind OF
            free : (next : link);
            ....
      END;
VAR
   freelist : link;
   ....
```

We define two procedures called *create* and *release*, each with a single
parameter of type *link*.

```
PROCEDURE create (VAR p : link);
   BEGIN
      IF freelist = NIL
         THEN new(p)
         ELSE
            BEGIN
               p := freelist;
               freelist := freelist↑.next
            END
   END; { create }

PROCEDURE release (p : link);
   BEGIN
      p↑.tag := free;
      p↑.next := freelist;
      freelist := p
   END; { release }
```

The initialization for the main program contains the statement

```
freelist := NIL
```

so that the free list is empty. At first, new records are obtained by
the procedure *new*, because *freelist = NIL*. As soon as some records
have been released by the program (using the procedure *release*), they
will appear on the free list, and will be re-used by the procedure
create. Note that because PASCAL binds a pointer to a particular
type, the free list can only contain records of one type.

In general, different variants of a record will require different
amounts of memory. When the procedure *new* is used to allocate space
for a new record, it will allocate enough memory for the largest
variant. In order to use memory efficiently, you should therefore
try to make the variants approximately equal in size, although this
may not be easy to do if you do not know how data structures are
represented by your computer. In particular, try to avoid the situation in which one variant is much larger than all the rest. PASCAL
does provide a mechanism which helps you to use memory efficiently.
The procedure *new* may be called with more than one parameter:

```
new(p,t)
```

where *t* is a constant tag field for the variant required. Values may
be assigned to the variable fields of this record in the usual way,
but the tag value must not be altered to any value other than *t*. A
record created in this way must be disposed by calling

```
dispose(p,t)
```

Program *circles* of Chapter 6 used variant records. Here are the declarations for the type *figure* used in that program:

```
TYPE
    shape = (point,line,circle,empty);
    coordinate =
        RECORD
            xcoor,ycoor : real
        END;
    figure =
        RECORD
            CASE tag : shape OF
                empty :
                    ( );
                point :
                    (position : coordinate);
                line :
                    (xcoeff,ycoeff,con : real);
                circle :
                    (center : coordinate;
                     radius : real)
        END;
VAR
    f : figure;
```

The call

```
new(f)
```

will create a record large enough to hold any variant. This record may be disposed by calling

```
dispose(f)
```

The call

```
new(f,point)
```

will create a record large enough to hold a figure of the kind *point*. This record may not be large enough to hold a figure of the kind *line* or *circle*. It must be disposed by calling

```
dispose(f,point)
```

We cannot change the kind of a record created in this way, and we cannot make assignments to the entire variable. We cannot write

```
new(g);
f↑ := g↑;
```

or

Exercises

$$f\uparrow.tag := circle$$

We can, however, make assignments to the components of $f\uparrow$, provided that these are consistent with the tag value with which it was created. For example, we can write

$$f\uparrow.position := coor$$

If the record type has nested variants, then a single variant is specified uniquely by a tag value at each level. In this case the calls to *new* and *dispose* take the form:

$$new(p,t_1,t_2,...,t_n)$$

and

$$dispose(p,t_1,t_2,...,t_n)$$

Exercises

9.1 Write two equivalent versions of a program, one using *GOTO* statements, and one without using *GOTO* statements. Choose a problem which makes the *GOTO* version shorter, simpler and faster than the *GOTO*-less version.

9.2 Write a function *max* such that

$$max(f,a,b)$$

finds the maximum value of $f(x)$ in the interval $a \le x \le b$ and returns the corresponding value of x.

9.3 Write a real function *integrate* such that

$$integrate(f,a,b)$$

returns an approximate value of

$$\int_a^b f(x)\ dx$$

9.4 Write a procedure *chop* which disposes every node of a binary tree. *Chop* has one parameter which is a pointer to the root node of the tree.

Program
Design

CHAPTER TEN

In the first chapter of this book we define a computer program to be a sequence of instructions. Most of the content of the following eight chapters is devoted to describing the various forms that these instructions may assume in PASCAL, and their effects. In this chapter, the last, we discuss various aspects of the programmer's task. Our starting point is the assumption that we have a problem to solve, and that we intend to write a computer program that is, in some sense, a solution to that problem. We will also assume that the problem is amenable to solution by a computer: output results are required which are a well-defined function of input data. Throughout this chapter, it is implicit that we are considering the design of a program of reasonable size. It is not difficult to write a perfect program that fits onto a page, but it is very difficult indeed to write a program of a hundred pages, and to be certain that it is entirely correct.

The computer does not *solve* the problem; this is the programmer's job. Solving the problem consists of finding an algorithm which will provide the required mapping from input to output. Writing the program consists of expressing this algorithm in a fashion acceptable to the computer. Since the computer is a machine without imagination or common sense, the algorithm must be presented to it in a clear and unambiguous manner. You do not have to be a mathematician to write computer programs, but you do have to be good at explaining things clearly.

It is well-known that some programs do not always yield correct
results. There are a number of possible reasons for this: the problem
may be stated incorrectly; the algorithm chosen may not be a true
solution of the problem; the program may not be an accurate implementation of the algorithm; or the program may be executed with the wrong
data. We are concerned here with only two of these sources of error:
the choice of an incorrect algorithm, and the inaccurate implementation of the algorithm. There are two ways of ensuring that the program
we produce is correct. We can employ a system of program development
that leads inevitably to correct programs, or we can devise a means of
demonstrating that a completed program contains no errors.

In many environments, the computer is used as a sophisticated toy,
and a hit or miss approach to programming can be tolerated because the
potential consequences of a programming error are not particularly
serious. Computers are being used more and more in environments where
the consequences of an error may be very serious, and in these environments a haphazard programming methodology is irresponsible and
dangerous. We do not accept engineers whose buildings do not often
collapse, or accountants whose books usually balance, and we should
not accept programmers whose programs occasionally fail.

10.1 Program Development

Modern techniques for program development are essentially formal
versions of the traditional method of programming, and so we start by
reviewing this method. There are three phases to constructing a
program by the traditional method: design, implementation, and testing. The design phase, usually carried out by an 'analyst', leads to
a specification in a natural language such as English. The specification is given to a 'programmer' who writes a program from it. Traditional programming techniques are shrouded in mystery, but a few
programmers have revealed their secrets, and so we know that the
techniques consist of a combination of guesses, hunches, tricks,
inspiration, and some programming principles. When the programmer
claims that the program is complete, it is tested, first by the
programmer, and then (sometimes) by the analyst. *Testing* consists of
running the program with input data carefully designed to exercise it
thoroughly. Later, tests may be carried out with 'real data' — that
is, by running the program in the environment in which it will eventually be used. Discrepancies between the program and the specification may be found, and if this is the case, the program is modified
and tested again. Sometimes the results delivered by the program
cast doubt upon the specification, and the whole cycle must be
repeated — revise the specification, modify the program, test it

again, and compare the results to the revised specification.

Under carefully controlled conditions, this technique can produce working programs. Occasionally, it fails altogether, and the project is abandoned. In many instances, perhaps the majority, it produces a program which works correctly most of the time, but which occasionally fails or gives incorrect results. The people who use a program frequently get to know its habits and learn to live with them, but to the people who use it rarely, the errors are very disconcerting.

Many people have expressed concern about the lack of rigor in traditional programming methods, and numerous ways of improving the situation have been suggested. Most of these suggestions involve the introduction of a formal programming system. Mathematicians have spent the last several hundred years trying to remove uncertainties from their theories and deductions, and they are familiar with many of the advantages of formal systems. For programmers there is an additional advantage to be gained from the construction of a formal programming system: if we can devise a set of rules for creating correct computer programs, then we can express these rules in the form of a computer program, and let the computer write our programs for us. The computer will never be able to do all of the work, but even if it only does some of the simple chores, we will have more time and energy to devote to more interesting and creative phases of program design.

The most important development to date in automatic program construction has been the introduction of high level programming languages and compilers for them. As we have seen, a program is an expression of a problem solution in a language acceptable to the computer, and programming is the process of translating the solution into such a language. A compiler can perform a significant proportion of the translation for us. High level languages, and compilers for them, extend the range of problems which we can solve with the aid of a computer. Another important development is the widespread use of standard functions and program libraries. It is better that one skilled programmer, or a skilled team, develop procedures to perform standard tasks, and that these procedures should be used by everybody, rather than that each programmer develop his own solution. Probably most PASCAL programmers who use standard functions such as *ln* and *sqrt* do not know how logarithms and square roots are calculated, and this is as it should be. Apart from the standard functions of a language, there are libraries of procedures and functions, and a programmer with no more than high-school algebra should have no difficulty computing matrix inverses or fast Fourier transforms in a modern computer installation. These well established tools are not, however, the subject of this chapter. Here we describe a popular contemporary method of program development, and some elementary ideas of program verification.

From the viewpoint of the program designer, the most important

fact about a computer program is that it is hierarchical. As we saw
in Chapter 4, hierarchical structure is obtained by the use of procedures. A program will require high-level procedures to carry out large
difficult tasks, such as 'solve a set of simultaneous equations', and
these will call procedures at lower levels in the hierarchy, down to
primitive procedures at the lowest level such as 'read a character.'
The high-level procedures will express the general and abstract features of the problem solution, and the low-level procedures will contain the details of the implementation. The first important decision
we must make when designing a new program is whether to start at the
top of the hierarchy (the most abstract level), or to start at the
bottom (most detailed level) and work up. Following the advice of a
number of distinguished authors, we advocate the former method: top-
down program development. Writing the program consists of proposing
a very abstract solution and then successively *refining* it until it is
entirely expressed in the chosen programming language.

   Procedures themselves do not refine the solution, they merely
enable us to express the refinements we have made in a convenient
notation.   There are three principal refinement techniques; appropriate mnemonics for them are 'divide and conquer', 'make finite progress',
and 'analyze cases'. We apply the first of these by *dividing* the
problem into disjoint parts, and then *conquering* each part in turn.
We use the word 'disjoint' to mean that the parts of subproblems are
independent of one another. For example, many problems in data
processing can be immediately divided into three steps:

> *read the data;*
> *perform calculations;*
> *print the results*

If there is more data than can be stored in memory at one time, then
this schema is unsuitable. If this is the case, the following schema
is more appropriate:

> *REPEAT*
>   *read some data;*
>   *perform calculations;*
>   *print results*
> *UNTIL no more data*

This is the second refinement technique: make finite progress. The
reasoning is that if we have a way of making finite progress towards
the solution, and we apply it repeatedly, we will eventually arrive
at the complete solution. The precise definition of 'finite progress'
is important, and we will return to it later in this chapter when we
discuss program verification. In the example above, suppose that the
items of data can be numbered $1, 2, \ldots, N$, say, and that the statement
read more data reads at least one item. Then we can assert that at
most N steps will be required to obtain the solution.

The third refinement technique is *case analysis*. Suppose that in the example above, the data can be divided into four classes: *sheep*, *pigs*, *goats*, and *donkeys*. It is then natural to use a different procedure for each class:

```
REPEAT
    read an item of data;
    CASE class OF
        sheep :
            process sheep;
        pig :
            process pig;
        goat :
            process goat;
        donkey :
            process donkey
    END;
    print results
UNTIL no more data
```

The refinement techniques are applied at each level until there is nothing more to be refined. In this example, we now have six subproblems:

```
read an item of data
process sheep
process pig
process goat
process donkey
print results
```

and the next step is to refine these into still simpler problems using any of the three refinement techniques.

Notice how naturally these methods of refinement relate to PASCAL statements. The result of dividing and conquering is a statement sequence or a compound statement. The iterative method (make finite progress) can be modelled by a *FOR*, *WHILE* or *REPEAT* statement, and case analysis can be modelled either by a *CASE* statement, or in situations where cases are most easily distinguished by boolean expressions, by an *IF* statement or a compound *IF* statement. We can moreover introduce procedures at any level we please. When procedures are used in top-down program development, the finished program retains traces of the design process which contribute to its intelligibility.

In practice, top-down development does not always proceed in the orderly manner which we have described here. Sometimes the refinement may lead to subproblems which are not disjoint, or which are insoluble. Before committing ourselves to a particular refinement, we should *look ahead* and attempt to forsee its consequences. Sometimes, despite looking ahead, we make a mistake, and we have to *backtrack,* undoing some of the refinements we have made. The amount of look ahead and backtracking that we will need to solve a problem depends on the complexity of the problem and our experience.

Top-down development is not the only systemmatic programming methodology. We have described it here because it is a method which is well-documented, reliable and safe. Top-down design does not always yield efficient solutions, and it does not always provide deep insight into the nature of the problem. Section 10.4 below demonstrates the application of top-down development to a typical programming problem.

10.2 Testing and Verification

A computer program, like any other product, should be tested before it is used. One way of testing a program would be to execute it once for each possible combination of input data. It is not difficult to see that in most cases this is impractical. A typical computer can represent perhaps a billion different integers, and so if we were to test exhaustively a program that read just one integer, we would have to execute it a billion times, and verify a billion sets of results. Clearly, we have to reduce the number of tests somehow. One way to reduce it would be to make random tests. Although random tests may reveal gross errors in the program — for example, that it invariably gives the wrong answer — it is extremely unlikely that random testing will reveal singularities in the behavior of a program. For example, a program which uses values of *tan(x)* might give unreliable results when $x \simeq \pi/2$, but random testing would probably not detect this.

If we were testing another product, say a car, we would consider neither exhaustive testing, which would presumably involve driving the car along every road in the country, nor random testing. Rather, we would classify the surfaces over which the car was expected to drive, and devise appropriate tests: we would use roads which were smooth or bumpy, straight or curved, level or inclined, and so on. In doing this, we would be considering parts of the car which might fail, and testing them to see if they did so. We would base our tests on what we know about the internal structure of the car. In a similar way, we have to study the internal structure of a program in order to construct test data for it.

Suppose that we have a program which contains the following statement, intended to assign to z the value of *max(x,y)*, the greater of x and y:

```
IF x > y
    THEN z := x
    ELSE z := y
```

A programmer designing test data for this program would observe that
there are two cases, $x > y$ and $x \leq y$, and would ensure that the test
data included values that would test both of these cases. In its
general form, this method ensures that every *path* of the program is
executed during testing. For example, program *quadratic* of Chapter 3
is shown with five sets of input data, corresponding to the five paths
of the program. The principle used here is that the decisions made
within the program divide the set of input data into five classes,
each class of input data resulting in the execution of a different
path in the program. In general it is not sufficient merely to test
all paths, or even all combinations of paths. A predicate may be in
error, as in this example:

```
VAR
    x,y : integer;
....
    IF ((x + y) DIV 2) = x
        THEN write('x = y')
        ELSE write('x ≠ y')
```

Both branches of this statement can be tested using test data (x = 2,
y = 2) and (x = 3, y = 2) without revealing the error, although the
statement fails for (x = 2, y = 3). Despite these difficulties,
systematic methods for finding a sufficient set of test data have been
proposed.

There are many large and complex programs which fail sometimes
despite apparently thorough testing. Compilers, for example, may be
used hundreds of times a day to the satisfaction of most of their
users, and yet occasionally reject a valid program. Many operating
systems run continuously for days, and then unexpectedly collapse.
In these cases, some rare combination of events has led the process
to a state unanticipated by the programmer. Programs as complex as
these can never be tested completely. A compiler, for example, must
accept any finite string of symbols, and if the string happens to
conform to the language definition, it must generate a semantically
equivalent object program. An operating system is even more difficult to test, because it must monitor many concurrent processes.
When an operating system fails, it is often impossible even to
recreate the circumstances which led to the failure.

A number of people have suggested that rather than testing programs, we should be attempting to *prove* that they function correctly.
Since a proven statement is no more reliable than the assumptions
underlying the proof, we must define the meaning of each construction
in the language before we attempt to prove the correctness of a program written in that language. It is feasible to do this only if we

assume the existence of an ideal processor, and so we cannot usually guarantee that a proven program will run correctly on an actual computer. We can, however, claim that the program is correct, even though the computer cannot execute it correctly.

A detailed study pf program proving, or program *verification* as it is also called, is beyond the scope of this book. We give an introductory treatment of program verification, based on an informal interpretation of the semantics of PASCAL. This is by no means a futile exercise, because an understanding of the techniques of program verification is an aid to clear programming. In fact, the concepts used to verify programs are no more than formal versions of ideas that are in the mind of any good programmer when he is writing a program.

Suppose that we write the statement

$$y := 1/x$$

in which x and y are real variables, in a program. When we write this statement, we must have reason to believe that x is not currently zero, because otherwise the expression $1/x$ cannot be evaluated, and we also expect that, after the statement has been executed, y will have the value $1/x$. The following account of program verification is a development of this concept. With each statement of the program we associate two boolean expressions. The first of these is called the *pre-condition* of the statement, and it expresses what we know to be true before the statement is executed. The second is called the *post-condition* of the statement, and it expresses what we know to be true after the statement has been executed. We write the conditions as comments before and after the statement.

> { *pre-condition* }
> *statement*
> { *post-condition* }

Suppose that at a point in the program where we know that $x > 0$, we write the statement

$$y := 1/x$$

Then we know that after the statement has been executed, $x > 0$, since the assignment does not alter the value of x, and also that $y = 1/x$. We can write

> { $X > 0$ }
> $y := 1/x$
> { $(X > 0) \wedge (Y = 1/X)$ }

We have written X and Y for the current values of the variables x and y. We will continue to use the convention of denoting current values by capital letters in the ensuing discussion. The operator '$\wedge$' is

AND, and in pre-conditions and post-conditions we will continue to use this symbol, and also the symbols 'V' meaning *OR* and '~' meaning *NOT*, because otherwise the conditions are rather cumbersome. We will assume that the program will be executed by an ideal processor, and we will ignore the possibility that the result of an assignment may be out of range or inaccurate.

In the example above, the statement added to our knowledge of the state of the process, but this does not always happen. In the following example, we know less about the value of *x* after the statement has been executed than before:

```
{ X = 0 }
read(x)
{ ? }
```

After the *read* statement, we know nothing at all about the value of *x*, and so the post-condition must be true for all values of *x*. One post-condition which is true for all values of *x* is the condition *true*. We can write:

```
{ X = 0 }
read(x)
{ true }
```

Although it may seem strange, *true*, in the context of program verification, is an expression of total ignorance about the state of the program.

It is not sufficient merely to write down the pre-conditions and post-conditions. In general, our task is to *prove* the post-condition, *assuming* that the pre-condition is true. In this way, we can proceed through the program statement by statement, ultimately proving that the first pre-condition implies the last post-condition. Since the first pre-condition and the last post-condition between them constitute the specification of the program, we have then proved formally that the program will function according to its specification.

As a simple example, consider this 'program':

```
c := a + b;
d := c * c
```

We express our ignorance about the initial values of the variables by writing the pre-condition *true*. The post-condition of the first statement is clearly

$$C = A + B$$

and this is also the pre-condition for the second statement. From the second statement we can deduce

$$D = C * C$$

and so the post-condition for the program is

$$(C = A + B) \land (D = C * C)$$

which we can simplify to

$$D = (A + B)^2$$

and so we can write

```
{ true }
c := a + b;
{ C = A + B }
d := c * c
{ D = (A + B)2 }
```

This may seem rather obvious. Verification becomes more interesting when we consider decisions and loops. Let us look first of all at the program above which calculated $max(x,y)$:

```
IF x > y
    THEN z := x
    ELSE z := y
```

Once again, we know nothing about the initial values of the variables, and so the first pre-condition is *true*. From our knowledge of the *IF* statement, we can derive pre-conditions for the *THEN* and *ELSE* clauses:

```
{ true }
IF x > y
    THEN
        { X > Y }
        z := x
    ELSE
        { ~ (X > Y) }
        z := y
```

The corresponding post-conditions are derived from our knowledge of the effect of the assignment statements:

```
{ true }
IF x > y
    THEN
        { X > Y }
        z := x
        { (X > Y) ∧ (Z = X) }
    ELSE
        { ~ (X > Y) }
        z := y
        { ~ (X > Y) ∧ (Z = Y) }
```

To obtain the post-condition for the whole statement, we note that exactly one branch of the *IF* statement is executed. Accordingly, exactly one of the two post-conditions must be true, and we have as the final post-condition

$$\{ (X > Y) \wedge (Z = X) \vee \sim (X > Y) \wedge (Z = Y) \}$$

which we may write in the form

$$Z = max(X,Y)$$

The next step is to attempt to verify a program with a loop, such as this one:

```
{ (X > 0) ∧ (Y > 0) }
u := x;
v := y;
WHILE u ≠ v DO
    IF u > v
        THEN u := u - v
        ELSE v := v - u
{ U = gcd(X,Y) }
```

We verify the loop by finding an expression whose truth value is unaltered during the execution of the loop; such an expression is called an *invariant* of the loop. Inspection of the program reveals that the idea involved is to reduce *U* and *V* while maintaining the truth of

$$gcd(U,V) = gcd(X,Y)$$

using the theorem

$$IF \ A > B \ then \ gcd(A - B,B) = gcd(A,B)$$

Furthermore, we note that *U* and *V* are initially positive, and the smaller is always subtracted from the larger, so that they both remain positive. This suggests the invariant

$$\{ (U > 0) \wedge (V > 0) \wedge (gcd(U,V) = gcd(X,Y)) \}$$

We can start by writing

```
{ (X > 0) ∧ (Y > 0) }
u := x;
v := y;
WHILE u ≠ v DO
    { (U > 0) ∧ (V > 0) ∧ (gcd(U,V) = gcd(X,Y)) }
```

The *IF* statement distinguishes the two cases $U > V$ and $U < V$. Note that $U = V$ is excluded by the *WHILE* condition. We have

```
IF u > v
    THEN
        { (U > V > 0) ∧ (gcd(U,V) = gcd(X,Y)) }
        u := u - v
    ELSE
        { (V > U > 0) ∧ (gcd(U,V) = gcd(X,Y)) }
```

For the case $U > V$, write $U' = U - V$. Since $U > V$, we know that $U - V > 0$, and hence $U' > 0$. Also,

$$gcd(U',V) = gcd(U - V,V) = gcd(U,V) = gcd(X,Y)$$

and therefore

$$\{ (U' > 0) \land (V > 0) \land (gcd(U',V) = gcd(X,Y)) \}$$

If we now write U for U', which is the effect of the assignment statement, then we have shown that the proposed invariant is still true after the *THEN* clause has been executed. Using a similar argument, we can show that the assignment

$$v := v - u$$

of the *ELSE* clause also preserves the truth of the proposed invariant. We have therefore established two things:

The first invariant is true at the beginning of the first cycle;

If the invariant is true at the beginning of a cycle, then it is still true at the beginning of the next cycle.

Using the principle of mathematical induction, we can now assert that the proposed invariant remains true for as long as the *WHILE* statement is executed. It is therefore the invariant which we sought.

The *WHILE* loop terminates when $U = V$, and so the post-condition for the *WHILE* statement is

$$(U > 0) \land (V > 0) \land (gcd(U,V) = gcd(X,Y)) \land (U = V)$$

From this we can deduce

$$gcd(X,Y) = gcd(U,V) = gcd(U,U) = U$$

as was required. We have now demonstrated that the program will find the value of $gcd(X,Y)$ if the loop terminates. We have not yet proved that the expression $u \neq v$ will not be true forever. In order to prove that eventually $U = V$, we note that

$$0 < min(U,V) \leq max(U,V)$$

in which $min(U,V)$ is the lesser, and $max(U,V)$ is the greater of U and V. During a cycle of the loop, we execute either

    $u := u - v$

or

    $v := v - u$

Whichever we execute, it is still true that

    $0 < min(U,V) \le max(U,V)$

but $max(U,V)$ must have diminished by at least 1, since $U \ne V$ and both are integers. Therefore, within a finite number of steps, we must have

    $0 < min(U,V) = max(U,V)$

and so $U = V$. It follows that the program will terminate after a finite number of steps.

We can verify a FOR loop by constructing an equivalent WHILE loop. This program sums the elements of an array a whose index type is $1 \mathrel{..} n$.

```
s := 0;
FOR i := 1 TO n DO
    s := s + a[i]
```

We write this in the equivalent form:

```
s := 0;
i := 1;
WHILE i ≤ n DO
    BEGIN
        s := s + a[i];
        i := i + 1
    END
```

Let s_i denote $\sum_{k=1}^{i} a[k]$ and define s_0 to be zero. Then on entry to the first cycle of the loop we have

    $(I = 1) \wedge (S = 0)$

Using the definition of S_0 we have

    $S = 0 = S_0 = S_{1-1} = S_{I-1}$

and so we can write the pre-condition for the WHILE statement as

$$(I = 1) \land (S = S_{I-1})$$

After the first assignment within the loop

$$S = S_{I-1} + A[I] = S_I$$

After the second statement, let the new value of I be I', and so

$$I' = I + 1$$

and

$$S_I = S_{I'-1}$$

The body of the WHILE statement now looks like this:

```
BEGIN
    { S = S_I-1 }
    s := s + a[i];
    { S = S_I }
    i := i + 1
    { S = S_I-1 }
END
```

Therefore $S = S_{I-1}$ is the correct loop invariant. On exit from the loop, we know that

$$I > N$$

and during the preceding cycle

$$I \leq N$$

and so now

$$I = N + 1$$

and

$$S = S_{I-1} = S_N$$

as required. We can now prove termination by noting that I starts at 1 and increases by 1 during each iteration. The loop will therefore terminate after exactly N cycles, in finite time.

We do not need any new concepts to verify procedures and functions. The pre-conditions for a procedure will define constraints on the values of its actual parameters. Well written procedures check the values of their parameters and have less restrictive pre-conditions. The post-condition of a procedure expresses the result it is expected to produce. These conditions are inserted in the

calling program wherever the procedure is invoked. If the procedure
has side-effects, these conditions will be much harder to write, and
this is one of the reasons why we try to avoid accessing or altering
global variables from procedures. Recursive procedures and functions
are more interesting and we will discuss the verification of a simple
recursive function. The factorial function $f(n) = n!$ may be defined
recursively:

$$0! = 1$$
$$n! = n * (n-1)! \quad for \ n > 0$$

The corresponding function for positive arguments may be written

```
FUNCTION f (n : integer);
    BEGIN
        { N ≥ 0 }
        IF n = 0
            THEN
                { N = 0 }
                f := 1
                { (N = 0) ∧ (F(0) = 1) }
            ELSE
                { N > 0 }
                f := n * f(n - 1)
                { (N > 0) ∧ (F(N) = N * F(N - 1)) }
        {(N = 0) ∧ (F(0) = 1) ∨ (N > 0) ∧ (F(N) = N * F(N - 1))}
    END;
```

The proofs required are straightforward. Note, however, that we must
include a proof that the call $f(n - 1)$ is valid. We know that $N > 0$
and so $N - 1 ≥ 0$, and so $n - 1$ is a permissible actual parameter for
f. We have proved that

$$f(0) = 1$$

and

$$f(n) = n * f(n - 1) \quad for \ n > 0$$

It follows from the definition of $n!$ that

$$f(0) = 0!$$

and

$$if \ f(n - 1) = (n - 1)! \quad then \ f(n) = n!$$

Using the second of these relations for $n = 1,2,3,...$ we have proved

$$f(1) = 1!$$
$$f(2) = 2!$$
$$f(3) = 3!$$
$$....$$

and hence, by the principle of induction, that

$$f(n) = n!$$

We can formulate general rules for deriving the post-condition from the pre-condition for each kind of statement. For the assignment statement,

$$v := E$$

the post-condition is obtained by substituting e for V in the pre-condition. For an *IF* statement we have

```
{ p }
IF b
    THEN
        { p ∧ b }
        S₁
        { q₁ }
    ELSE
        { p ∧ ~ b }
        S₂
        { q₂ }
    { q₁ ∨ q₂ }
```

We must prove that executing S_1 with pre-condition $p \wedge b$ gives post-condition q_1, and executing statement S_2 with pre-condition $p \wedge \sim b$ gives post-condition q_2. Since exactly one of S_1 and S_2 is executed, the post-condition for the *IF* statement is $q_1 \vee q_2$. The *CASE* statement is treated analogously, one proof being required for each case label. Loops are verified inductively. If we have

```
{ p }
WHILE b DO
    { i }
    S
{ i ∧ ~ b }
```

then we have to prove that p implies i and that S preserves the truth of i. For the *REPEAT* statement

```
{ p }
REPEAT
    { i }
    S₁; S₂; .... Sₙ
UNTIL q
```

290

$$\{ \ i \wedge q \ \}$$

we must prove that p implies i and that the statement sequence $S_1; \ S_2; \dots S_n$ preserves the truth of i. We have already seen how to construct a *WHILE* loop from a *FOR* loop.

A useful rule for proving termination is to look for a function with the following properties:

Initially $f = f_0 > 0$;

During each iteration, f decreases by at least 1; the process terminates when $f \le 0$.

If such a function can be found, then it is easy to prove that the loop will be executed at most f_0 times. In the precious example, we could have chosen $f = N - I$. The importance of choosing a suitable function can be seen from the following example:

```
VAR
    term,sum : real;
BEGIN
    term := 1;
    sum := 0;
    REPEAT
        term := term / 2;
        sum := sum + term
    UNTIL sum ≥ 1
END
```

Assuming that we have a computer with unlimited precision, a finite quantity will be added to *sum* during each iteration, and yet the termination condition will never be satisfied. On an actual computer, either *term* would eventually become zero and the program would continue to loop until the operating system intervened, or at some point the division would produce an underflow condition, and this would cause the operating system to abort the program.

We have only skimmed the surface of program verification in this section. We have not considered the difficulties of verifying programs which use real variables, which make assignments to components of arrays, which use pointers, or which use *GOTO* statements. In fact, the program fragments which we have verified have all been rather trivial. Verifying non-trivial programs is difficult and tedious, and large programs will probably not be verified until automatic verification techniques are available. However, there are some lessons to be learned. If you try verifying a few programs for yourself, you will discover that program proving gives valuable insight into the nature of program construction. If you consider, as you write a program, how you would set about proving it correct, your programming style will become clearer. Important pre-conditions and post-conditions,

inserted as comments, will make your programs easier to read.
Finally, learn to use proven algorithms rather than *ad hoc* devices
for standard programming tasks.

10.3   Debugging

The intention of structured programming, top-down design and
program verification is to produce programs without errors.   Consequently, 'debugging' has become something less than a polite word.
Unfortunately, bugs do not go away simply because we do not speak of
them.   The most dutiful structured programmer, carefully verifying
each line, may still write '-' where he meant to write '+', or *sqr*
where he meant to write *sqrt*, and then his program will have a bug.

In this book, we have frequently made suggestions for improving
the readability of programs.   For example, we have recommended the
use of good layout, declarations for all constants, meaningful names
for variables, tag values to discriminate variants, and the avoidance
of side-effects.   If you follow these recommendations, not only will
your programs be more readable, but also they will tend to have fewer
bugs.   Moreover, when they do fail, the bugs will be easier to find.
There are no general rules for finding bugs: each bug is unique.
Debugging requires intuition, inspiration and experience.   Here we
offer a few hints for debuggers, some of them general, the rest
specific to PASCAL.

When your program has a bug, examine *all* of the evidence.   The
'evidence' consists of the text of the program itself, the input data
that it reads, the output that it generates, and diagnostic information provided by the run-time system if the failure led to abnormal
termination.   You should consider anything which is not exactly as
you expect it to be as an aid to finding the bug.   If there is not
enough evidence, then you can generate some more: you can re-run the
program with different data, or you can insert *write* statements into
it to check intermediate results and re-run it with the same data.
If you think that you have identified the section of the program that
contains the bug, but there appears to be nothing wrong with it, then
look somewhere else.   In particular, look at the parts of the program
which were executed *before* the suspect area.   If you cannot find anything wrong with the program, then show it to a friend.   Do *not*
explain how you think the program should work to your friend, because
by doing so you may prevent him (or her) from seeing the error, by
communicating your mental 'set'.   When you have found the bug, make
sure that it accounts for *all* of the anomalous behavior of the program.   If it does not, then look for more bugs.

There are a few PASCAL constructions which frequently are involved in obscure errors. Check that compound *IF* statements are constructed correctly, and do not be misled by incorrect layouts, such as

> *IF p*
> > *THEN*
> > > *IF q*
> > > > *THEN S$_1$*
> > >
> > > *ELSE S$_2$*

the effect of which is correctly expressed by the layout

> *IF p*
> > *THEN*
> > > *IF q*
> > > > *THEN S$_1$*
> > > > *ELSE S$_2$*

Loops controlled by *WHILE* and *FOR* may not be executed at all. The statement *S* in either of the constructions

> *WHILE p DO*
> > *S*

and

> *FOR i := j TO k DO*
> > *S*

will never be executed if *p* is *false* or $j > k$ respectively. On the other hand, the body of a *REPEAT* statement is always executed at least once.

Check that formal variable procedure parameters are prefixed by *VAR*: omission of *VAR* can lead to very puzzling errors! Finally, if you are using records with variants, check that the fields you access are consistent with the tag values.

10.4 Example: A Cross-Reference Generator

This section is devoted to the development of a useful program using some of the techniques described in this chapter. We use strict top-down development for both the algorithm and the data structures of the program. We do not attempt to prove that the program is correct. The program is a cross-reference generator, and this is its specification:

> *Read a source text containing up to 999 lines. Print a list*

Example: A Cross-Reference Generator

> *consisting of one entry for each distinct word in the text.*
> *Each entry consists of the word itself, followed by a list*
> *of the numbers of the lines on which it appears. A 'word'*
> *is a string of consecutive letters. Letters after the*
> *twentieth letter of a word may be ignored. The words are*
> *listed in ascending sequence. If a word occurs twice in*
> *one line, the line number should be printed once only. The*
> *output must be formatted for pages of 60 lines and no line*
> *may contain more than 80 characters.*

This program is somewhat similar to the concordance program of
chapters 6 and 8, but more information must be stored in each word
entry. We first 'divide and conquer.' The program falls naturally
into two steps: construct the table of words, and then print it. The
alternative construction (read a little, print a little, and repeat)
is inappropriate because we must scan the entire source text before
we can start printing. We will assume that there is sufficient
memory available to store all of the necessary information. This
assumption is reasonable in view of the limit of 999 lines of text.
We require a data structure into which we can insert words and from
which we can later print the words in alphabetical order. A binary
search tree is an appropriate choice of data structure. We can now
write the first, and most abstract, version of the program.

```
PROGRAM crossreference (input,output);
    TYPE
        treepointer = ↑node;
        node =
            RECORD
                entry : entrytype;
                left,right : treepointer
            END;
    VAR
        wordtree : treepointer;
    BEGIN
        wordtree := NIL;
        buildtree(wordtree);
        printtree(wordtree)
    END.
```

This program is manifestly correct, so far as it goes. We cannot
execute it yet, because *entrytype*, *buildtree* and *printtree* are
undefined.

   We use two principles to refine *buildtree*. The first is repetition: in each cycle we process one word of the text. This guarantees
that we will finish building the tree in finite time. The second
principle is again divide and conquer: first get the word, then put
it into the tree.

Example: A Cross-Reference Generator

```
PROCEDURE buildtree (VAR tree : treepointer);
    VAR
        currentword : wordtype;
        currentline : counter;
    BEGIN
        currentline := 1;
        WHILE NOT eof DO
            BEGIN
                getword(currentword,currentline);
                IF NOT eof
                    THEN
                        entertree(tree,currentword,currentline)
            END { while }
    END;
```

This procedure has introduced four new undefined entities: the types *wordtype* and *counter*, and the procedures *getword* and *entertree*. We can define the new types without much difficulty.

```
CONST
    maxlines = 999;
    maxwordlen = 20;
TYPE
    counter = 1 .. maxlines;
    wordindex = 1 .. maxwordlen;
    wordtype = PACKED ARRAY [wordindex] OF char;
```

With this established, we can proceed with the refinement of *getword*, which is based on similar procedures which have appeared previously in this book.

```
PROCEDURE getword (VAR word : wordtype;
                   VAR line : counter);
    VAR
        currentchar : char;
        index, blankindex : 0 .. maxwordlen;
    BEGIN
        currentchar := blank;
        WHILE NOT (eof OR (currentchar IN letters)) DO
            getchar(currentchar,line);
        IF NOT eof
            THEN
                BEGIN
                    index := 0;
                    WHILE currentchar IN letters DO
                        BEGIN
                            IF index < maxwordlen
                                THEN
                                    BEGIN
                                        index := index + 1;
                                        word[index] := currentchar
```

295

```
                                    END;
                        IF eof
                            THEN currentchar := blank
                            ELSE getchar(currentchar,line)
                    END; { while }
                IF index < maxwordlen
                    THEN
                        FOR blankindex := index + 1
                                        TO maxwordlen DO
                            word[blankindex] := blank
            END
    END;
```

The procedure *getchar*, called by *getword*, provides the next character from the input file and maintains the line counter. Procedure *getchar* is developed using case analysis. The cases to consider are end of file, end of line, and neither of these. *Getchar* inserts a blank character between lines to ensure that the program does not concatenate the first word of a line with the last word of the previous line. Both *getchar* and *getword* may return with *eof = true*.

```
    PROCEDURE getchar (VAR ch : char;
                       VAR lin : counter);
        BEGIN
            IF eof
                THEN ch := blank
            ELSE IF eoln
                THEN
                    BEGIN
                        ch := blank;
                        lin := lin + 1;
                        readln
                    END
            ELSE read(ch)
        END;
```

We continue with the refinement of *buildtree* by elaborating the call

```
    entertree(tree,word,line)
```

In order to do this we must first consider in more detail the refinement of *entrytype*, which is the type we are using for entries in the word tree. An entry must be able to store a word and some line numbers. Looking ahead to the printing phase, we see that we have to print the line numbers in ascending sequence. This, however, is exactly the order in which the program will encounter them. The structure should therefore permit first-in, first-out access, and a queue is suitable. As we saw in Chapter 8, a queue can be implemented as a list with a pointer to its head and another pointer to its tail. We can therefore write:

Example: A Cross-Reference Generator

```
TYPE
    entrytype =
        RECORD
            wordvalue : wordtype;
            firstinqueue, lastinqueue : queuepointer
        END;
```

The queue items each contain a line number and a pointer to the next
item in the queue:

```
TYPE
    queuepointer = ↑queueitem;
    queueitem =
        RECORD
            linenumber : counter;
            nextinqueue : queuepointer
        END;
```

At this point it is convenient to summaraize the constants and types
we have introduced so far.

```
CONST
    maxlines = 999;
    maxwordlen = 20;
TYPE
    counter = 1 .. maxlines;
    wordindex = 1 .. maxwordlen;
    wordtype = PACKED ARRAY [wordindex] OF char;
    queuepointer = ↑queueitem;
    queueitem =
        RECORD
            linenumber : counter;
            nextinqueue : queuepointer
        END;
    entrytype =
        RECORD
            wordvalue : wordtype;
            firstinqueue, lastinqueue : queuepointer
        END;
    treepointer = ↑node;
    node =
        RECORD
            entry : entrytype;
            left, right : treepointer
        END;
```

The procedure entertree is derived by case analysis. On entry, one of
its parameters is a pointer to the word tree or one of its subtrees.
If this pointer is NIL, we create a new entry and set the pointer to
it. Otherwise, we compare the word stored in the node to the word we
have just read. If they are equal, we have only to add the current

297

Example: A Cross-Reference Generator

line number to the list, unless it is there already, in which case
lastinqueue must point to it. Otherwise, we search either the left
or the right subtree of this node by calling *entertree* recursively.
This is the conventional algorithm for binary tree insertion.

```
PROCEDURE entertree (VAR subtree : treepointer;
                     word : wordtype;
                     line : counter);
BEGIN
   IF subtree = NIL
      THEN create a new entry
   ELSE IF word = subtree↑.entry.wordvalue
      THEN append line number to list
   ELSE IF word < subtree↑.entry.wordvalue
      THEN entertree(subtree↑.left,word,line)
      ELSE entertree(subtree↑.right,word,line)
END;
```

The actions *create a new entry* and append *line number to list* are
developed using standard algorithms.

```
{ create a new entry }
BEGIN
   new(subtree);
   WITH subtree↑ DO
      BEGIN
         left := NIL;
         right := NIL;
         WITH entry DO
            BEGIN
               wordvalue := word;
               new(firstinqueue);
               lastinqueue := firstinqueue;
               WITH firstinqueue↑ DO
                  BEGIN
                     linenumber := line;
                     nextinqueue := NIL
                  END { with firstinqueue↑ }
            END { with entry }
      END { with subtree↑ }
END

{ append a list item }
WITH subtree↑, entry DO
   IF lastinqueue↑.linenumber ≠ line
      THEN
         BEGIN
            new(nextitem);
            WITH nextitem↑ DO
               BEGIN
                  linenumber := line;
```

298

Example: A Cross-Reference Generator

```
                    nextinqueue := NIL;
                END; { with nextitem↑ }
              lastinqueue↑.nextinqueue := nextitem;
              lastinqueue := nextitem
          END
      ELSE { word is on same line }
```

This completes the development of the input phase, and we can turn to the refinement of

printtree(wordtree)

Since we will be printing entries from a binary search tree, we can anticipate that we will use binary tree traversal to print the entries and subtrees of a node. It is useful to look ahead a little, and consider how the output will be arranged. The paging can be controlled by a procedure, *printline*, which keeps track of the current position on the page. We decide at this stage how many line numbers will be printed on a line. The word may occupy up to 20 positions. Since the maximum line length is 80 characters, this leaves 60 print positions for line numbers. The largest line number is 999, which has three digits, and so if we leave five print positions for each number there will be at least two blanks between each pair of numbers. It follows that we can print 12 numbers on a line. The program can perform these calculations itself, and is better if it does so. Accordingly, we define some constants and subrange types:

```
CONST
    maxlinelen = 80;
    maxonpage = 60;
    numbergap = 2;
    radix = 10;
TYPE
    pageindex = 1 .. maxonpage;
    lineindex = 1 .. maxlinelen;
```

and proceed to the first version of procedure *printtree*.

```
PROCEDURE printtree (tree : treepointer);
    VAR
        pageposition : pageindex;
        numberwidth, maxonline : lineindex;
    BEGIN
        numberwidth := trunc(ln(maxlines)/ln(radix))
                        + 1 + numbergap;
        maxonline := (maxlinelen - maxwordlen) DIV numberwidth;
        pageposition := maxonpage;
        printentry(tree,pageposition)
    END;
```

We do not pass *numberwidth* and *maxonline* as parameters to *printentry*.

Example: A Cross-Reference Generator

Since their values are constant, we simply ensure that *printentry* is within their scope. The procedure *printentry* performs an inorder traversal of the word tree, using this schema:

> *print nodes in the left subtree;*
> *print the current node;*
> *print nodes in the right subtree*

An entry is printed by printing the word in it, and then traversing the list of items containing the line numbers. The procedure *print-line* controls the paging, and the constant *entrygap* determines the number of blank lines between successive words.

```
{    Cross-Reference Generator

     Author:          Peter Grogono
     Date Written:    24 September 1977
     Last Modified:   30 September 1977

     Purpose:

         Generate a cross-reference listing from a text-file.

     Specification:

         The program reads a text-file from file 'input' and
         writes a cross-reference listing to the file 'output'.
         The cross-reference listing contains one entry for each
         distinct word in the source text.  A word is a string of
         letters.  An entry displays the word and the number of
         each line on which it occurred.  For restrictions, see
         the constant declaration section.    }

PROGRAM crossreference
  ( { read text from } input,
    { write listing to } output);

CONST
    maxlines = 999;      { longest document permitted }
    maxwordlen = 20;     { longest word read without truncation }
    maxlinelen = 80;     { length of output line }
    maxonpage = 60;      { size of output page }
    headingsize = 3;     { number of lines for heading }
    entrygap = 1;        { number of blank lines between entries }
    numbergap = 2;       { number of blanks between line numbers }
    radix = 10;
    blank = ' ';
    cha = 'a';
    chz = 'z';
    heading = 'cross-reference listing';
```

Example: A Cross-Reference Generator

```
TYPE
  counter = 1 .. maxlines;
  wordindex = 1 .. maxwordlen;
  pageindex = 1 .. maxonpage;
  lineindex = 1 .. maxlinelen;
  wordtype = PACKED ARRAY [wordindex] OF char;

  queuepointer = ↑queueitem;
  queueitem =
    RECORD
      linenumber : counter;
      nextinqueue : queuepointer
    END;

  entrytype =
    RECORD
      wordvalue : wordtype;
      firstinqueue, lastinqueue : queuepointer
    END;

  treepointer = ↑node;
  node =
    RECORD
      entry : entrytype;
      left, right : treepointer
    END;

VAR
  wordtree : treepointer;
  letters : SET OF char;

PROCEDURE buildtree (VAR tree : treepointer);
  VAR
    currentword : wordtype;
    currentline : counter;

  PROCEDURE getword (VAR word : wordtype;
                     VAR line : counter);
    VAR
      currentchar : char;
      index, blankindex : 0 .. maxwordlen;

    PROCEDURE getchar (VAR ch : char;
                       VAR lin : counter);
      BEGIN { getchar }
        IF eof
          THEN ch := blank
          ELSE IF eoln
            THEN
              BEGIN
                ch := blank;
```

```
              lin := lin + 1;
              readln
          END
      ELSE read(ch)
    END; { getchar }

  BEGIN { getword }
    currentchar := blank;
    WHILE NOT (eof OR (currentchar IN letters)) DO
      getchar(currentchar,line);
    IF NOT eof
      THEN
        BEGIN
          index := 0;
          WHILE currentchar IN letters DO
            BEGIN
              IF index < maxwordlen
                THEN
                  BEGIN
                    index := index + 1;
                    word[index] := currentchar;
                  END;
              IF eof
                THEN currentchar := blank
                ELSE getchar(currentchar,line)
            END; { while }
          IF index < maxwordlen
            THEN
              FOR blankindex := index + 1 TO maxwordlen DO
                word[blankindex] := blank
        END
  END; { getword }

PROCEDURE entertree (VAR subtree : treepointer;
                     word : wordtype;
                     line : counter);
  VAR
    nextitem : queuepointer;
  BEGIN { entertree }
    IF subtree = NIL
      THEN
        BEGIN { create a new entry }
          new(subtree);
          WITH subtree↑ DO
            BEGIN
              left := NIL;
              right := NIL;
              WITH entry DO
                BEGIN
                  wordvalue := word;
                  new(firstinqueue);
```

```
                        lastinqueue := firstinqueue;
                        WITH firstinqueue↑ DO
                          BEGIN
                             linenumber := line;
                             nextinqueue := NIL
                          END { with firstinqueue↑}}
                       END { with entry }
                   END { with subtree↑ }
            END
          ELSE { append a list item }
            WITH subtree↑, entry DO
              IF word = wordvalue
                THEN
                  BEGIN
                    IF lastinqueue↑.linenumber ≠ line
                      THEN
                        BEGIN
                          new(nextitem);
                          WITH nextitem↑ DO
                            BEGIN
                               linenumber := line;
                               nextinqueue := NIL
                            END; { with nextitem↑ }
                          lastinqueue↑.nextinqueue := nextitem;
                          lastinqueue := nextitem
                        END
                  END
                ELSE IF word < wordvalue
                  THEN entertree(left,word,line)
                  ELSE entertree(right, word, line)
       END; { entertree }

  BEGIN { buildtree }
    currentline := 1;
    WHILE NOT eof DO
      BEGIN
        getword(currentword,currentline)
        IF NOT eof
          THEN entertree(tree,currentword,currentline)
      END { while }
  END; { buildtree }

PROCEDURE printtree (tree : treepointer);
  VAR
    pageposition : pageindex;
    numberwidth, maxonline : lineindex;

  PROCEDURE printentry (subtree : treepointer;
                        VAR position : pageindex);
    VAR
      index : wordindex;
```

303

```
    itemcount : 0 .. maxlinelen;
    itemptr : queuepointer;

  PROCEDURE printline (VAR currentposition : pageindex;
                           newlines : pageindex);
    VAR
      linecounter : pageindex;
    BEGIN { printline }
      IF currentposition + newlines ≥ maxonpage
        THEN
          BEGIN
            FOR linecounter := 1 TO newlines DO
              writeln;
            currentposition := currentposition + newlines
          END
        ELSE
          BEGIN
            page(output);
            writeln(heading);
            FOR linecounter := 1 TO headingsize - 1 DO
              writeln;
            currentposition := headingsize + 1
          END
    END; { printline }

  BEGIN { printentry }
    IF subtree ≠ NIL
      THEN
        WITH subtree↑ DO
          BEGIN
            printentry(left,position);
            printline(position,entrygap + 1);
            WITH entry DO
              BEGIN
                FOR index := 1 TO maxwordlen DO
                  write(wordvalue[index]);
                itemcount := o;
                itemptr := firstinqueue;
                WHILE itemptr ≠ NIL DO
                  BEGIN
                    itemcount := itemcount + 1;
                    IF itemcount > maxonline
                      THEN
                        BEGIN
                          printline(position,1);
                          write(blank : maxwordlen);
                          itemcount := 1
                        END;
                    write(itemptr↑.linenumber : numberwidth);
                    itemptr := itemptr↑.nextinqueue
                  END { while }
```

```
            END; { with entry }
          printentry(right,position)
        END { with subtree↑ }
    END; { printentry }

  BEGIN { printtree }
    numberwidth := trunc(ln(maxlines)/ln(radix)) + 1 + numbergap;
    maxonline := (maxlinelen - maxwordlen) DIV numberwidth;
    pageposition := maxonpage;
    printentry(tree,pageposition)
  END; { printtree }

 BEGIN { crossreference }
   letters := ['a' .. 'z'];
   wordtree := NIL;
   buildtree(wordtree);
   printtree(wordtree)
 END. { crossreference }
```

An Appraisal of PASCAL

The languages that we use have a profound effect on the way we think. While it may be true that our inspirations are not the result of linguistic mental processes, most of our conscious thoughts are linguistic in nature. Although we can translate from one language to another, the flavor of the message is often lost in the translation. The same is true of programming languages: we think of programmed solutions to problems in our favorite programming language. A problem will seem easier to us if it is simple to program its solution in that language. Professional programmers generally know several programming languages, and when confronted with a problem, they will select the most appropriate language for its solution at an early stage.

In this book, we have been concerned exclusively with PASCAL. The example programs have been selected to perform calculations for which PASCAL is appropriate, and problems for which PASCAL is inappropriate have not been considered. We now consider PASCAL in a more objective way, looking first at its strengths, and then at its weaknesses.

An important feature of PASCAL is its sparseness. There is a relatively small number of basic constructions, but the language is powerful because these can be combined in many ways. In particular, both algorithms and data structures can be constructed hierarchically. The sparse nature of PASCAL is its most important asset and it benefits the language in at least four different ways. First, PASCAL is relatively simple to compile and PASCAL programs run efficiently on

most computers. Second, well-written PASCAL programs are easy to read
and understand. Third, the recursive nature of PASCAL structures
permits top-down development techniques to be applied in a natural and
simple way. Fourth, with a few exceptions, PASCAL control structures
are easy to verify, because their semantics are simple. On the other
hand, PASCAL is not *too* sparse. There is a number of languages with
fewer constructions than PASCAL, and although these languages are
capable of expressing any algorithm that can be expressed in PASCAL,
the resulting programs may be very obscure. In PASCAL, a compromise
has been achieved: there is enough variety to express most basic algorithms concisely, but not so many that the language is baroque.

There are three criticisms frequently directed at PASCAL. The
first is that the file handling capabilities of PASCAL are inadequate.
PASCAL provides automatic conversion facilities for text files, but
these cannot be used in real programs because no provision is made for
error conditions. Although PASCAL is the best language we have for
teaching programming, the important techniques of random file access
cannot be taught with it. The second criticism refers to PASCAL
arrays: the size of an array is determined at compile-time. It is
very difficult to write useful programs for numerical analysis or
string manipulation in PASCAL because there are no dynamic arrays.
The third objection is that there is no loop construction with an
exit. There are many situations in which we want to jump out of a
loop from its middle, and the only way we can do this in PASCAL is to
introduce spurious boolean variables or use *GOTO* statements.

Finally, the quest for efficiency in PASCAL has led to a lack of
portability. The designer of a programming language specifies standards which must be respected by any implementation of the language.
These standards should be sufficient to make programs written in the
language portable. (A program is *portable* if it can be run without
change on different computers.) We will illustrate the connection
between standards and efficiency with a simple example. It is
reasonable for a language designer to require that *real* arithmetic be
provided, because most computers have either hardware or a standard
software package for performing *real* calculations. It would be
unreasonable for a language designer to insist that the results of
real calculations be accurate to exactly ten places of decimals (no
more and no less), however, because this would give rise to serious
inefficiency on almost all computers. In the case of PASCAL, some of
the standards are too lenient. The fact that PASCAL does not specify
a representation for characters, for example, makes it very difficult
to write programs which are completely independent of the character
set of a particular computer. The most useful data structure we have
for writing character set independent programs is *SET OF char*, but
this type is illegal in many PASCAL implementations!

The drawbacks of PASCAL are minor when considered in the perspect-
ive of its advantages over other contemporary languages. PASCAL has
a secure place in the handful of programming languages which have

Exercises

achieved widespread implementation and which have won worldwide
popularity. PASCAL notation is used in a large and increasing proportion of the papers published in the programming literature; PASCAL
is being used more and more at both academic and industrial computer
installations; there is a new generation of languages which acknowledge their debt to PASCAL; and each year more schools choose PASCAL
as the first computer language that they teach to students. PASCAL
is already almost ten years old, and it is possible that the language
in its present form may not be used for many more years. There is no
doubt, however, that its concepts will be used by programming language
designers for many years to come. It can be truly said that, at the
present time, a thorough knowledge of PASCAL is indispensable for any-
one who aspires to be a professional computer programmer.

Exercises

10.1 If you know a high-level language other than PASCAL, write a
      comparison of the two languages. Consider, amongst other factors:

      (a) Constant, type and variable declarations
      (b) The scope of variables
      (c) Dynamic data structures
      (d) Input and output

      Write programs in PASCAL and in the other language that you know
      and compare

      (e) Ease of coding
      (f) Ease of debugging
      (g) Ease of verification
      (h) Compilation and execution times
      (i) Memory used by the object programs

10.2 Select a PASCAL program, either from this book or elsewhere, and
      prove that it is correct.

10.3 The procedure below performs a binary search of the ordered
      array *v*. Find an invariant for the *REPEAT* loop.

```
TYPE
    vector = ARRAY [min .. max] OF real;
PROCEDURE binarysearch ( v : vector;
                         key : real;
                         VAR found : boolean;
                         VAR mid : integer);
    VAR
        lo,hi : integer;
```

307

```
BEGIN
    { v[min] ≤ key ≤ v[max] ∧ v ordered }
    lo := min;
    hi := max;
    REPEAT
        mid := (lo + hi) DIV 2;
        IF key > v[mid]
            THEN lo := mid + 1
            ELSE hi := mid - 1
    UNTIL (v[mid] = key) OR (lo > hi);
    found := lo ≤ hi
END;
```

10.4 Program *crossreferences* can be used to provide a cross-reference
listing for PASCAL programs. However, to perform this function
usefully, it should read identifiers rather than words, it should
not reference reserved words, and it should ignore comments.
Modify it to do this.

10.5 Write a non-recursive program that lists the operations necessary to move the tower of Hanoi (Section 4.3). Describe the
development of your program in detail.

10.6 Write a program that accepts as input a syntactically correct
PASCAL program in any format and generates a listing of the same
program with the layout conventions of Appendix D.

10.7 Develop Program *calculator* of Chapter 4 into a useful software
tool. Some examples of the facilities you could add to it are:

(a) function evaluation (e.g. *sin*, *cos*, *sqrt*, *exp*, *ln*);
(b) radix conversion (enable calculations to be performed in
     binary, octal, etc.);
(c) control of output format;
(d) complex number calculations.

Do *not* 'patch up' the original program. Write a complete specification of your calculator, and use top-down development techniques
to implement it.

F̲urther Reading

The most important source book for PASCAL programmers is the PASCAL User Manual and Report by Jensen and Wirth [1976]. Wirth has written two other books which use PASCAL notation but are not intended to teach PASCAL: Systematic Programming — An Introduction [1973] emphasizes formal aspects of programming, and Algorithms + Data Structures = Programs [1976a] is a more advanced book which contains PASCAL versions of many useful algorithms. Two PASCAL textbooks other than this one have been published: Conway, Gries and Zimmerman [1976] and Webster [1976]. Many of the ideas that lead to PASCAL can be found in the classic book Structured Programming by Dahl, Dijkstra and Hoare [1972].

Related Books

You do not become a good programmer simply by learning a programming language: you have to know some theory as well. Knuth [1973] provides a detailed and thorough background for the theory of algorithms and data structures. Aho, Hopcroft and Ullman [1974] offer a more advanced treatment of algorithm theory, but they expect a certain amount of mathematical expertise on the part of the reader. If you are interested in the complexities of calculations with real variables, glossed over in Chapter 2 of this book, you could try

Further Reading

Dahlquist and Bjorck [1974], Knuth [1969] or Sterbenz [1974].

Program *update* of Chapter 7 is based on an example given by Dijkstra [1976] (he attributes the algorithm to Feijen) in a book which demonstrates a formal approach to program design and contains many elegant algorithms.

Program *circles* of Chapter 6 is based on an example given by Birtwistle, Dahl, Myhrhaug and Nygaard [1973] in their book on the beautiful but neglected language SIMULA.

Papers

The standard reference for PASCAL is Wirth's [1971a] paper. Although this paper contains a useful account of the aims of PASCAL, some details of the language have been changed since it was written, and so it should not be used for its definition of PASCAL. In an interesting dialogue, Habermann [1973] makes some critical remarks about PASCAL, and Lecarme and Desjardins [1974] reply to them. More recently, Conradi [1976] has criticized PASCAL. Wirth [1975] has published his own criticism of PASCAL.

The 'official' Zurich compiler has been described by Wirth [1971c] and Amman [1973, 1977]. Other PASCAL compilers have been described by Welsh and Quinn [1972], Thibault and Manuel [1973], Feiereisen [1974], Bron and deVries [1976], Desjardins [1976] and Grosse-Lindemann and Nagel [1976]. Bates and Cailliau [1977] describe some of the diffi- culties PASCAL implementors may encounter, and give an account of their experiences in implementing PASCAL using the Zurich P-Compiler. (The P-Compiler is a machine-independent compiler which generates code for a hypothetical stack machine.) Correspondence about these and many other PASCAL implementations has appeared in PASCAL News (see below). Brinch-Hansen [1975, 1976] has described a minicomputer operating system written in a dialect of PASCAL.

Hueras and Ledgard [1977] have written an automatic formatting program for PASCAL source text. They have also proposed a set of standards for PASCAL programs [Singer, Hueras and Ledgard, 1976].

Program measurement is an important topic not discussed in this book. Techniques for performance analysis of PASCAL programs have been described by Yuval [1975] and Matwin and Missala [1976].

If you are interested in the continuing discussion about the merits and demerits of structured programming, there is a large selection of reading material. Some of the better known papers are: Wirth [1971b], Ledgard [1973], Peterson, Kasami and Tokura [1973], Lecarme [1974], Wirth [1974], Zahn [1974], Abrahams [1975], Dijkstra [1975], Ledgard and Marcotty [1975], Weinberg, Geller and Plum [1975],

Further Reading

Shneidermann [1976] and Atkinson [1977]. The specific topic of *GOTO* statements, mentioned in Chapter 9 of this book, has been discussed by many authors, including Dijkstra [1968], Wulf [1971], Bochman [1972] and Knuth [1974].

Many people have suggested improvements to PASCAL. Dynamic arrays are felt to be an important omission by McLennan [1975], Conradi [1976], Pokrovsky [1976], Condict [1977] and Kittlitz [1977]. Wirth [1976b] has commented upon the implementation of dynamic arrays. Other revisions have been proposed by Kittlitz [1977] and Biedl [1977]. Numerous suggestions for enhancing PASCAL have appeared in PASCAL News (see below).

There are many new languages which acknowledge PASCAL as part of their foundations. Some of them are described by Ambler et al [1977], Geschke et al [1977], Lamson et al [1977], Shaw et al [1977] and Travis et al [1977].

PASCAL News

PASCAL News is the official publication of the PASCAL User's Group. It is sent to all members of the PASCAL User's Group, and it contains a wealth of information about PASCAL in the form of letters, articles and implementation notes. If you are interested in the present state of PASCAL, the future of PASCAL, or in implementing PASCAL on your own computer, then PASCAL News is essential reading. PASCAL News appears four times a year, usually in September, November, February and May. Write to one of the addresses below.

Europe, North Africa, Middle East, Near East: (₤4.00)

    Pascal User's Group (UK)
    c/o Computer Studies Group
    Mathematics Department
    The University
    Southampton SO9 5NH
    United Kingdom

    Telephone: 44-703-559122 ext 700

Australia, New Zealand, Indonesia, Malaysia: ($A8)

    Pascal User's Group (AUS)
    c/o Arthur Sale
    Department of Information Science
    University of Tasmania
    GPO Box 252C
    Hobart
    Tasmania 7001

Further Reading

Australia

Telephone: 23-0561

Everywhere Else: ($US6.00)

Pascal User's Group
c/o Andy Mickel
University Computer Center: 227 EX
208 SE Union Street
University of Minnesota
Minneapolis
MN 55455
USA

Telephone: 1-612-376-7290

Abbreviations used in the Bibliography

ACM   Association for Computing Machinery
CACM   Communications of the ACM
DECUS   Digital Equipment Corporation Users' Society
IEEE   Institute of Electrical and Electronic Engineers
IFIP   International Federation for Data Processing
SIGPLAN   Notices of the Special Interest Group on Programming
           Languages of the ACM
SP&E   Software: Practice and Experience
           (published by Wiley and Sons, Chichester, England)
TSE   Transactions in Software Engineering
           (published by IEEE)

Abrahams, P.W. [1975]
   Structured Programming Considered Harmful
   SIGPLAN, Vol 10, #4, April 1975

Aho, A.V., Hopcroft, J.E. and Ullman, J.P. [1974]
   The Design and Analysis of Computer Algorithms
   Addison-Wesley, 1974

Ambler, A.L., et al [1977]
   GYPSY: A Language for Specification
   SIGPLAN, Vol 12, #3, March 1977, p1-10

Amman, U. [1973]
   The Method of Structured Programming Applied to
   the Development of a Compiler
   Proceedings of the ACM International Computing Symposium
   at Davos, ed. Gunther et al, 1973, p93-9

Further Reading

Amman, U. [1977]
   On Code Generation in a PASCAL Compiler
   SP&E, Vol 7, 1977, p391-423

Atkinson, G. [1977]
   The Non-Desirability of Structured Programming in
   User Languages
   SIGPLAN, Vol 12, #7, July 1977, p43-50

Bates, D. and Cailliau, R. [1977]
   Experience with PASCAL Compilers on Minicomputers
   SIGPLAN, Vol 12, #11, Nov 1977, p10-22

Biedl, A. [1977]
   An Extension of Programming Languages for Numerical
   Computation in Science and Engineering with Special
   Reference to PASCAL
   SIGPLAN, Vol 12, #4, April 1977, p31-3

Birtwistle, G.M., Dahl, O-J., Myhrhaug, B. and Nygaard, K. [1973]
   SIMULA Begin
   Auerbach, 1973

Bochmann, G.W. [1972]
   Multiple Exits from a Loop Without GOTO
   CACM, Vol 16, #7, July 1972, p443-4

Brinch-Hansen, P. [1975]
   The Programming Language Concurrent PASCAL
   TSE, Vol Se-1, #2, 1975, p199-207

Brinch-Hansen, P. [1976]
   The SOLO Operating System
   SP&E, Vol 6, 1976, p139-205

Bron, C. and deVries, W. [1976]
   A PASCAL Compiler for the PDP-11
   SP&E, Vol 6, 1976, p109-16

Condict, M.N. [1977]
   The PASCAL Dynamic Array Controversy and a Method
   for Enforcing Global Assertions
   SIGPLAN, Vol 12, #11, Nov 1977, p23-7

Conradi, R. [1976]
   Further Critical Comments on PASCAL, Particularly
   as a System Programming Language
   SIGPLAN, Vol 11, #11, Nov 1976, p8-25

Further Reading

Conway, R., Gries, D. and Zimmerman, E.C. [1976]
   A Primer on PASCAL
   Winthrop, 1976

Dahl, O-J., Dijkstra, E.W. and Hoare, C.A.R. [1972]
   Structured Programming
   Academic Press, 1972

Dahlquist, G. and Bjorck, A. [1974]
   Numerical Methods
   (translated by Ned Anderson)
   Prentice-Hall, 1974

Desjardins, P. [1976]
   A PASCAL Compiler for the Xerox Sigma 6
   SIGPLAN, Vol 8, #6, June 1976, p34-6

Dijkstra, E.W. [1968]
   GOTO Statement Considered Harmful
   CACM, Vol 11, #3, March 1968, p147-8

Dijkstra, E.W. [1975]
   Guarded Commands, Nondeterminacy, and Formal Derivation
   of Programs
   CACM, Vol 18, #8, August 1975, p453-7

Dijkstra, E.W. [1976]
   A Discipline of Programming
   Prentice-Hall, 1976

Feiereisen [1974]
   Implementation of PASCAL on the PDP11/45
   DECUS Conference, Zurich, Sept 1974, p259

Geschke, M. et al
   Early Experience with MESA
   CACM, Vol 20, #8, Aug 1977, p540-552

Grosse-Lindemann, C.O. and Nagel, H.H. [1976]
   Postlude to a PASCAL Compiler for the DEC System 10
   SP&E, Vol 6, 1976, p29-42

Habermann, A.N. [1973]
   Critical Comments on the Programming Language PASCAL
   Acta Informatica, Vol 3, #1, 1973, p45-57

Hoare, C.A.R. and Wirth, N. [1973]
   An Axiomatic Definition of PASCAL
   Acta Informatica, Vol 3, 1973, p335-355

Hueras, J. and Ledgard, H.F. [1977]
An Automatic Formatting Program for PASCAL
SIGPLAN, Vol 12, #7, July 1977, p82-4

Jensen, K. and Wirth, N. [1976]
PASCAL User Manual and Report (Second Edition)
Springer-Verlag, 1976

Kittlitz, E.N. [1976]
Block Statements and Synonyms in PASCAL
SIGPLAN, Vol 11, #10, Oct 1976, p32

Kittlitz, E.N. [1977]
Another Proposal for Variable Size Arrays in PASCAL
SIGPLAN, Vol 12, #1, Jan 1977, p82

Knuth, D.E. [1969]
The Art of Computer Programming, Vol 2, Seminumerical Algorithms
Addison-Wesley, 1969

Knuth, D.E. [1973]
The Art of Computer Programming, Vol 1, Fundamental
Algorithms (Second Edition)
Addison-Wesley, 1973

Knuth, D.E. [1974]
Structured Programming with Goto Statements
ACM Computing Surveys 6, 1974, p261-301

Lampson, B.W. et al [1977]
Report on the Programming Language EUCLID
SIGPLAN, Vol 12, #2, Feb 1977, p1-77

Lecarme, O. [1974]
Structured Programming, Programming Teaching and the
Language PASCAL
SIGPLAN, Vol 9, #7, July 1974, p15-21

Lecarme, O. and Desjardins, P. [1974]
Reply to a Paper by A.N. Habermann on the Programming
Language PASCAL
SIGPLAN, VOl 9, #10, Oct 1974, p21

Ledgard, H.F. [1973]
The Case for Structured Programming
BIT, 13, 1973, p45-57

Ledgard, H.F. and Marcotty, M. [1975]
A Genealogy of Control Structures
CACM, Vol 18, #11, Nov 1975, p629-639

Further Reading

Matwin, S. and Missala, M. [1976]
    A Simple Machine Independent Tool for Obtaining
    Rough Measurements of PASCAL Programs
    SIGPLAN, Vol 11, #8, Aug 1976, p42

McLennan, B.J. [1975]
    Note on Dynamic Arrays in PASCAL
    SIGPLAN, Vol 10, #9, Sep 1975, p39-40

Mohilner, P.R. [1977]
    Using PASCAL in a FORTRAN Environment
    SP&E, Vol 7, 1977, p357-362

Peterson, W., Kasami, T., and Tokura, N. [1973]
    On the Capabilities of While, Repeat and Exit Statements
    CACM, Vol 16, #8, Aug 1973, p503-512

Pokrovsky, S. [1976]
    Formal Types and their Application to Dynamic Arrays
    in PASCAL
    SIGPLAN, Vol 11, #10, Oct 1976, p36

Shaw, M. et al [1977]
    Abstraction Mechanisms in CLU
    CACM, Vol 20, #8, Aug 1977, p564-576

Shneiderman, B. [1976]
    A Review of Design Techniques for Programs and Data
    SP&E, Vol 6, 1976, p555-567

Singer, A., Hueras, J. and Ledgard, H.F. [1977]
    A Basis for Executing PASCAL Programmers
    SIGPLAN, Vol 12, #7, July 1977, p101-5

Sterbenz, P.H. [1974]
    Floating Point Computation
    Prentice-Hall, 1974

Thibault, D. and Manuel, P. [1973]
    Implementation of a PASCAL Compiler for the CII Iris 80
    Computer, SIGPLAN, Vol 8, #6, June 1973, 189-90

Travis, L. et al [1977]
    Design Rationale for TELOS, a PASCAL based AI Language
    SIGPLAN, VOl 12, # 8, Aug 1977, p67-76

Webster, C.A.G. [1976]
    Introduction to PASCAL
    Heyden and Son, 1976

Further Reading

Weinberg, G.M., Geller, D.P. and Plum, T.W. [1975]
    If-Then-Else Considered Harmful
    SIGPLAN, Vol 10, #8, Aug 1975, p34-43

Welsh, J. and Quinn, C. [1972]
    A PASCAL Compiler for the ICL 1900 Series Computer
    SP&E, Vol 2, 1972, p73-7

Wirth, N. [1971a]
    The Programming Language PASCAL
    Acta Informatica, Vol 1, 1971, p35-63

Wirth, N. [1971b]
    Program Development by Stepwise Refinement
    CACM, Vol 14, #4, April 1971, p221-7

Wirth, N. [1971c]
    Design of a PASCAL Compiler
    SP&E, Vol 1, 1971, p309-33

Wirth, N. [1973]
    Systematic Programming — An Introduction
    Prentice-Hall, 1973

Wirth, N. [1974]
    On the Construction of Well Structured Programs
    ACM Computing Surveys, Vol 6, #4, Dec 1974, p247-59

Wirth, N. [1975]
    An Assessment of the Programming Language PASCAL
    TSE, Vol SE-1, #2, June 1975, p192-8

Wirth, N. [1976a]
    Algorithms + Data Structures = Programs
    Prentice-Hall, 1976

Wirth, N. [1976b]
    Comment on a Note on Dynamic Arrays in PASCAL
    SIGPLAN, Vol 11, #1, Jan 1976, p37

Wulf, W.A. [1971]
    Programming without the GOTO
    Proceedings IFIP Conference, 1971

Yuval, G. [1975]
    Gathering Run-Time Statistics without Black Magic
    SP&E, Vol5, 1975, p105-8

Zahn, C.T. [1974]
    A Control Statement for Natural, Top-Down Structured
    Programming, Symposium on Programming Languages, Paris, 1974

The Vocabulary of PASCAL

APPENDIX A

PASCAL programs are written using letters, digits, and other characters. Many of the other characters are present on all type-writers and computer peripherals and present no problems. Some of these characters are not always available, and so synonyms are defined.

We have used both upper and lower case letters in PASCAL programs in this book. Many computers do not have facilities for reading and printing lower case characters, and if this is true of your computer then obviously you can only use upper case letters for PASCAL programs. If your installation does permit lower case letters to be used, then you should find out how lower case letters are processed by the PASCAL compiler.

A.1 Reserved Words

The following reserved words are treated in PASCAL as indivisible symbols. They cannot be used for anything other than the purpose for which they are defined in the language, except in comments.

Identifiers

AND	ARRAY	BEGIN	CASE	CONST
DIV	DO	DOWNTO	ELSE	END
FILE	FOR	FUNCTION	GOTO	IF
IN	LABEL	MOD	NIL	NOT
OF	OR	PACKED	PROCEDURE	PROGRAM
RECORD	REPEAT	SET	THEN	TO
TYPE	UNTIL	VAR	WHILE	WITH

A.2 Identifiers

Identifiers are names chosen by the programmer to denote constants, types, variables, procedures and functions. An identifier consists of a letter followed by any combination of letters and digits. The compiler will regard two identifiers which differ in their first eight characters as distinct. There are some standard identifiers which will be recognized by the compiler without a definition in the program. A standard identifier may be redefined within a program, globally or locally. The following is a list of the standard identifiers.

Standard Constants:

false	true	maxint

Standard Types:

integer	boolean	real	char
text			

Standard Files:

input	output

Standard Functions:

abs	arctan	chr	cos
eof	eoln	exp	ln
odd	ord	pred	round
sin	sqr	sqrt	succ
trunc			

Standard Procedures:

get	new	pack	page
put	read	readln	reset
rewrite	unpack	write	writeln

A.3 Punctuation Marks

The remaining PASCAL symbols are listed in the table below. The first column in the table contains the standard symbol; the second column, if present, contains a synonym that may be used if the standard symbol is not available; and the third column contains a very brief (and not necessarily complete) description of the function of the symbol. These symbols and synonyms are not universally accepted, and so room has been left in the table for you to write the symbols used at your installation.

+		plus
−		minus
*		times
/		divide
<		is less than
≤	<=	is less than or equal to
=		is equal to
≠	<>	is not equal to
≥	>=	is greater than or equal to
>		is greater than
∧	*AND*	boolean conjunction
∨	*OR*	boolean inclusive disjunction
~	*NOT*	boolean negation
:=		becomes
,		separates items in a list
;		separates statements
:		separates variable name and type
'		delimits character and string literals
.		decimal point, record selector and program terminator
..		subrange specifier
↑		file and pointer variable indicator
(		starts parameter list or nested expression
)		end parameter list or nested expression
[	(.	starts subscript list or set expression
{	(*	starts a comment
}	*)	ends a comment
]	.)	end subscript list or set expression

PASCAL Syntax

APPENDIX B

This appendix includes a complete set of syntax diagrams for PASCAL. In the event of a discrepancy between these syntax diagrams and the syntax diagrams in the body of the text, assume that these diagrams are correct.

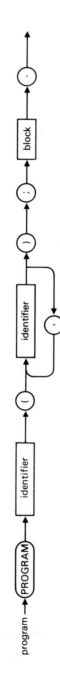

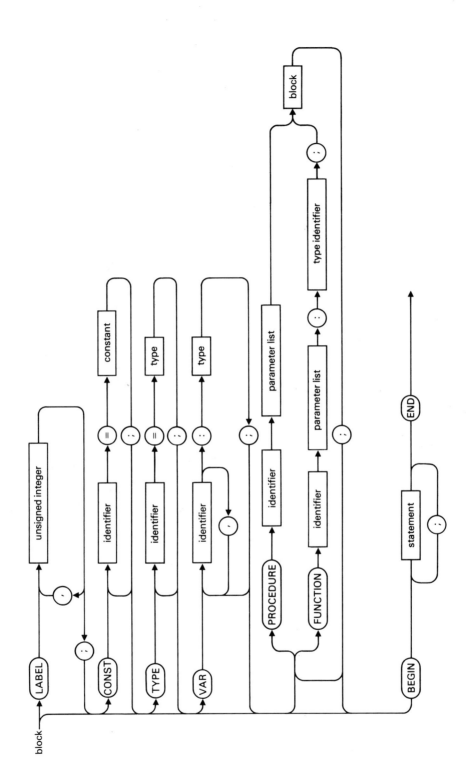

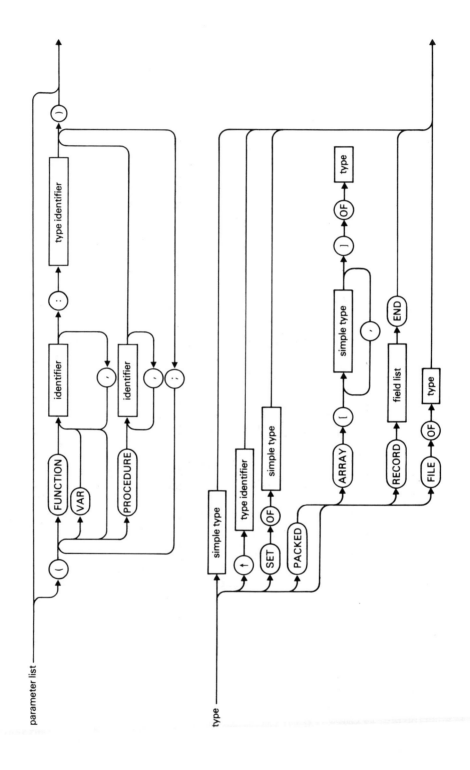

326

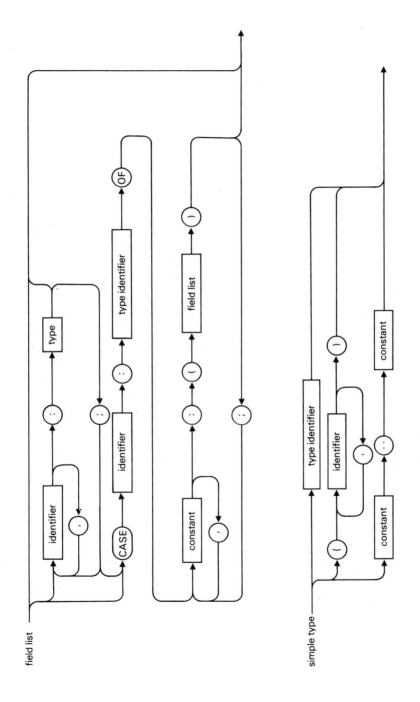

field list

simple type

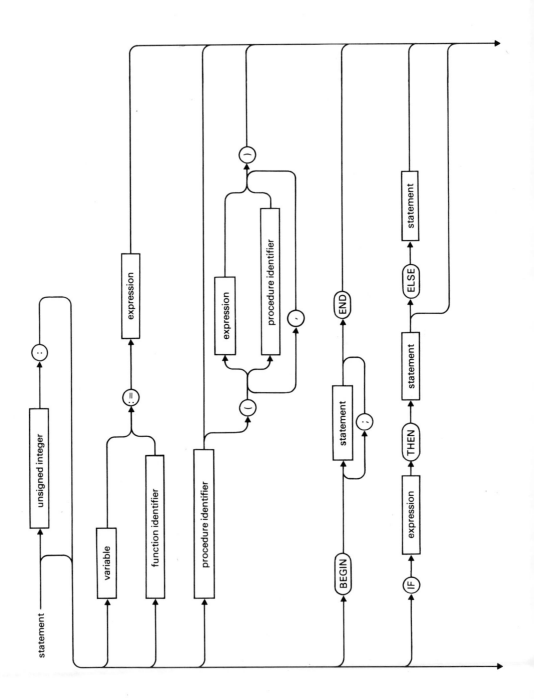

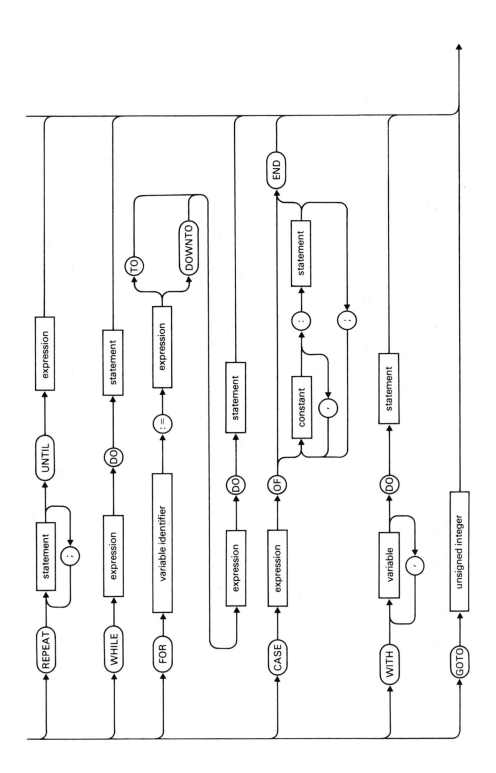

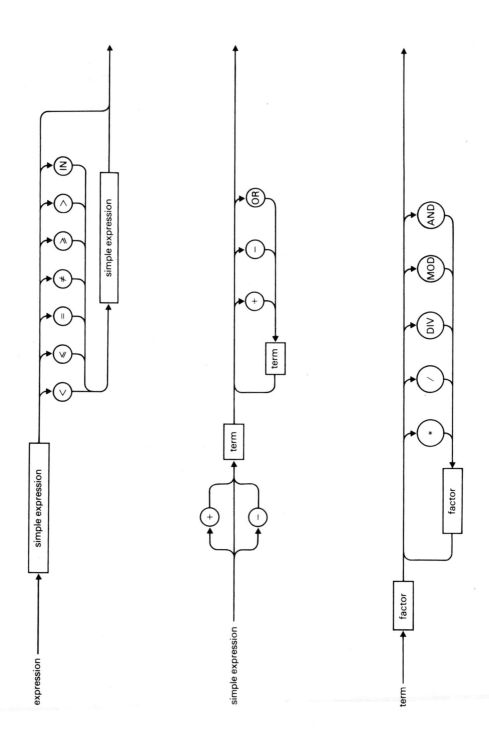

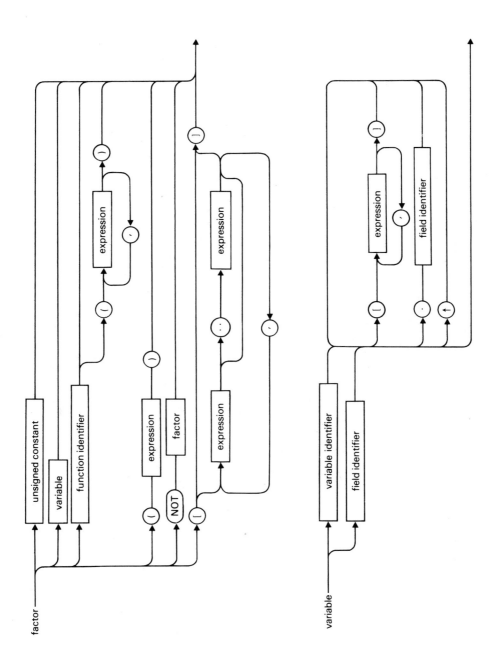

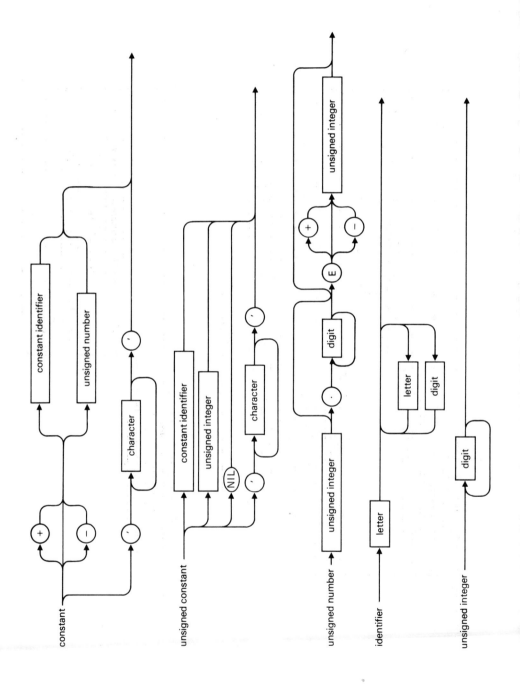

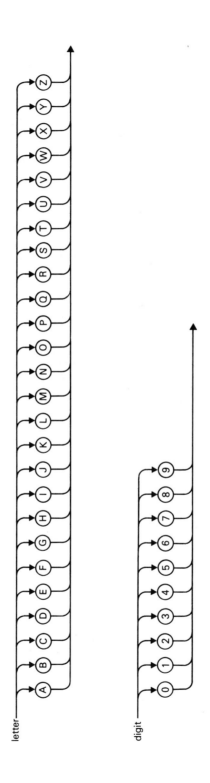

333

A PASCAL
Implementation

APPENDIX C

In this appendix, we review one particular implementation of
PASCAL. A study of this appendix will help you to appreciate the
distinction between the abstract language definition, which we have
used throughout the book, and an implementation for a specific class
of computers. The implementation we have chosen to describe is CDC
6000 PASCAL. Although there are many other implementations of
PASCAL, this one is in widespread use, particularly at universities.
It is also the 'official' version of PASCAL, in that the compiler
was written by Urs Amman under the guidance of Niklaus Wirth at ETH
in Zurich.

The CDC 6000 and CYBER 170 series of computers are all identical,
as far as the programmer is concerned, to the original CDC 6600
designed in the early sixties. The 6600 was intended for the scientific community, and since FORTRAN was the most widely used scientific
programming language at that time, its principal aim in life is to
execute FORTRAN programs rapidly. Rather more than a decade later,
the 6600 and its descendants are in widespread use, and, unfortunately, so is FORTRAN. The question of how suitable the 6000 series of
machines are as host machines for a PASCAL system has been discussed
by Wirth [1971] and Amman [1973, 1977]; in this appendix we describe
only the effects of this particular computer on the language.

C.1 Standard Types

The 6000 computers have a word length of 60 bits. This may be divided into 1 bit sign, 11 bit exponent and 48 bit fraction for numerical calculation, or into 10 groups of 6 bits each for character storage. Consequently:

(a) *Maxint* = 2^{48} - 1 = 281474976710655;

(b) If *x* is real, then either *x* = *0* or

$$10^{-293} < |x| < 10^{322} \quad \text{approximately;}$$

(c) Real numbers have a precision of about 14 places of decimals;

(d) There are 64 different characters. Several different character sets are available, and so no one particular set is given here. The character *ch* for which *ord(ch)* = *0* may not be usable because the operating system employs 12 zero bits (0000_8) to signify end of line. Unfortunately, on many systems, this character is the colon, and so another character (for example, '%') must be used in place of ':'. The character available, and their ordering, differ from one installation to another, and sometimes from one peripheral to another. Usually,

$$'a' < 'b' < 'c' \ldots 'z' < ' '$$

which has rather startling consequences if you try to sort lexicographically. One solution to this problem is to replace blanks by *chr(0)*, but be careful to convert *chr(0)* back to blank again before attempting to print it.

(e) Sets may have up to 59 members. A set variable can therefore be stored in a 60 bit word. The character *ch* cannot be a member of a set if *ord(ch)* > 58. This is an unfortunate sacrifice to efficiency. In particular, the type

    SET OF char

is not allowed, which is seriously inconvenient. For example, the expression used in Program *contingencies* of Chapter 6:

    [thischar,prevchar] ≤ *[cha .. chz]*

cannot be used in 6000 series PASCAL because the program will fail if *ord(thischar)* > *58* or *ord(prevchar)* > *58.*

(f) The type *alfa* is standard and is equivalent to

PACKED ARRAY [1 .. 10] OF char

The Zurich compiler uses *alfa* variables to store identifiers during compilation. Consequently, two identifiers whose first ten characters are the same are considered to be identical. The PASCAL Report states that the compiler must distinguish identifiers whose first eight characters are not identical, and so the Zurich compiler meets the standard. Most of the more recent compilers follow the preferable convention that all characters of an identifier are significant.

(g) Octal (base 8) constants may be written in a program in the form

ddd ... ddb

where each d is a digit in ['0' .. '7']. For example

100B   7777777777777777B

are octal constants representing 64_{10} and *maxint* respectively.

C.2 Arithmetic

The CDC 6000 processor gives no indication that an integer operation has yielded a result greater than *maxint*. Moreover, numbers *N* such that

$$2^{48} <= |N| < 2^{59}$$

can be added and subtracted but not multiplied, divided or printed. The expression

abs(n) > maxint

will, under these circumstances, have the value *true*.

The CDC 6000 processor uses special codes to denote infinite and indefinite values of real variables. A calculation leading to a result too large to be represented will give an indefinite value, and a division by zero will give an infinite value. If the real number *f* has an infinite or indefinite value, then the boolean function

undefined(f)

will be *true*.

C.3   Standard Procedures and Functions

In addition to the standard procedures and functions defined in Appendix A, the following are predefined:

PROCEDURE date (VAR d : alfa);
  { *sets d to today's date in the format YY/MM/DD* }

PROCEDURE time (VAR t : alfa);
  { *sets t to the time now in the format HH.MM.SS.* }

PROCEDURE message (m : PACKED ARRAY [1 .. 40] OF char);
  { *writes a message of up to 40 characters to the dayfile* }

PROCEDURE linelimit (VAR textfile : text; num : integer);
  { *abort the program when num lines have been written*
    to the file textfile }

PROCEDURE halt;
  { *abort the program and print a post-mortem* }

FUNCTION card (s : SET OF T) : integer;
  { *returns cardinality of s, that is, the number of members of s* }

FUNCTION clock : integer;
  { *returns the number of milliseconds of processor time used by*
    the job (NOT the program) so far }

FUNCTION expo (f : real) : integer;
  { *returns the contents of the exponent field of the real*
    number f }

FUNCTION undefined (f : real) : boolean;
  { *returns true if the value of f is infinite or indefinite*
    otherwise false }

The additional procedures *getseg* and *putseg*, and the function *eos*, are defined in Section C.6.

C.4 Input and Output

If *a* is an *alfa* variable, then the statement

    write(a)

is permitted and will write the value of *a* as a string of 10 characters, but the statement

    read(a)

is not permitted, and so you must read *alfa* values one character at a time.

Integers may be printed in octal format; if *i* is an integer variable, then the statement

    write(i : fieldwidth OCT)

will write the value of *i* as an octal number (without a postfixed 'B') with *fieldwidth* digits. Leading zeros are not blanked. If *fieldwidth* ≥ 20 then *fieldwidth* - 20 blanks and 20 digits will be printed. If *fieldwidth* < 20, the rightmost *fieldwidth* digits only will be printed, even if non-zero digits are thereby lost. For example,

    bignum := 40000000000000005555;
    write(bignum : 4 oct)

will write

    5555

to the output file. *Fieldwidth* = 0 has the same effect as *fieldwidth* = 20.

The default field widths used by *write* for other types are:

    10 for *integer*
    22 for *real*
    10 for *boolean*
     1 for *char*

A real number for which no filed width or precision is specified will be printed in the form

    d.dddddddddddddE±ddd

where each d is a decimal digit (there are 13 after the decimal point). The first digit (before the decimal point) is non-zero.

A line of text file is stored as an integral number of words of 10 characters each. The end of a line is represented by 12 zero bits in the last word of the line, and character positions between the last non-blank character of a line and the end of line marker are filled with blanks. Consequently, an input procedure should be prepared to find as many as eight blanks at the end of a line.

The procedure *reset* has no effect on the file *input*, and the procedure *rewrite* has no effect on the file *output*.

C.5   Files

CDC filenames must not contain more than seven characters. Files may be given longer names than this in a PASCAL program, but only the first seven characters will be used for communication with the operating system. As far as the operating system is concerned, a program which starts

> PROGRAM *filehandler*
> > *(primarydatafile, secondarydatafile,output)*

uses the files *primary*, *seconda* and *output*.

The type *FILE OF FILE* is not permitted. A file may, however, be a component of an array or record.

CDC operating systems support several different kinds of file organization. Most files containing characters are organized in the manner that is called *text* in PASCAL. In fact, the operating system converts card-files to this format, to avoid storing trailing blanks. You should therefore not expect a card image to have 80 columns; rather, you should read a card image one character at a time, testing *eoln* at each character.

The type

> *cardfile* =
> > *RECORD*
> > > *PACKED ARRAY [1 .. 80] OF char*

can be used, but it employs a different kind of file organization, in which each component of the file contains exactly 80 characters. Program *copydeck* of Chapter 7 will work correctly with this kind of file, but it will not work with a text file, such as *input*.

C.6 Segmented Files

A file may be declared as *SEGMENTED*. For example, we may write

> *TYPE*
> *tty = SEGMENTED FILE OF char;*

A segmented file is composed of *segments*. The standard procedures
putseg and *getseg*, and the boolean function *eos*, are used for accessing segmented files. In the examples below, *segfile* is a segmented
file, and *num* is an integer.

rewrite(segfile)

Prepare the file for rewriting from the beginning.

rewrite(segfile,num)

Prepare the file for rewriting segment *num*, counting from the
current position. Note that *rewrite(segfile,1)* means 'prepare to
rewrite starting at the next segment' and is not the same as
rewrite(segfile).

putseg(segfile)

Terminate a segment. This procedure is called after information
has been written to a segment using *write* or *put*.

getseg(segfile)

Position the file at the beginning of the next segment. *segfile↑*
becomes the first component of this segment, or, if the segment
is empty, *eos(segfile)* becomes true. The segment is read by
calling *get(segfile↑)* or *read(segfile,buffer)* until *eos(segfile)*
becomes true. At the end of the last segment of the file, both
eos(segfile) and *eof(segfile)* are true.

getseg(segfile,num)

Skip *num* segments forward (*num* > 0) or backwards (*num* < 0).
getseg(segfile,0) positions the file at the beginning of the
current segment. *getseg(segfile,1)* is equivalent to *getseg(segfile)*.

There is a very important application of segmented files, apart
from the obvious one of speeding up access to very large files. This
is the use of segmented files for interactive programs. A PASCAL
program using the standard files *input* and *output* will not accept more

than one line of input when it is run from a terminal. An interactive program should be written in this way:

```
PROGRAM interact (ttyin,ttyout, output);
    TYPE
        ttyfile = SEGMENTED FILE OF char;
    VAR
        ttyin, ttyout : ttyfile;

    PROCEDURE getchar (VAR ch : char);
        BEGIN
            IF NOT eof(ttyin)
                THEN
                    IF eos(ttyin)
                        THEN
                            BEGIN
                                putseg(ttyout);
                                getseg(ttyin);
                                ch := ' '
                            END
                        ELSE read(ch)
        END;

    BEGIN
        ....
    END.
```

At some installations the Zurich compiler has been modified to
enable non-segmented files to be used interactively. You should find
out what the local conventions are at your installation before you
write a large interactive program.

C.7 External Procedures

Procedures which are not defined in a program are said to be
external to the program. If a program calls external procedures (or
functions: everything we say about procedures in this section applies
to functions as well) then the object program will contain *external
references* which must be satisfied before it can be executed. The
loader satisfies external references by looking up the procedure
definitions in a *library*. The definitions of the standard procedures
of PASCAL are contained in a library, and the loader will always scan
this library while loading a PASCAL program. The PASCAL 6000 compiler
may be asked to look for procedure definitions in other libraries too.
The procedures are declared in the program, but instead of writing a
procedure body, we write *extern* or *fortran*. For example:

342

> *PROCEDURE eat (firstcourse,secondcourse : real;*
> *VAR replete : boolean);*
>   *extern;*
>
> *FUNCTION cosh (VAR x : real) : real;*
>   *fortran;*

The compiler uses the words *extern* and *fortran* to choose the appropriate *calling sequence* for the procedure. The calling sequence used by PASCAL and FORTRAN are incompatible, and therefore it is important to use the correct mode. Note also that the calling sequence generated by *fortran* corresponds to the calling sequence used by the FTN compiler, and so this compiler must be used to create the FORTRAN subroutine library.

The PASCAL compiler will not compile an incomplete program, and so we must use a trick to generate a library of PASCAL procedures. The compiler generates a multi-record file containing one record for each module, where a module is a procedure that may contain nested procedures, and one record (the last) for the main program. You should therefore write a program containing all the procedures you want in your library, followed by a dummy main program:

> *BEGIN*
> *END.*

Compile this program, and then copy all of the records except the last into another file, which becomes your library file.

The principal hazard of using library procedures is that the compiler cannot check for agreement between formal and actual parameter lists. This means that it is up to you to ensure that the parameters lists agree in both number *and type* of parameters. It is best *not* to use structured types other than unpacked arrays as parameters of library procedures. If you are using FORTRAN subroutines, note the following:

(1) FORTRAN *INTEGER* and *REAL* correspond to PASCAL *integer* and *real*, except that FORTRAN may return -0 which PASCAL does not understand. Fortunately

$$-0 + 0 = 0$$

and so you can prevent problems by adding zero to FORTRAN results before returning them.

(2) FORTRAN *LOGICAL* is *not* the same as PASCAL *boolean*. A FORTRAN *LOGICAL* variable is represented by an integer, and

> *.FALSE.* ≥ 0
> *.TRUE.* < 0

(3) FORTRAN *COMPLEX* and *DOUBLE PRECISION* use two words each and can
be represented in PASCAL by an array or record containing two *real*
components. PASCAL has no facilities for double precision arithmetic,
and so it cannot do anything with double precision variables except
store them.

Libraries of compiled programs evolved at a time when compilers
were cumbersome and slow and loaders were simple and fast. Compilers
have since become more efficient, and loaders have grown into baroque
monstrosities. Therefore there is less advantage in storing libraries
in compiled form than there was, and storing libraries in source form
is increasingly attractive. This is particularly true for PASCAL,
because PASCAL can be compiled efficiently by a one-pass compiler.

C.8 Compiler Options

The CDC 6000 PASCAL Compiler recognizes directives written in the
form

{ $ <option sequence> <comment string> }

The *option sequence* consists of options separated by commas. An
option consists of one of the letters B, E, L, P, T, U or X followed
by a symbol. For the options B and X this symbol is an integer, and
for the other options the symbol is "+' or '-'. All the options have
default settings, and if you do not provide any directives, the compiler will use the default values. The default values are sensibly
chosen, and it is strongly recommended that you do not use any
compiler directives unless you have good reason. The default options
setting is

{$B4,E-,L+,T+,U-,X4}

The effect of each option is described below. The effect of the
default setting is described first.

B4 File buffers will contain at least 512 words.

Bn File buffers will contain at least 128 * n words, $1 \leq n \leq 9$

E- The compiler generates unique symbols for local module names.
That is, the identifiers which you give to procedures and functions are translated by the compiler into names like C000001.
Note that this translation is invisible to you unless you examine
the relocatable object program generated by the compiler. This
translation is done because the CDC operating system only recognizes seven character identifiers as entry points, and therefore

PASCAL identifiers which differed in the eighth character only would be ambiguous. Note that this does not apply to procedures or functions declared as 'extern' or 'fortran': these get an entry point name equal to the procedure or function identifier truncated to seven characters.

E+ The first seven characters of the local module name are used as the entry point name. If you use this option, you have to make sure that your procedure and function identifiers differ in their first seven characters.

L+ Send a listing of the source text of the program to the output file.

L- Print error diagnostics only on the output file.

P+ Generate the code necessary for a post-mortem after the program fails or after the procedure halt has been called.

P- Do not generate code for post-mortem.

T+ Include execution time tests. These check array indexes and sub-ranges to make sure that the variable is within range; divisions to make sure that the divisor is not zero; integer to real conversions, which is necessary because conversion fails for integers i such that $abs(i) > maxint$; CASE statements to ensure that the case selector corresponds to a case label.

T- Do not include any run-time tests. This should be used for large slow programs that have been exhaustively tested and are run hundreds of times daily. (Such as the PASCAL Compiler.)

U- A line of the program may contain up to 120 characters. Characters after this are treated as comments.

U+ A line of the program may contain 72 characters only. Characters after this are treated as comments.

X4 The registers X0, X1, X2 and X3 are used for passing parameters to procedures and functions. This option produces fast and compact code with the risk that the compiler will report an error saying 'running out of registers'. In practice, this error does not occur with reasonable programs. In general, Xn means use the registers X_0, X_1,...,X_{n-1} for passing parameter descriptors, for $1 \leq n \leq 6$.

X0 Use the stack for parameter descriptors. This is a bit slower, and will use more memory, but there is no risk of running out of registers.

These directives may be used anywhere in the program. It is

therefore possible to list selected parts of a program only, or to compile run-time tests only into new sections of a large program.

Program
Standards

APPENDIX D

There is no definitive standard for writing a computer program.
Many organizations establish a standard and insist that their programmers use it, and from time to time individuals publish their own
standards in the hope that others will follow their example. By
programming according to a standard you make your own programs more
readable to other people in your organization or to the programming
community in general. The standards given in this appendix should be
regarded as recommendations, not commands. If you use them, you can
be sure that any PASCAL programmer anywhere will find your programs
readable, and you will probably find that you make fewer mistakes
while writing your programs.

You may notice that the example programs in this book are not
written according to the standards given here. The example programs
are not model programs: rather, they were designed to illustrate
particular points. Comments are omitted from them because the
explanations in the surrounding text make further comments super-
fluous. Blank lines are omitted from example programs simply to save
space. Input validation and output formatting have not been attempted, also to save space.

Comments

D.1 Program Description

All programs commence with a comment which must include at least
the following information:

A brief title for the program;

The name of the programmer (or chief programmer);

A description of what the program does;

A description of the input required by the program, and the
output that it produces.

If the program employs complicated algorithms which require
lengthy explanation, give references, either to your own documentation
or to the book or journal in which you found the algorithm. For
example:

The symbol table is a balanced binary tree. See 'The Art
of Computer Programming', Volume 3, 'Sorting and Searching',
by D.E. Knuth. Algorithm A, Page 455 (Addison-Wesley, 1975)

Each procedure should be introduced by a description using the
same model. When the program is written by one person, he does not
need to put his own name before each procedure, but if the program is
written by a team, then the name of the author of the procedure should
be given. Procedure documentation should describe what the procedure
does, how it does it, and the role of each parameter.

D.2 Comments

Use comments to clarify potentially obscure sections of the program. Do not clutter up the program with unnecessary comments, and
above all, do not write comments that contain nothing that is not
obvious from the program. Do not, for example, write:

num := num + 1   { increment num }

Organize comments neatly. When comments occupy several lines, each
line should start in the same column, even it there are no program
statements to the left of the comment. For example:

Declarations

```
VAR
    sum1, sum2,              { sums of samples }
    sumsq1, sumsq2,          { sums of squared samples }
    sumprod                  { sums of products }
        : real;
```

D.3 Declarations

Constants should have global scope. It is easier to locate a constant definition if there is one constant declaration section at the beginning of the program than if constants are declared in every procedure. The program should not contain literals other than *0* and *1* outside the constant declaration section. Literal strings, however, may be used in *write* statements.

Types should also have global scope in most cases. However, if a type is used in one procedure only, it may be declared as a local type for that procedure.

Variables should be declared according to their usage. A procedure should access only its parameters and local variables. If a non-local variable must be accessed by a procedure, provide suitable comments. Functions should not access non-local variables at all.

Procedures and functions may be declared locally (that is, nested) but the program is not necessarily more readable if this is done. Some compilers may in fact limit the number of nesting levels.

Choose descriptive names for constants, types, variables, procedures and functions.

D.4 Layout

Leave one blank line before a label, constant, type or variable declaration section. Leave two or more blank lines before a procedure or function declaration, and before the beginning of the main program. Use blank lines to divide complicated sections of the program into chunks small enough to be easily assimilated by the reader.

In the following, S_1, S_2, $\ldots, S_n$ are statements, (possibly compound statements), b is a boolean expression, i is a scalar variable, and $expr_1$ and $expr_2$ are scalar expressions.

Layout

Layout for a compound statement:

```
BEGIN
    S_1;
    S_2;
    ...
    S_n
END
```

Layout for an *IF* statement:

```
IF b
    THEN S_1
    ELSE S_2
```

If S_1 and S_2 are compound statements use:

```
IF b
    THEN
        S_1
    ELSE
        S_2
```

Layout for the *REPEAT* statement:

```
REPEAT
    S_1;
    S_2;
    ...
    S_n
UNTIL b
```

Layout for the *WHILE* statement:

```
WHILE b DO
    S_1
```

Layout for the *FOR* statement:

```
FOR i := expr_1 TO expr_2 DO
    S_1
```

Layout for the *CASE* statement (c is the case selector, and $a_1, a_2, \ldots a_n$ are case labels):

```
CASE c OF
    a_1 :
            S_1;
    a_2 :
            S_2;
    ....
```

$$a_n :$$
$$S_n$$
$$END \{ \ case \ \}$$

Layout for the *WITH* statement (*v* is a record identifier):

WITH v *DO*
    S_1

When the statement controlled by a *WHILE, FOR* or *WITH* clause is compound, annotate the final end. For example:

WHILE b *DO*
    BEGIN
        S_1;
        S_2;
        ...
        S_n
    END { *while* }

Leave one blank on each side of operators, '=' and ';' in declarations and ':=' in assignment statements (unless there isn't room). Leave one blank after '{' and one blank before '}' in comments.

PROGRAM is always written in the left margin. In this book we have indented *CONST, TYPE, VAR, PROCEDURE* and *FUNCTION* according to the nesting level, but it is acceptable to write these in the left margin too, provided that the result is not confusing. Procedure nesting should, however, be indicated by indentation.

D.5 Portability

A program is *portable* if it can be run without alteration on systems other than the one for which it was written. Whenever you write a program you should consider the possibility that it will one day be run at another installation. If there is a chance that it will be, then you should write it in a machine independent way as far as possible. Unfortunately, PASCAL has not been defined in a way which makes it easy to write portable programs. The rules which follow are intended as a guide to writing portable programs, but they do not guarantee portability.

Do not assume properties of the character set. Safe assumptions are

    'a' < 'b'   ... < 'z'
    '0' < '1'   ... < '9'

Portability

If the program is to convert numbers, you may want to use

$$ord('n') - ord('0') = n, \quad 0 \leq n \leq 9$$

but it is safer to use

```
CASE n OF
   '0' : value := 10 * value;
   '1' : value := 10 * value + 1;
   ....
```

Do not assume that

```
succ('a') = 'b'
succ('b') = 'c'
etc
```

because this is not true of at least one character set.

Do not use the type *SET OF char*, and do not use character subranges. The subrange

```
'0' .. '9'
```

is reasonably safe, but subranges such as

```
'+' .. '/'
```

may have quite the wrong effect or even be illegal.

Do not use variant records without tag-fields, and do not use undiscriminated unions for tricks such as writing pointer values.

Include fieldwidth and precision parameters whenever you are writing the values of integers or reals.

Do not use standard procedures or standard functions as actual parameters of procedures or functions.

Do not use standard identifiers which are not defined in the PASCAL Report.

Do not assume unrealistically high precision for the results of real calculations. Use constants (not literals) to establish convergence criteria, and define them at the beginning of the program with appropriate comments.

Document carefully any parts of the program that you think might not be machine independent.

D.6 Automatic Formatting

Many computer installations have a program which will format a PASCAL program automatically. This is relatively easy to do in PASCAL because the nesting level, and hence the required indentation, can be determined from the reserved words in the program. Whether or not you use a formatting program is largely a matter of taste. Programmers who write programs with good intelligible layouts should never be compelled to use a formatting program. Many programmers, however, feel that counting blanks is something that the computer can do better than they can, and they will prefer to use a formatting program. Sometimes the compiler itself will provide a formatted listing, in which case you have no choice in the matter.

There are two good reasons for using a formatting program, even if you are justifiably proud of your own layouts. First, formatted programs are consistent, and so if a group of programmers all use the same formatting program, they will find each other's programs easy to read. Second, although entering a new program neatly is not difficult, revising a program while preserving the layout can be extremely tedious.

Index

Index